From Story Interpretation to Sermon Crafting

From Story Interpretation to Sermon Crafting

A Structured-Repetition Approach for Exegesis and Sermon Crafting of Old Testament Narratives

CHARLES R. DICKSON

WIPF & STOCK · Eugene, Oregon

FROM STORY INTERPRETATION TO SERMON CRAFTING
A Structured-Repetition Approach for Exegesis and Sermon Crafting
of Old Testament Narratives

Copyright © 2011 Charles R. Dickson. All rights reserved. Except for brief quotations in critical publications or reviews, no part of this book may be reproduced in any manner without prior written permission from the publisher. Write: Permissions, Wipf and Stock Publishers, 199 W. 8th Ave., Suite 3, Eugene, OR 97401.

Wipf & Stock
An Imprint of Wipf and Stock Publishers
199 W. 8th Ave., Suite 3
Eugene, OR 97401

www.wipfandstock.com

ISBN 13: 978-1-61097-274-1

Manufactured in the U.S.A.

Scripture quotations taken from the New American Standard Bible®, Copyright © 1960, 1962, 1963, 1968,1971, 1972, 1973, 1975,1977, 1995 by The Lockman Foundation used by permission. (www.Lockman.org).

Contents

Preface / vii

1. Introduction to the Structured-Repetition Approach / 1
2. The Process of Uncovering the Structure of a Narrative Text / 29
3. Other Approaches to Narrative Analysis / 45
4. Describing and Illustrating the Five Basic Narrative Structures / 56
5. Exegesis and Interpretation of the Narrative Structure / 101
6. Sermon Construction Based on the Exegetical, Theological, and Preaching Ideas / 153
7. Sermon Formats and the Structured-Repetition Approach / 172

Conclusion / 238

Bibliography / 241

Scripture Index / 247

Subject Index / 249

Preface

STUDIES ABOUT THE LITERARY nature of Old Testament historical narrative and its implications for exegesis and interpretation abounds. This is a consequence of the impact that literary studies had on biblical studies, which started in the 1930s, and resulted in a definite shift in the 1960s and 1970s from a diachronic approach to a synchronic approach to biblical narratives. *A Study of Two Ways: Thirty Years of Old Testament Scholarship in South Africa*[1] traces this shift as it took place in South Africa. Many books on methods and approaches that apply this shift to biblical narratives have been published, for example, *Fishing for Jonah* (1995) and *Fishing for Jonah (anew): Various Approaches to Biblical Interpretation* (2005). This publication is practical and introduces theological students to the various approaches and methods for a literary reading of the Bible. Louis Jonker's work, *Exclusivity and Variety: Perspectives on Multidimensional Exegesis* (1996), also gives attention to this shift and its implications for exegesis, although the main thrust of the work is the development of a multidimensional approach to exegesis.

There are a plethora of international publications, both journals and books that have made contributions towards a better understanding of the literary nature of Old Testament historical narrative. Some classic examples include: Meir Steinberg, *The Poetics of Biblical Narrative* (1987), Adele Berlin, *Poetics and Interpretation of Biblical narrative* (1994), Jan P. Fokkelman, *Reading Biblical Narrative* (trans. 1999), Robert Alter, *The Art of Biblical Narrative* (1981), Richard L Pratt Jr. *He Gave Us Stories* (1990), J. L. Ska, "Our Fathers Have Told Us: Introduction to the Analysis of Hebrew Narrative" (2000), Daniel Marguerat and Yvan Bourquin, *How to Read Bible Stories* (trans. 1999), to name a few. Of particular relevance for this book is Simon Bar-Efrat, "Some Observations on the Analysis of Structure in Biblical Narrative,"[2] and David A Dorsey,

---

1. J. H. Le Roux, *A Study of Two Ways*, Pretoria: Verba Vitae, 1993.
2. Bar-Efrat, "Observations," 154–73.

The Literary Structure of the Old Testament: A Commentary on Genesis–Malachi (1999).

Work has also been done to apply this literary approach to Old Testament historical narrative to preaching; one of the main tasks of the Church's ministry and the work of the pastor. One is reminded of Eugene Lowry, *The Homiletical Plot* (1980), Thomas G. Long, *Preaching the Literary forms of the Bible* (1989), John C. Holbert, *Preaching Old Testament Narrative: Proclamation & Narrative in the Hebrew Bible* (1991), Steven Mathewson, *The Art of Preaching Old Testament Narrative* (2002), Joel B. Green and Michael Pasquarello III (eds.), *Narrative Reading, Narrative Proclamation: Reuniting New Testament Interpretation and Proclamation* (2003), and Robert B. Chisholm Jr., *Interpreting The Historical Books: An Exegetical Handbook* (2006), to name a few.

There is still a need for practical ways of making this relatively new approach to biblical narrative benefit the pastoral ministry, and much still needs to be done to translate this wealth of research and information to enhance and enrich the preaching ministry of the church. By doing this, the historical narratives will continue to speak to Christian believers in contemporary society; to show how historical narrative can and still does address the issues, concerns and struggles the church and Christians face on a daily basis.

This book seeks to make a contribution in this regard, presenting an approach to the exegesis of Old Testament historical narrative that forms the foundation for sermon crafting, based on Old Testament narrative that is rooted in the text, shaped by the text, and is also characterized by sound and controlled exegesis.

The book owes an enormous debt to the work of Bar-Efrat (1980) and Dorsey (1999). Bar-Efrat's concept of levels of repetition and Dorsey's concepts of repetition and structure have made an important contribution to the development of the approach to Old Testament historical narrative explored here. It is hoped that by working through this volume, students preparing for pastoral ministry will be encouraged to spend time exploring the narrative, and would focus on the literary richness of the text before consulting commentaries.

This book also has in mind the pastor who desires to preach from the historical books more regularly, taking into account the particular challenges of the pastoral ministry: the constraint of time for preparation; the need for an exegetical approach that takes seriously and respects

Preface ix

the literary nature of the narratives; interpretation that is theologically and biblically sound; and the preparation and preaching of sermons that are fresh and innovative. The approach presented in this book seeks to help the pastor with these challenges.

This book started out as a reader, and has been developed and used over the last seven years in classes for undergraduate students and in a workshop for Master of Theology students at the Cape Town Baptist Seminary in South Africa.

The introduction looks at the dominance of narrative in the Old Testament and the reason for this prevalence. It also sketches the history of the approaches used to access the narratives for use in the life and ministry of the church. It concludes with a discussion about the shift towards a literary approach to biblical narrative, the understanding of narrative text that informed the approaches used historically, and the application of this literary shift to sermon preparation and proclamation.

Chapter 1 introduces the structured-repetition approach to narrative structural analysis, exegesis, and interpretation of a narrative text. The understanding of narrative text that informs this approach is also discussed. It also discusses the importance of structure in communication, and the way structure and repetition relates to Old Testament narrative.

In chapter 2, a selection of narrative passages from Judges are used to illustrate the process of uncovering the structure of a narrative text, paying particular attention to the role of narrative constituents and repetition in this process. It also introduces the very important issue of closure; the first step in a structured-repetition approach.

Chapter 3 discusses and evaluates a number of approaches used to analyze a narrative text, pointing out similarities and differences between these methods and the approach presented in this book.

Chapter 4 explains the five basic narrative structures used by Old Testament story tellers (writers) to communicate their message. Each of the basic structures is then illustrated with a few narrative passages. Other narrative structures are developed from these basic structures.

Chapter 5 is a very important chapter, illustrating the exegesis and interpretation of the structure of narrative texts. It explains the role of the focus point and demonstrates the formulation of the main point of a narrative unit. The latter is an important step in the process of the transition from exegesis and interpretation to sermon crafting.

Chapter 6 sees the culmination of the work done in the previous chapters. Exegetical, theological, and preaching ideas are explained and their formulation illustrated.

In chapter 7, sample sermon manuscripts are presented. Use is made of the didactic, third person, frame story, and story-reflection-story formats. The chapter illustrates practically the transition from story structuring and analysis to sermon crafting.

If this book enables some pastors to acquire and use an additional tool for preaching, enhances their ability to preach sermons from Old Testament narratives regularly and responsibly, that are exegetical and theological but still refreshing and relevant, it would have been a worthwhile effort. Michael Fishbane, in reviewing Bar-Efrat's *Literary Modes and Methods in Biblical Narrative in View of 2 Sam 10–20; 1 Kings 1–2*; Fokkelman's *Narrative Art in Genesis: Specimens of Stylistic and Structural Analysis,* and Licht's *Storytelling in the Bible,* remarked, "I, for one, would not like to see the eventual sophistication of the literary study of the Bible obscure the religious truths which the Bible itself seeks to teach. I would rather hope that interest in the literary dimension of texts might elicit new means of apprehending religious truths."[1] His hope is our aim. So this book is sent forth with the prayer that it will enrich the preaching ministry of pastors for whom the call to biblical preaching burns like a fire within.

---

1. Fishbane, "Reviews," 103.

1

Introduction to the Structured-Repetition Approach

INTRODUCTION

THE LITERARY APPROACHES TO Old Testament historical narrative discussed in the Preface are synchronic, working with the text as it stands. The focus is on the individual narratives or episodes in a narrative, or scenes or units of an episode. A key aspect of these approaches is the exegesis of the narrative text by structural analysis, focusing on the surface structure of the text.

The use of literary approaches in Old Testament studies began in the 1930s, becoming more popular in the 1970s and firmly establishing itself from the 1980s as biblical scholars increasingly applied the approach in the structural analysis of various Old Testament narrative texts. This is represented in the works of Alter (1981), Fokkelman (1975 and 1999), Light (1978), Milne (1998), Pratt (1990), Marguerat and Bourquin (1999), Dorsey (1999), Walsh (2001), and Schutte (1989).

Biblical scholars did not clarify the basis for their structural analyses, that is, the *elements in the narrative text* which were used as the basis for the structure of the narrative. Bar-Efrat[1] responded to this issue by examining a number of structural analyses, giving special attention to the constituents and varieties of the narrative structures. He identified four different elements on which narrative structure is based, referred to as *levels*:

---

1. Bar-Efrat, "Observations," 154–73.

1. Verbal level—words or phrases
2. Narrative technique level—narration vs. character speech, scenes vs. summary, narration vs. description, explanation, comment, etc.
3. Narrative world level—characters, events [action], place, time
4. Conceptual content level—themes and ideas[2]

Bar-Efrat found four basic structure types: parallel (A A'); ring (A X A'); chiastic (ABB'A') and concentric (A BXB'A').[3] I add a fifth one, namely, linear (A B C D E . . .).[4]

Finally, Bar-Efrat suggests that "these patterns are created by repetition of certain elements of the structure . . . The repeated elements belong to any of the structural levels discussed above—the verbal level, the level of narrative technique, the level of narrative world, or the level of conceptual content."[5]

Bar-Efrat analyzed Old Testament narrative texts, and it is appropriate to look at the understanding of narrative text that informed these analyses. Basic constituent elements must be present in a narrative for it to be defined as such. Miller, for example, says:

> . . . there must be, first of all, an initial situation, a sequence leading to a change or a reversal of that situation, and a revelation made possible by the reversal of the situation. Second, there must be the use of personification whereby character is created out of signs—for example the words on a page in a written narrative, the modulated sounds in the air in an oral narrative. However important plot may be, without personification there can be no story telling . . . Third, there must be some patterning or repetition of key elements, for example, trope or system of tropes, or a complex word . . . Any narrative, to be narrative, I claim, must have some version of these elements: *beginning, sequence*, reversal; *personification*, or, more accurately and technically stated, prosopopeia, bringing protagonist, antagonist, and witness 'to life'; some patterning or *repetition* of elements surrounding a nuclear figure or complex word (my emphasis).[6]

2. Ibid., 154–62.
3. Ibid., 163.
4. See Dorsey, *Structure*, 26.
5. Bar-Efrat, "Observations," 163.
6. Miller, "Narrative," 75.

Introduction to the Structured-Repetition Approach

The emphasized phrases are the fundamental elements necessary to form a narrative. Brink, building on Todorov and others, describes narrative as follows, "iets gebeur met iemand op 'n sekere tyd en plek" (translation: "something happens to someone at a particular time and place and in a particular set of circumstances").[7] Ryken says that "[t]hese three [i.e., *setting*, plot or *action*, and *character*] make up the narrative that we enter when we sit down and read a biblical story."[8] Arp, writing about the aim of *Perrine's Story and Structure*, comments " . . . the book examines the major elements of fiction . . . the elements discussed are to be found in all fiction [and these elements are] *plot, character, theme, point of view, symbol* and *irony, emotion* and *humor* and *fantasy*."[9] These elements are by no means an exhaustive list; they are the essentials without which a story cannot be a story. Marguerat and Bourquin, quoting Ecco, put it this way: " . . . to tell a story you must first construct a world, furnished as much as possible, down to the smallest detail . . . The second feature consists in linking together *actions* within a causal relationship . . . The third feature is *time*. Paul Riceour's basic intuition . . . is the recognition of the link between *causality* and *temporality* as elements of narrativity. Everything that is recounted occurs in time, takes time, unfolds temporally, and what unfolds in time can [be] recounted" (my emphasis).[10] Similarly, Amit quotes Polak as follows: "A story relates what is happening to *people*, and describes *objects, places* and *events*" (my emphasis).[11] This understanding of narrative text is presented in the diagram below:

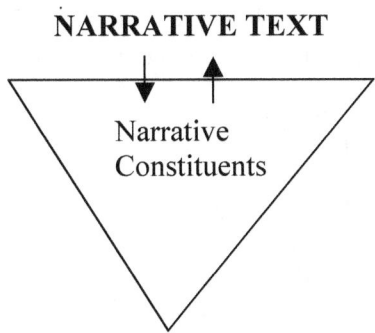

---

7. Brink, *Vertelkunde*, 38.
8. Ryken, *Words*, 53.
9. Arp, *Story and Structure*, v–vi.
10. Marguerat and Bourquin, *How To Read Bible Stories*, 15–16.
11. Amit, *Reading*, 46.

When comparing Bar-Efrat's four levels with the narrative constituents mentioned above, it is clear that they are the same. Bar-Efrat says that "these patterns [i.e., parallel (A A'); ring (A X A'); chiastic (ABB'A') and concentric (A BXB'A')] are created by repetition of certain elements of the structure."[12] If the *elements of the structure* (Bar-Efrat) are the same as *the narrative constituents constituting a narrative* (definitions above), then in effect *the repetition of narrative constituents create the structures.* There is a very close link between the structure of a narrative and the narrative constituents. This means that identifying the narrative constituents that are repeated in the narrative will reveal the structure of a text. Consequently, there is a slight difference with Bar-Efrat at this point, in that the patterns are not created by "repetition of certain elements of the structure,"[13] but by the repetition of certain narrative constituents. One could argue that the constituents are elements of the narrative text, and since the structure is an essential element of a narrative text, the constituents of the narrative are also the constituents of the structure. But the difference in formulation has a practical consequence for sermon crafting, which will be illustrated later on. This reformulation of Bar-Efrat's description of the relation between patterns of structure and the repeated elements of structure is clear from an examination of his examples.

Example 1

Before Bar-Efrat discusses the micro-levels of repetition in small sections of a narrative, he shows how the narrative of Ruth as a whole (on a macro-level) is structured.[14] The emphasis is mine.

A 1		*People* who died before main action		
	B	*Ruth + Orpah* Women of Bethlehem		
2		C	*Naomi-Ruth*	
			D	*Boaz-servant*
				F *Boaz-Ruth*
			D	*Boaz-servants*
		C	*Naomi-Ruth*	

12. Bar-Efrat, "Observations," 163.
13. Ibid.
14. Ibid., 157.

3		Naomi-Ruth
		Boaz-Ruth
		Naomi-Ruth
4	B	*Boaz + redeemer*
		Women of Bethlehem
	A 1	*People* who were born after main action[15]

The structural elements that are repeated above fall under the category "level of the narrative world." Each of the elements italicized[16] are a narrative constituent. In this structural pattern, three narrative constituents are the basis for the structure of the narrative as a whole, namely: character, place (space/geography), action (event), and they are repeated throughout the structure above. A close reading of the narrative provides further details of place (space), as place refers not just to the name of a town, Bethlehem, but also to the field, the house, Moab, and the city gate. But, as illustrated in the structure above, the dominant narrative constituent is *character*.

This type of narrative structure is concentric, because when the matching units are connected there are four circles: A+A, B+B, C+C, and D+D.

Example 2

(2) THE LEVEL OF NARRATIVE TECHNIQUE

> The analysis of structure on this level is based on variations in narrative method, such as narrator's account as opposed to character's speech (dialogue), scenic presentation versus summary, narration as against description, explanation, comment, etc. For example, the narrative about David and Achish at Aphek (1 Sam 29) is constructed in the following manner: first, the narrator relates that the Philistines gathered their armies together to Aphek, not far from the Israelite encampment in Jezreel, and that David and his men passed on with Achish in the rear of the lords of the Philistines. Following that, there are two rather elaborate dialogues, one between the commanders of the Philistines and Achish, and the other between Achish and David; both dia-

---

15. Ibid.

16. See Fokkelman, *Reading*; Walsh, *Style and Structure*; Trible, *Rhetorical Criticism*; Dorsey, *Structure*; and Klaus, *Patterns*.

logues are concerned with the question of David's loyalty to the Philistines and his presence in their camp. The narrative concludes with the narrator's statement that David departed early in the morning to return to the land of the Philistines, whereas the Philistines went up to Jezreel. Thus the bulk of the narrative is made up of two dialogues of considerable length, which are framed by two short communications by the narrator.

> A Narrator's account (verses 1–2)
>   B Dialogue (verses 3–5)
>   B Dialogue (verses 6–10)
> A Narrator's account (verse 11)[17]

Here, the structural analysis is based on the narrative constituent of speech—*character speech* and *narrator speech* (description).

Example 3

The story of Samuel's birth (1 Sam 1:1—2:11) is composed mainly of three scenes. The first and largest scene takes place at the House of God in Shiloh and it shows Hannah before the birth of her son. The second scene takes place at Elkanah's home in Ramathaim and it shows Hannah after the birth of Samuel. The third scene takes place again at the House of God in Shiloh and it shows Hannah presenting her son at the sanctuary. These three scenes are preceded, joined and concluded by brief summaries. The first summary, by way of introduction, supplies the necessary background information about the participating characters and tells of their custom to go up to Shiloh every year. The second summary reports that Elkanah and his family returned to their home at Ramathaim, where Hannah conceived and gave birth to Samuel. The third summary relates that Hannah sucked her son until she weaned him and the last summary informs us that Elkanah went to his house, while Samuel remained at Shiloh. Thus we find that the narrative is organized in the following way:

> A Summary (1:1–3)
>   B Scene (verses 4–18)
>   C Summary (verses 19–20)
>   D Scene (verses 21–23a)
>   C Summary (verse 23b)
>   B Scene (1:24—2:10)
> A Summary (verse 11)

---

17. Bar-Efrat, "Observations," 158–59.

Introduction to the Structured-Repetition Approach

The alternation of scenic presentation and summary account is closely related to the handling of time. As is well known the author can vary the relations between narrated and narration time freely according to his wish. In scenic presentation narrated time flows rather slowly, whereas in summary it runs quickly, relative to narration time.[18]

Ska[19] describes "narrated time" as the duration of action and events in the story measured in real time, that is, measured in seconds, minutes, hours, days, months, years, centuries, etc.; it refers to chronological time and narration time as the duration of the story measured in terms of words, phrases, sentences, verses, paragraphs, pages, and chapters.

The narrative constituent technique uses the following elements as the basis for the structural analysis: summary, scene, the narrative elements *place/space* (the alternation between the house of God=Elkanah's house=the house of God), *character* (each of the summaries has at its center the main characters of the story), and *time* (the alternation of scene and summary is used to slow down or speed up the story).

Example 4

Thus we find in the story of David and Bathsheba (2 Sam 11) that the opening and concluding parts of the narrative, which are concerned with Bathsheba—David seeing her from his roof and lying with her and in the end bringing her to his house and making her his wife—are told in such a manner as to make narrated time flow very fast. On the other hand, the two sections in the middle of the narrative, which are concerned with Uriah—David's attempts to make him go down to his house and lie with his wife and the messenger's report of Uriah's death—contain a large amount of direct speech, with the result that time passes relatively slowly. Only the factual account by the narrator of Uriah's death itself is related rather quickly. So in this case the narrative displays the following construction in terms of time-velocity:

A   *Quick (time):*   A Bathsheba   (verses 2–5)
     B   *Slow(time):*   B Uriah   (verses 6–15)
         C   *Quick(time):*   B Uriah   (verses 16–17)
     B   *Slow(time):*   B Uriah   (verses 18–25)
A   *Quick(time):*   A Bathsheba   (verses 26–27)

---

18. Ibid., 159.
19. Ska, "Our Fathers," 7–8.

The molding of time in narrative pertains not only to its (relative) rate of progress, but also to its order. The author can begin his story at the beginning, in the middle or at the end; he can introduce flashbacks, anticipations, etc. In biblical narrative events are arranged as a rule in successive order and time flows in one direction only. However, in a number of cases flashbacks can be found.[20]

Character and *time* are the basis for the structural analysis here; the units above are linked to each other based on the repetition of some aspect of time or a particular character.

Example 5

For example, the narrative dealing with the armed conflict between *David and the Amalekites* [my emphasis] (1 Sam 30) *begins with a flashback* by the narrator relating what had happened at Ziklag before David returned there from Aphek: "And it came to pass when David and his men came to Ziklag on the third day, the Amalekites had made a raid upon the Negeb and upon Ziklag and smitten Ziklag and burned it with fire. And had taken captive the women that were in it; small or great, they killed no one, but carried them off and went their way" (verses 1–2).

As against this reversal to the past at the beginning of the narrative, there is a *leap into the future* at the end of the narrative: "And it was so from that day forward, he made it a statute and an ordinance for Israel to this day" (verse 25).

In the narrative of *David and Abigail* (1 Sam 25), *several brief flashbacks* are to be found, which all occur at central points and function as markers of the structure (my emphasis). These flashbacks are clearly indicated by the use of the . . . verb denoting the past perfect tense...The flashbacks are all located at the points of transition.

The first section of the narrative dealing with David ends with the statement that David set out with 400 men, all girded with swords, towards Nabal (verse 13). The second section telling of Abigail begins with a flashback: "Now Abigail, Nabal's wife, had been told by one of the servants, 'Behold, David sent messengers from the wilderness to salute our master . . .'" (verse 14). This section concludes as follows: "Now as she was riding on the ass

---

20. Bar-Efrat, "Observations," 159–60.

and coming down under the cover of the mountains, behold, David and his men coming down toward her, and she met them" (verse 20). At this point—the beginning of the third section—when the meeting between the two chief characters is about to materialize, we are again *carried back in time [flashback]*: "And David had said, 'Surely in vain have I guarded all that belongs to this one in the wilderness . . .'" (verse 21). At the end of the third section, just as the meeting between David and Abigail is brought to an end and she is about to return to Nabal, *another flashback* occurs: "And to her he had said, 'Go up in peace to your house, see I have listened to your voice and I have lifted up your countenance'" (verse 35). In view of the foregoing it hardly comes as a surprise to find flashbacks at the end of the last section and the conclusion of the narrative as a whole: "And Ahinoam had been taken by David from Jezreel, and so both of them became his wives. But Saul had given Michal his daughter, David's wife, to Palti the son of Laish, who was of Gallim" (verses 43–44) (emphases all mine).[21]

In this example, *time* is the basis for the structural analysis; the units are linked to each other based on the repetition of time through flashbacks.

Example 6

(3) *The level of the narrative world/narrative content*
The analysis of structure on this level is based on the narrative content as created by the language and the techniques. The two chief components of narrative content are *characters and events* (other components are *setting, clothes, arms* and similar items).

(3a) *Characters*
Several aspects of the characters, such as their identity, their nature, and their function in the story, may serve as a basis for structural analysis of the narrative.

With regard to structure based upon the identity of the characters it is instructive to re-examine the narrative of Samuel's birth (1 Sam 1–2) referred to above. In the first scene of that narrative Elkanah talks to Hannah and afterwards Eli talks to Hannah, following her prayer to God. In the second and third scenes Hannah talks to Elkanah and subsequently she talks to Eli, this

---

21. Ibid., 160–61.

time preceding her prayer to God. This gives us the following scheme:

```
A    B              A    B
Elkanah-Hannah      Eli-Hannah (following Hannah's prayer)
  x    x
B    A              B    A
Hannah-Elkanah      Hannah-Eli (preceding Hannah's prayer)
[emphases all mine]²²
```

In example 5, the narrative constituent technique was the basis for the chiastic structure of the narrative. In this example, a different narrative constituent, namely *character*, is the basis for the concentric structure. The same narrative has produced two different types of structures based on different narrative constituents, which demonstrates the richness of the meaning possibilities of the biblical narrative.

Example 7

A striking illustration of structure based upon identity of characters is provided by the narrative of Amnon and Tamar (2 Sam 13). This narrative is constructed in the manner of a chain: in each link composing the chain two characters are to be found. The narrative begins with an opening section introducing the main participating characters. Afterwards, in the first link of the story proper, Jonadab and Amnon appear, in the second link Amnon and David, in the third David and Tamar, in the fourth Tamar and Amnon, in the fifth Amnon and the servant, in the sixth the servant and Tamar, and in the seventh Tamar and Absalom. Following the seventh link there is a short concluding section.

The joining together of the links is effected by means of the second character in each link, who is invariably the first character in the next link:

```
Jonadab-Amnon (verses 3–5) A
    Amnon-David (verse 6) B
        David-Tamar (verse 7) C
            Tamar-Amnon (verses 8–16) D
                Amnon-servant (verse 17) C
                    servant-Tamar (verse 18) B
                        Tamar-Absalom (verses 19–20) A
```

22. Ibid., 161–62.

Introduction to the Structured-Repetition Approach

It should be observed that Amnon is found in the first two links, whereas Tamar is found in the last two. Moreover, Tamar is also found in the third link from the beginning and Amnon in the third link from the end. In the middle link, which is much larger in size than any of the other ones (9 verses), Amnon and Tamar meet and here the climax of the story is reached.

It is noteworthy too that Amnon is present in links 1 and 2, Tamar in links 3 and 4, Amnon in links 4 and 5, and Tamar again in links 6 and 7. *An additional contribution to the symmetry of the structure is achieved by means of the fact that Jonadab, who is close to Amnon and his ally, is mentioned in the first link, whereas Absalom, who is close to Tamar and her ally, is mentioned in the last link. However, this last symmetry no longer belongs to the aspect of the identity of the characters, but to the aspect of their function in the story* [my emphasis].

The aspect of the function of the characters includes distinctions such as hero and opponent, assistants to either side, instigators, obstacles, pursuer and pursued, etc. The aspect of the nature of the characters comprises characteristics such as virtuous versus vicious, hospitable versus inhospitable, loyal versus disloyal, fruitful versus barren. *Analysis of structure may be based on any of these matters* [my emphasis].[23]

The narrative constituent character is the basis of the narrative structure.

Example 8

(3b) Events
The events of the story in their mutual [causal] relationships make up the plot. The plot always has a *structure* [my emphasis]. Contrary to real life no accidental and irrelevant facts are included and the incidents are connected with each other both temporally and causally... Along with dramatic structure mention should be made of *spatial and temporal structure of the plot*... The narrative of Job's trial, to which reference has just been made, provides a very clear example of spatial structure. After the introduction, telling of Job and his piety, the action takes place alternately *in heaven, on earth*, in heaven and on earth again. The scenes in heaven are very similar to each other, and so are the scenes on earth. In this way a very pronounced sym-

---

23. Bar-Efrat, "Observations," 162–63.

> metry is achieved . . . In numerous biblical narratives the scene of action is not confined to one single place, but it *shifts from one region to another*, thus creating a distinct structure. For instance, in the story of the suing for Rebekah (Gen 24) the introductory and concluding scenes are located in and near Abraham's dwelling place in Canaan, whereas the two main scenes in the middle of the narrative are situated near and in the city of Nahor in Mesopotamia (at the well and in the house of Bethuel respectively).
>
> A Canaan   (verses 1–10)
>   B Mesopotamia   (verses 11–31)
>   B Mesopotamia   (verses 32–61)
> A Canaan   (verses 62–67)[24]

The narrative constituents *place/space and events* (my emphasis) (happenings) form the structure of this narrative. Events and action (happenings) have a temporal and geographic element attached to them. Put differently, an event happens in a particular place and time and cannot be identified and described without also identifying and describing the temporal (time) and geographic (place) elements, because they are conceptually interlinked.

> *The temporal structure* of the plot is established using dates and by stating when the action took place and how long it lasted. Those indications of time are not at all uncommon in biblical narrative, and are particularly evident in the story of Noah and the Flood (Gen 6–8).
>
> Most of the dates in the narrative refer to the 600th year of Noah. The flood began on the seventeenth day of the second month (7:11) and the earth became completely dry on the twenty-seventh day of the second month one year later (8:14). The flood lasted 365 days, or one solar year in total. On the seventeenth day of the seventh month, exactly five months into the flood, the ark rested on the mountains of Ararat (8:4). The mountain tops were seen on the first day of the tenth month (8:5). On the first day of the first month (in the 601st year), exactly three months later, the waters had dried from the ground (8:13).
>
> In addition to dates, periods of time are also mentioned. The flood began seven days after God had commanded Noah to enter the ark with his family and all the animals (7:10). It rained for forty days (7:12, 17) and the waters prevailed for 150 days (7:24;

---

24. Ibid., 163, 167.

8:3). Noah opened the window of the ark forty days after the mountain tops had become visible (8:6). Noah waited seven days (twice) until he sent the dove out again (8:10, 12). This gives us the following scheme of periods of time:

A 7 days
   B 40 days
      C 150 days
   B 40 days
A 7 days[25]

"Another example of temporal structure can be found in the Book of Judges, where periods of distress and warfare are separated by spells of peace and quiet, lasting forty years each (once eighty years) (Judg 2:11, 30, 31; 8:28)."[26]

In this case, *chronological time* (my emphasis) is the basis for the structural analysis.

Example 9

(4) *The level of conceptual content*
On this level the analysis of structure is based on the themes of the narrative units or the *ideas* contained therein. Themes and ideas are closely related. *But themes are usually formulated in the form of short phrases, ideas in the form of complete sentences.* Themes define the central issues of the narrative. They [themes] are embodied in the various narrative elements discussed before and serve as their focal point and as a unifying and integrating principle. Ideas are the meanings and lessons contained in the narratives, their message or "philosophy." In the majority of cases neither themes nor ideas are stated explicitly. They are implied in the narrative and have to be abstracted by interpretation.

A basic theme to be discerned in 1 Samuel and functioning as a cornerstone of its structure is the transference of leadership—from Eli to Samuel, from Samuel to Saul, and from Saul to David. The process is carried out smoothly and harmoniously in the case of Eli; it is accompanied by discord and conflict in the case of Samuel; and it leads to outbreaks of violence and undisguised hostility in the case of Saul. This theme is a determining factor in the overall composition of the book. The book can be divided

---

25. Bar-Efrat, "Observations," 168.
26. Ibid., 167–68.

roughly into three parts. The first quarter (chapters 1–7) deals with Eli and Samuel, the second quarter (chapters 8–15) with Samuel and Saul, while the third and fourth quarters of the book (chapters 16–31) are devoted to Saul and David. The theme mentioned is accompanied of course by other themes.

Another example can be found in the narratives of David, Bathsheba and Uriah (2 Sam 11), Amnon and Tamar (2 Sam 13), Absalom's rebellion (2 Sam 15–19) and Adonijah's attempt at the throne (1 Kgs 1–2). These four narratives are brought into close relationship by means of a thematic structure which is shared by all of them. Just as in the case of David sexual offence is followed by murder, so in the case of Amnon, Absalom, and to a certain extent Adonijah too, sexual offense is followed by murder:

David x Bathsheba	—killing of Uriah
Amnon x Tamar	—killing of Amnon
Absalom x David's concubines	—killing of Absalom
(Adonijah x Abishag) [emphases all mine]27	—killing of Adonijah

The *content/idea (killing)* (my emphasis) is the basis for this structural analysis.

Every narrative has a message, a main idea it wants to communicate. Each narrative structure has a focus point, and the main idea of the narrative is identifiable through this focus point.

"A word of warning should be uttered here. Since themes or ideas are not stated overtly, but have to be extracted by means of interpretation, one should exercise a good deal of self-restraint and self-criticism before proceeding to the delineation of thematic or ideational structures... So in order to steer clear of undue arbitrariness themes and ideas should be borne out by the facts of the narrative as clearly and unambiguously as possible. Also, vague and general formulations should be avoided."28

It is important to note that the structure uncovered in the narratives above is based on a very limited number of combined narrative constituents, not more than three, which are found *throughout the narrative* and in *all the units of the structure*. This conforms to the concern expressed by Bar-Efrat who remarks "what should be avoided, however, is the mixing of miscellaneous elements. It is definitely undesirable to

---

27. Ibid., 168–69.
28. Ibid., 169–70.

base the structural analysis partly on verbal elements, partly on elements of technique, and partly on characters, on events, on themes, or on other varieties of narrative or conceptual content."[29]

It will be observed that the elements of the structure, or narrative constituents identified above are repeated in the narrative text. When these elements are identified and marked, the structure of the narrative emerges. The discussion here is represented diagrammatically below:

RELATIONSHIP BETWEEN NARRATIVE TEXT

AND

NARRATIVE STRUCTURE

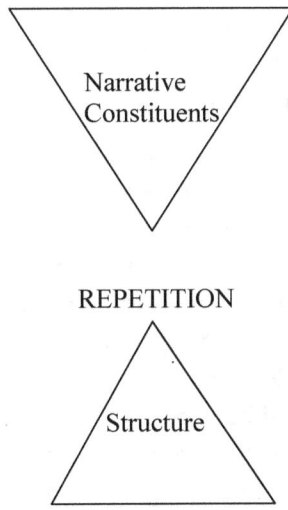

This discussion and analysis of Bar-Efrat's examples demonstrates a very close link between narrative structure, narrative constituents, and repetition in a narrative text, illustrating that a text is not a disorganized collection of words in sentences and paragraphs. Moreover, it shows that by marking and labeling the narrative constituents repeated in the text, the structure of the narrative can become clear. In the words of Trible, "only the ipsissima verba [narrative constituents] of the text can yield the structure."[30]

29. Ibid., 172; cf. Fokkelman, *Reading*, 118.
30. Trible, *Criticism*, 105.

Based on this discussion of the link between Bar-Efrat's elements of structure and the general description of narrative in literature, a close link emerges between narrative constituents and narrative structure, and we can say that a narrative text is: a piece of writing (written text) in which narrative constituents are used by the story teller (narrator) in various ways, through repetition, to create a story.

REPETITION AND STRUCTURE

Repetition is universally recognized as a dominant constituent of Old Testament narratives, and any type of communication, whether oral or written, must be structured if it is to have meaning and make sense. It follows then that the elements of repetition and structure are indispensable for meaningful communication, whether oral or written. The basis for this dominance is explored below.

1. *The Dominance of Repetition*

When we read Old Testament stories we come across the phenomenon of repetition. The simplest reason for this is the dominance of narrative material in the Bible as a whole. Some estimates put it at 75 percent of the Bible. Trible speaks about "repetition as a prominent feature of Hebrew rhetoric."[31] Sometimes a story is repeated more than twice, for example, the deception of a foreign ruler is repeated three times in Genesis: 12, 20, and 26. Moreover, words, phrases, sentences, and complete paragraphs are also often repeated within stories.

Rauber, quoted by Ryken, remarks, "more and more I become convinced that the great key to the reading of Hebraic literature is sensitivity to pattern; [while Ryken himself says that] much of the pattern of Biblical narrative consists of repetition."[32] Parunak writes, "the study of literary architecture [structure] is, in simplest terms, the study of patterns of repetition in a text."[33] Borgman states, "Genesis is a narrative that relies on ancient story-telling techniques of repetition. Miss the repetition; miss the story—and any chance of objectivity. From echoing word sounds to parallelism and double episodes, Genesis plays very se-

---

31. Ibid., 28–29.
32. Ryken, *Words*, 47.
33. Parunak, "Axioms," 4.

riously with the possibilities of repetition. Herein lays a buried treasure of meaning and disclosure of character, including God's."[34]

What is said about Genesis applies to narrative in the Old Testament in general. Although repetition is found from the smallest linguistic unit to the larger units, for example: panels, repetition usually occurs on the narrative-constituent level of the text, both in episodes and scenes.

Fokkelman[35] points out that repetition is not just dominant, but varied too. Writers use repetition with variation and in a number of different ways by employing literary techniques and devices such as foreshadowing, parallelism, echoing, the doublet, back-flash, type-scenes, anaphora, anadiplosis, allusions, chiasm, inclusio, alliteration, and refrain, to name a few. The common denominator in all these devices is repetition; and they are variations of repetition. These devices are found in abundance in stories, which underscores the point that repetition is a dominant feature of Old Testament narrative. Moreover, repetition is used in Hebrew narrative on two levels: stylistic and organizational or compositional. Some of the types of repetition mentioned by Fokkelman (1999) are stylistic, for example, anaphora, anadiplosis, allusions, back-flash, foreshadowing, alliteration, and refrains, and others are organizational, for example, chiasm and inclusio. This begs the question: why is repetition so dominant in biblical narrative?

The prominence of repetition in Old Testament narrative could be related to its temporal / historical nature; it is about both the past and the future. A brief look at the term "history" will help to demonstrate this point.

History as an academic discipline has basically two meanings: history as *the past* and history as *a record of the past*. Bebbington writes:

> a visitor to the Tower of London may well buy a copy of its history. When "history" is used in this way it means something different from "history" in the claim that history repeats itself. A history of the Tower of London is written history, *a record of the past*. The history that may or may not repeat itself, on the other hand, is *the past itself*, not a record of what really happened. In the English language the word "history" can mean either what people write about of time gone by, that is *historiography*; or else it can mean what people have done or suffered, that is *the historical process* . . . about how such works as a history of the

---

34. Borgman, *Genesis*, 18.
35. Fokkelman, *Reading*, 112.

Tower are written as well as about the great configurations that has been discerned in the past ... the grand patterns of history [my emphasis].³⁶

We can sum up these two definitions of the word history as preserving time and the past and "abolishing" time and the past. "Abolishing" is used here in the sense of transcending, going beyond time and the past. We can think about the past as repeated, on the one hand, and the past as static or fixed, on the other hand. The two interpretations of history stated above are explained by Kawin as follows: historical events are normally viewed as those events which can be described as unique events,

> ... those "once in a lifetime," extraordinary, unrepeatable experiences that we consider the true or interesting material of our life histories ... Our belief is in history, the recording of unique events occurring in linear time—time, that is, which moves from time-point A to time-point A+1 to time-point A+2 ... without doubling back [or repeating itself], and which can conveniently be organized into past, present, and future. Events [that are not unique] do not seem worth recording; in fact hardly seem worth noticing. We rest secure in the uniqueness of our experience and identity ... What is true, however, is that many of the experiences we call extraordinary [i.e., unique and unrepeatable] take on their personal importance [i.e., become repeatable] either because they approximately repeat earlier experiences, or because they fulfill earlier expectations long rehearsed in fantasy; so that in both instances an event may have an air of familiarity about it even as it is occurring [cf. the expression Déjà vu].³⁷

The implication is that what is thought to be a unique event is in fact a repetitive event. For example, in 1994 Nelson Mandela became the first black president of South Africa. This was described as a unique and historic event because South Africa was a country governed by a white minority. Then in 2009, Barack Obama became the first black president of the United States of America, which was also described as a unique and historic event, because the country, which has a white majority, has never had a black president. Yet these "unique" events have a repetitive dimension: "what is true ... is that [both these events] ... take on their uniqueness and historical importance in that they repeat earlier

---

36. Bebbington, *Patterns*, 1, 17.
37. Kawin, *Telling It*, 1–2.

experiences, or because they fulfill earlier expectations long rehearsed."[38] The point is that Barack Obama becoming the first black president of America is a repetition of Nelson Mandela becoming the first black president of South Africa. Moreover, their uniqueness lies in the fact that *each event has meaning and significance for a particular group of people in the present.*

The historic uniqueness of an event therefore lies not in its unrepeatableness, but in its significance, and the scope of that significance. The wider the scope and reach of the significance, the more unique, and therefore more historic, the event is. Put differently, the greater the number of people for whom the event has significance and meaning, the more unique the event, and the greater the historic nature of the event. This is the second meaning of the term history; an "abolishing" of the past through repetition. The word "abolishing" is in quotation marks because repetition does not literally abolish the past, it brings the past into the present, decreasing the "pastness" of the past so that an event that happened is no longer stuck in the past; the event moves on to the present through repetition.

The first meaning of "history" is encapsulated in the axiom "the only thing we learn from history is that we never learn from history," that is, history (the past) is preserved through repetition. This is the everyday meaning of history. It is in this sense that history has a profound effect on life, as Kawin comments: "life takes its tone and character from repetition . . . Every day the sun comes up, stays up, goes down. We experience this cycle of light and warmth 26,000 times in an average lifetime, and find that not enough. What is more important for our purposes here: we do not find the cycle boring. It has rhythmic sympathy with the way we function. It is important. It is dependable. It is like us."[39] Repetition makes the past present, preserving history.

Old Testament narratives demonstrate both these senses of history, because time is an important part of literature and repetition is a very important device for time in literature. Events encountered in Old Testament narratives are historical, especially in the first sense of the word. These stories are not just a record of past events, but repetitions of the past as a written record of a *historical process*. The moment the historical process is repeated by memory or recall, orally narrated or

38. Ibid., 2.
39. Ibid., 1–3.

written down, it becomes a record of a historical process. Without this repetition, an event remains a mere occurrence or happening. Since Old Testament narratives share in this understanding of history, it is not surprising to find that they are dominated by repetition. It is this element of repetition that gives the narratives their temporal and historical dimension. The relationship between repetition and time accounts for the dominance of repetition in biblical narratives and which makes them historical in both senses of the word mentioned above. In literature, time and repetition are closely related because time shares three important attributes with repetition: *directionality, duration,* and the *causal ordering of events.* In this regard, Kawin remarks, "clearly repetition is felt to have the power to negate time just as it has the power to punctuate, create, or transfigure time. Its very quality of being *the same thing again* makes us doubt that this thing was ever not here or that there was ever any time in which it could have not been here" (my emphasis).[40]

Simplistically, one could say: *events plus time plus repetition is history.* Hahn writes "for the Israelite, time and history were inseparably connected. Time interested him only in so far as it was qualified by a particular event. This is the case above all with regards to Yahweh's dealings with his people or their representatives."[41]

Moreover, repetition makes it possible to re-experience the past. Thus the past becomes meaningful and relevant in the present.[42] This is important, especially for biblical narrative which has a theological dimension, dealing with the God who created time, is outside time, enters and acts in time, and who speaks with and to every generation. Repetition implodes the past, disorganizing past-present-future and making the story a present experience. Repetition is a key entry point to the narrative, as one of the main ways in which the writer structures a story[43] is through repetition, and structure is essential to meaningful communication.

As discussed earlier, biblical narratives in general and Old Testament narratives in particular are narrations of past events, occurring in time. In this regard, Long commenting on Robert Scholes's multi-choice test for defining a story, says "we can try to answer this question by first

---

40. Ibid., 104.
41. Hahn, "Time," 841.
42. Kawin, *Telling It*, 90-94; Judges 2:6–10.
43. Kawin, *Telling It*, 1–7, 104; Kubler, *Shape of Time*, 13–24, 71–77, 96–122.

asking what is it about the narrative that signals to us as readers that it is a miniature story? First, it involves the passing of time. A story is not like a still life painting . . . because [something] happens . . . there is movement [events] through time."[44] This is true of biblical narratives too. The narration that happens is about events inside time, but also outside of time, as it transcends time. For example, primordial time, which occurs in the Genesis stories. Against this background, we can say that *repetition underscores the historical nature of Old Testament narratives.* Therefore the study, analysis, exegesis, and interpretation of Old Testament narrative requires paying serious attention to the historical dimension of the narrative, which means paying serious attention to repetition in Old Testament narratives.

2. The Importance of Structure for Communication

Literature speaks! It was, is, and will continue to be created and preserved for the purpose of communication. And of crucial importance to literature's ability to communicate is *structure*. In this study, structure refers to the surface structure of the literary text. So structure is inherent to all forms of oral and written communication because it gives communication *coherence*[45] and coherence is crucial for understanding. This is true of both oral and written communication. The basic types of structures we find in biblical narrative (linear, chiastic, concentric, ring, and parallel) perform this function, be it in the whole narrative, the episode, the narrative unit, or narrative cycles.

Ancient Near Eastern and Mediterranean societies were oral societies. Transmission and communication of cultural folklore took place orally, even when it was in written form. Structure played an important role in Near Eastern and Mediterranean literature, and its use in the exegesis and interpretation of literary texts is ancient. It has been used for the study of both biblical and classical literature for more than 100 years,[46] which underscores the importance of structure. Sailhamer says that one difference between a text and a non-text is "texts are made of words, phrases, clauses, sentences, paragraphs, and the like—that is, texts are composed of language. They are *structured . . .*" (my emphasis).[47]

44. Kawin, *Telling It*, 70.
45. Erickson, *Beginner's Guide*, 56–68, 82–85.
46. Talbert, *Patterns, Themes and Genre*.
47. Sailhamer, *Pentateuch*, 8.

Regarding language, structure involves the choice and *ordering* of words in sentences, and when applied to narratives it refers to the ordering "*of events in stories*" (my emphasis).[48] The reference to "arrangements of literary components" and the "ordering . . . of events in stories" refers to Stylistics (the old term for literary structure). And because Old Testament narratives are largely based on oral tradition, it is therefore not surprising that the discussion on structure above applies to these narratives too.

3. *The Interrelation between Structure and Repetition*

The English word structure comes from the Latin noun *structura*, which derives from the verbal forms *structus* and *struere*—which refer to the acts of "scattering," "piling up," or "to build." The English words structure and strew are closely linked to these Latin terms.[49]

The concepts of time and space are basic to the words structure and strew. Rowe says[50] "in modern thought after Kant and Einstein, it is impossible to think *space* apart from some form of *temporality*. Virtually every twentieth-century theorist uses 'structure' as a key term to recognizes the interrelation of time and space as fundamental to the concept of structurality." Along with *time and space, activity* is also intrinsic to the concept of structure. When structuring happens, an activity takes place in time and involves the occupation or extension of space. The difference between "structure" and "scatter" lies in the space that is involved. In "scatter" there is a relationship between pre-existing space and what is scattered, whereas in structure the elements each "constitute their own self-subsisting space." In scattering, the elements need not belong to the same set, while in structure they must belong to the same set. In the example: "I scatter my thoughts to the wind," thoughts (mental) and wind (nature) are different sets. In the example "the stones of this building," stones and building belong to the same set. Based on this distinction, Rowe theorizes "that 'structure' suggests an abstract conception of temporality, albeit capable of very specific applications to historical circumstances, whereas 'strew' depends upon a specific temporal act that can be imitated but not repeated." Thus "structure" can be repeated

---

48. Ibid., 8.
49. Rowe, "Structure," 23.
50. Ibid., 24.

and "strew" can be imitated, but not repeated. This concept of structure is the foundation of structuralism. The term "structure" in structuralism can be defined as follows, "... a set of *relations* among *elements* shaped by a *historical* situation" (my emphasis).[51] This concept of structure has been influential in European structuralism, which in turn impacted a number of disciplines like linguistics, anthropology, and sociology. It was also used for literature in general, including Old Testament narrative literature, despite the fact that the Old Testament is historical and theological in nature too.

When the term *structure* is applied to Old Testament narrative literature, the four basic elements: *activity, time, space, and repeatability* are present and interrelating. This is evident from descriptions of structure applied to biblical narrative by scholars. For example, Bar-Efrat writes, "structure can be defined as the network of relations among the parts of an object or a unit."[52] Conradie, in discussing the disciplines that study the literary aspects of the text says of style that it "can be defined as the artistic choice and *arrangement of literary components*" (my emphasis).[53] I use the phrase narrative constituents for Conradie's literary components.

The question of how repetition is utilized to give structure to a narrative, episode, or narrative unit in Old Testament narrative literature is an important one. Because written narrative is structured in order to be meaningful, and repetition is inherent in the concept of structure, repetition obviously plays an important part in narrative structuration. Old Testament narrative is given structure through the repetition of the basic narrative constituents time, place (space/geography), character, action (events), content, dialogue, and language.[54] So the main function of repetition in biblical narrative is *structuration*. "Repetition helps listeners perceive literary structure ... much of the repetitiveness in biblical literature serves to create such structural schemes..."[55] And Kawin says that "... repetition with variation serves to emphasize, echo, label, abstract from, falsify, and *organize past experience*" (my emphasis).[56]

51. Rowe, "Structure," 1995:25.
52. Bar-Efrat, "Observations," 155.
53. Ibid., 115.
54. Miller, "Narrative," 75; Brink, *Vertelkunde*, 38; Ryken, *Words*, 53; Arp, *Story and Structure*, v-vi; Marguerat and Bourquin, *How To*, 15–16; Amit, *Reading*, 46.
55. Dorsey, *Literary Structure*, 43; Parunak, "Axioms," 4.
56. Kawin, *Telling It*, 90.

Trible quotes Toni Craven, who says that the book of Judith "is structured along the lines of a Hebrew narrative with repetition serving as the cornerstone of its composition."[57] Biblical storywriters used repetition to give effect to that element that is inherent and key to all forms of communication: structure. In this way they help the reader to grasp the message and meaning of what they have written.

The structure of Old Testament narratives can be revealed by a technique called matching units, based on the repetition of narrative constituents, which results in a narrative text divided into units or paragraphs. Parunak's third axiom for literary architecture states that "biblical writers wrote in paragraphs."[58] Dorsey, writes "any piece of literature written or oral is made up of a number of parts, or units, that constitute the basic building blocks of the composition."[59] Repetitions of narrative constituents occurring in narrative material are marked and labeled, which divides the narrative into units. When the labeled narrative units that match each other are linked, the narrative structure is uncovered.

But repetition performs another important interpretive function. It connects the past with the present and the future; it enables the story to speak from the past, into the present and to look forward to the future. This function of repetition fits into the concept of time in ancient Mediterranean societies. In these societies, time was not conceived as chronological time, but rather as "event time,"[60] this means that something happens when the time is right; it happens when it happens and the right time is the time it happens (see Galatians 4:4–5). This understanding of time meant that ancient Mediterranean societies focused on the present time (see Matthew 6:25–34). The people are people of the present. As Malina et al. says,

> Mediterranean man was therefore someone who strongly bound himself to the present. That was most important. Then the past followed. The past, however, directly influenced the present. Only after that the future became relevant, when the emphasis would be place even more on the past . . . The past was the testing ground for the present . . . [the past] determined his present and bore him into the future . . . the past has to clarify what hap-

---

57 Trible, *Rhetorical Criticism*, 36, n. 29.

58. Parunak, "Axioms," 5; Parunak, "Techniques," 526–27.

59. Dorsey, *Literary Structure*, 16.

60. Malina et al., *Time Travel*, 97.

pens in the present . . . If something happens now, the past is the framework within which the present can and must be explained.[61]

Given this understanding of time, it is not surprising that both *repetition* and *narrative* dominated communication in ancient Near Eastern societies, and therefore the Old Testament.

By connecting the story with the past, present, and future, repetition gives the story what Borgman[62] calls an "organic unity"; it gives it coherence and organization, making the story hang together from beginning to end. And very importantly, the organic unity that characterizes the story as a result of repetition helps to unlock the meaning of the story, as structure and meaning are closely linked. Deist, in talking about the composition and structuring of Genesis remarks, "there is an obvious attempt to give the divine addresses their own structure, so that an extra layer of meaning is subtly written into the narrative . . . The 'concealed' structure of the divine addresses forms part of the narration technique employed in the Hexateuch and shapes the meaning of the narrative."[63]

So, by helping to uncover the structure of the narrative, repetition serves the very important function of making the message and meaning of the narrative clear.

Finally, the dominant presence of repetition in the Old Testament stories means that these narratives are characterized by two elements: things stay *the same* and yet things *change*; the interplay between sameness and change makes the story the ideal vehicle for human transformation.[64] This interplay not only enables the readers to identify the structure of the story, but also allows them to identify with the story, see themselves in the story, and make the story their own. Structure gives the sense of something that is fixed and immoveable, and repetition gives it movement, breathing life into structure.

A STRUCTURED-REPETITION APPROACH

Based on this concept, I have developed a structured-repetition approach to Old Testament narrative texts. The approach is delineated below.

---

61. Ibid., 101–3.
62. Borgman, *Genesis*, 17, 14–15.
63. Bosman et al., *Story-Tellers*, 14, 15.
64. Borgman, *Genesis*, 19–21.

1. Determine the limits of the narrative: establish where the narrative begins and ends.

   Details in the narrative determine the beginning and ending. This step in the process is known as closure. It is very important because it has a huge influence on the meaning and message of the narrative. Dorsey[65] describes some helpful techniques used by biblical writers to determine closure.

2. Identify and mark the narrative constituent(s) repeated in the narrative text.

   To identify and mark the narrative constituent(s), the text is read a number of times. As the narrative is read, a narrative constituent(s) will begin to stand out because it is repeated. The narrative constituents that would normally be repeated are: time, space (place, geography), character, speech/dialogue, action (event), an idea, a word, phrase (language), because these are the primary narrative constituents of an Old Testament narrative text. The narrative constituent identified in this way is then marked wherever it recurs or is repeated in the narrative text. A narrative structure with a "high degree of probability and convincing power" should not be based on more than three narrative constituents.[66] What is involved in marking the narrative text for the purpose of narrative structure is ". . . the necessity to single out among a multitude of diverse phenomena those elements with which a significant structure can be realised."[67] And because a choice must be made from a "multitude of diverse phenomena" using narrative constituents to identify and determine narrative structure, further ensures that a highly probable and convincing narrative structure is the end result. For the purposes of marking the narrative constituent(s), a legend is developed.[68] For the purpose of marking the text we will make use of italics.

---

65. Dorsey, *Literary Structure*, 21–23.
66. Bar-Efrat, "Observations," 172–73.
67. Ibid., 169–70.
68. See Trible, *Rhetorical Criticism*, 32–38, 105, 129, 140, 142.

Introduction to the Structured-Repetition Approach

3. After completing the marking, a note explaining the marking process is written at the end of the marked narrative text.
4. The marked narrative units are now labeled A, B, C, D, E, etc., or in terms of the marking legend developed (see Example 1, pp. 4–5). For the purpose of marking the text, a narrative unit will constitute a half-verse, verse, or number of verses (v/vv). The label is written at the top of the marked unit.
5. The narrative units (i.e., vv) which match each other are given the same label.
6. The result of 4–5 above is the division of the narrative text into units (vv) labeled A, B, C, D, E, etc. The labeled narrative passage is set out in the form of a diagram that represents the structure of the narrative text.
7. The diagrammatic structure has the following format:
    7.1 The narrative units resulting from 4–5 above are written down chronologically.
    7.2 A label is written in front of the verse(s) making up the narrative unit.
    7.3 A phrase summarizing the content of the verse(s) are written next to the narrative unit.
8. The focus point of the narrative structure is marked in bold.

    This approach has good potential for sermon crafting. To realize these possibilities, attention must be given to the steps listed below.

9. Once the structure has been outlined as set out in 1–8 above, the next phase in the process can begin, which is the *exegesis and interpretation* of the structure:
    9.1 The structure is described briefly.
    9.2 Exegesis of the focus point is completed, which is summarized in a main point.
    9.3 Exegesis of the remaining narrative units is completed and summarized in a main point.
    9.4 All the main points are written down chronologically.
    9.5 The exegetical idea is formulated by summarizing all the main points using the past tense.

- 9.6 The theological idea is formulated using the exegetical idea and writing it in the present tense.
- 9.7 The preaching idea is formulated using the theological idea and writing it in language that is situation specific and contemporary.

10. Transition to the sermon

- 10.1 A decision is made about which sermon format will be used for the sermon. (For example, didactic, third person narrative, first person narrative, frame-story, and story-response; see chapter 7.)
- 10.2 The transition from the exegetical task to the homiletic task is the movement from exegesis to interpretation to application, showing the relevance for the listener through the use of personal and contemporary language. The exegetical content is not merely copied over to the sermon, but is rather rewritten in personal and contemporary language and based on how it will be presented or preached. The rewriting process conforms to the person's preaching style. This stage of the process leaves a lot of room for creativity and personal style.

In the rewriting process, the interrelationship between the exegetical idea, the focus point, and the main points are examined. Careful attention is given to the manner in which the focus point and the main points develop the exegetical idea. The question should be asked: what contribution do the focus point and the main points make to the development of the exegetical idea? Does each of the main points develop a particular aspect of the exegetical idea? Mathewson[69] is helpful in this regard.

---

69. Mathewson, *Art*, 93.

2

The Process of Uncovering the Structure of a Narrative Text

INTRODUCTION

CHAPTER 1 INTRODUCED THE structured–repetition approach and demonstrated the very close link between narrative constituents, repetition, and structure using Simon Bar-Efrat's[1] examples. In addition, it was demonstrated that the four levels identified by Bar-Efrat correspond to the basic narrative constituents of biblical stories found in many definitions of narrative.

This chapter explains the process of uncovering the structure of a narrative text based on the approach presented in this book. A few passages from the book of Judges are used to show that by identifying and marking the narrative constituents repeated in a text via bold italics, narrative units are formed. The narrative units are then labeled. The narrative units with the same labels are called matching units,[2] which lead to the uncovering of the narrative structure.

Bar-Efrat comments on the structural analysis of 2 Samuel 17:8–13: "in this example the analysis is based on verbal and thematic elements. These reinforce each other, thus providing a firm foundation for the analysis. But structural analysis may very well be based on one type of element only and yet have a high degree of plausibility. What should be avoided, however, is the mixing of miscellaneous elements. It is definitely undesirable to base the structural analysis partly on verbal elements, partly on elements of technique, and partly on character, on events, on

---

1. Bar-Efrat, "Observations," 154–79.
2. Dorsey, *Literary Structure*, 32.

these, or on other varieties of narrative or conceptual content."[3] The examples used in this chapter practically affirm the wisdom of this advice and provide a firm foundation for a sound structural analysis of Old Testament narrative.

Passages were randomly selected to illustrate the process. The words representing the narrative constituents in the text are marked with bold italics.

Uncovering of the Structure of a Narrative Text or Narrative Unit

∽ JUDGES 9:8–15

1. Narrative Passage

> [8] The trees once went forth to anoint a king over them. And they said to the olive tree, "Reign over us!"
> [9] But the olive tree said to them, "Should I cease giving my oil, With which they honor God and men, And go to sway over trees?"
> [10] Then the trees said to the fig tree, "You come and reign over us!"
> [11] But the fig tree said to them, "Should I cease my sweetness and my good fruit, And go to sway over trees?"
> [12] Then the trees said to the vine, "You come and reign over us!"
> [13] But the vine said to them, "Should I cease my new wine, Which cheers both God and men, And go to sway over trees?"
> [14] Then all the trees said to the bramble, "You come and reign over us!"
> [15] And the bramble said to the trees, "If in truth you are anointing me as king over you, Then come and take shelter in my shade; But if not, let fire come out of the bramble And devour the cedars of Lebanon!"

2. Identifying and Marking Narrative Constituents

A

[8] The ***trees*** once went forth to anoint a king over them.
And they ***said to the olive tree***, "Reign over us!"
[9] But ***the olive tree said*** to them, "Should I cease giving my oil, With which they honor God and men, And go to sway over trees?"

---

3. Bar-Efrat, "Observations," 172.

B

¹⁰ Then ***the trees said to the fig tree***, "You come and reign over us!"
¹¹ But ***the fig tree said*** to them, "Should I cease my sweetness and my good fruit, And go to sway over trees?"

C

¹² Then ***the trees said to the vine***, "You come *and* reign over us!"
¹³ But ***the vine said*** to them, "Should I cease my new wine, Which cheers both God and men, And go to sway over trees?"

D

¹⁴ Then ***all the trees said to the bramble***, "You come *and* reign over us!"
¹⁵ And ***the bramble said*** to the trees, "If in truth you anoint me as king over you, Then come and take shelter in my shade; But if not, let fire come out of *the bramble* And devour the cedars of Lebanon!"

Note:
1. The narrative constituent(s) is marked in **italics**.
2. The marking of this passage is based on the narrative constituents of *character* and *speech*.
3. There are no matching units.

3. Structure

Linear Structure

A vv8–9		The olive tree turns down the invitation to reign over the trees
B vv10–11		The fig tree turns down the invitation to reign over the trees
C vv12–13		The vine turns down the invitation to reign over the trees
D vv14–15		***The bramble tree accepts the invitation to reign over the trees***[4]

---

4. The bold unit is the Focus Point of the structure.

From Story Interpretation to Sermon Crafting

∽ Judges 11:4–11

1. Narrative Passage

> ⁴ It came to pass after a time that the people of Ammon made war against Israel.
> ⁵ And so it was, when the people of Ammon made war against Israel that the elders of Gilead went to get Jephthah from the land of Tob.
> ⁶ Then they said to Jephthah, "Come and be our commander that we may fight against the people of Ammon."
> ⁷ So Jephthah said to the elders of Gilead, "Did you not hate me, and expel me from my father's house? Why have you come to me now when you are in distress?"
> ⁸ And the elders of Gilead said to Jephthah, "That is why we have turned again to you now, that you may go with us and fight against the people of Ammon, and be our head over all the inhabitants of Gilead."
> ⁹ So Jephthah said to the elders of Gilead, "If you take me back home to fight against the people of Ammon, and the Lord delivers them to me, shall I be your head?"
> ¹⁰ And the elders of Gilead said to Jephthah, "The Lord will be a witness between us, if we do not do according to your words."
> ¹¹ Then Jephthah went with the elders of Gilead, and the people made him head and commander over them; and Jephthah spoke all his words before the Lord in Mizpah.

2. Identifying and Marking Narrative Constituents

A

⁴ ***It came to pass after a time*** that the people of Ammon made war against Israel.
⁵ ***And so it was***, when the people of Ammon made war against Israel that the elders of Gilead went to get Jephthah from the land of Tob.

B

⁶ Then **they said to Jephthah**, "Come and be our commander, that we may fight against the people of Ammon."
⁷ So **Jephthah said to the elders** of Gilead, "Did you not hate me, and expel me from my father's house? Why have you come to me now when you are in distress?"

⁸ And ***the elders of Gilead said to Jephthah***, "That is why we have turned again to you now, that you may go with us and fight against the people of Ammon, and be our head over all the inhabitants of Gilead."
⁹ So ***Jephthah said to the elders of Gilead***, "If you take me back home to fight against the people of Ammon, and the Lord delivers them to me, shall I be your head?"
¹⁰ And ***the elders of Gilead said to Jephthah***, "The Lord will be a witness between us, if we do not do according to your words."

A

¹¹ ***Then Jephthah went*** with the elders of Gilead, and the people made him head and commander over them; and Jephthah spoke all his words before the Lord in Mizpah.

Note:
1. The narrative constituents are marked in **italics**.
2. The marking is based on the narrative constituents of *narrator speech* which is normally past tense description and *character speech / dialogue*.
3. There are two matching units, vv4–5 (A) and v11 (A). Matching units are units which repeats the same narrative constituent(s).

3. Structure

Ring Structure

A vv4–5   Narrator's speech

   B vv6–10   Character speech, in bold italics

A v11   Narrator's speech

∽ Judges 8:22–25

1. Narrative Passage

> ²² Then the men of Israel said to Gideon, "Rule over us, both you and your son, and your grandson also; for you have delivered us from the hand of Midian."
> ²³ But Gideon said to them, "I will not rule over you, nor shall my son rule over you; the Lord shall rule over you."

²⁴ Then Gideon said to them, "I would like to make a request of you, that each of you would give me the earrings from his plunder." For they had gold earrings, because they were Ishmaelites. ²⁵ So they answered, "We will gladly give them." And they spread out a garment, and each man threw into it the earrings from his plunder.

2. Identifying and marking narrative constituents

A

²² Then ***the men of Israel said to Gideon***, "Rule over us, both you and your son, and your grandson also; for you have delivered us from the hand of Midian."

B

²³ But ***Gideon said to them***, "I will not rule over you, nor shall my son rule over you; the Lord shall rule over you."

B

²⁴ Then ***Gideon said to them***, "I would like to make a request of you, that each of you would give me the earrings from his plunder." For they had gold earrings, because they were Ishmaelites.

A

²⁵ So ***they [the men of Israel] answered [said to Gideon]***, "We will gladly give them." And they spread out a garment, and each man threw into it the earrings from his plunder.

Note:
1. The narrative constituents are marked in **italics**.
2. The marking is based on a combination of *characters* and *speech / dialogue*.
3. There are two sets of matching units, v22 (A) and v25 (A); v23 (B) and v24 (B) the first based on the character "men of Israel"; the second based on the character "Gideon."

3. Structure

Chiastic Structure

***A* v22**   Israel invited Gideon to rule over them
    B v23   Gideon refused the invitation

B	v24	Gideon requested jewelry from the people
A	*v25*	The people gave the jewelry asked for by Gideon

∽ JUDGES 9:1–21

1. Narrative Passage

¹ Then Abimelech the son of Jerubbaal went to Shechem, to his mother's brothers, and spoke with them and with all the family of the house of his mother's father, saying,

² "Please speak in the hearing of all the men of Shechem: 'Which is better for you, that all seventy of the sons of Jerubbaal reign over you, or that one reign over you?' Remember that I am your own flesh and bone."

³ And his mother's brothers spoke all these words concerning him in the hearing of all the men of Shechem; and their heart was inclined to follow Abimelech, for they said, "He is our brother."

⁴ So they gave him seventy shekels of silver from the temple of Baal-Berith, with which Abimelech hired worthless and reckless men; and they followed him.

⁵ Then he went to his father's house at Ophrah and killed his brothers, the seventy sons of Jerubbaal, on one stone. But Jotham the youngest son of Jerubbaal was left, because he hid himself.

⁶ And all the men of Shechem gathered together, all of Beth Millo, and they went and made Abimelech king beside the terebinth tree at the pillar that was in Shechem.

⁷ Now when they told Jotham, he went and stood on top of Mount Gerizim, and lifted his voice and cried out. And he said to them: "Listen to me, you men of Shechem, That God may listen to you!

⁸ᵃ The trees once went forth to anoint a king over them.

⁸ᵇ And they [the trees] said to the olive tree, 'Reign over us!'

⁹ But the olive tree said to them, 'Should I cease giving my oil, With which they honor God and men, And go to sway over trees?'

¹⁰ Then the trees said to the fig tree, 'You come and reign over us!'

¹¹ But the fig tree said to them, 'Should I cease my sweetness and my good fruit, And go to sway over trees?'

¹² Then the trees said to the vine, 'You come and reign over us!'

¹³ But the vine said to them, 'Should I cease my new wine, Which cheers both God and men, And go to sway over trees?'

¹⁴ Then all the trees said to the bramble, 'You come and reign over us!'

¹⁵ And the bramble said to the trees, 'If in truth you anoint me as king over you, Then come and take shelter in my shade; But if not, let fire come out of the bramble And devour the cedars of Lebanon!'

¹⁶ Now therefore, if you have acted in truth and sincerity in making Abimelech king, and if you have dealt well with Jerubbaal and his house, and have done to him as he deserves—

¹⁷ for my father fought for you, risked his life, and delivered you out of the hand of Midian;

¹⁸ but you have risen up against my father's house this day, and killed his seventy sons on one stone, and made Abimelech, the son of his female servant, king over the men of Shechem, because he is your brother—

¹⁹ if then you have acted in truth and sincerity with Jerubbaal and with his house this day, then rejoice in Abimelech, and let him also rejoice in you.

²⁰ But if not, let fire come from Abimelech and devour the men of Shechem and Beth Millo; and let fire come from the men of Shechem and from Beth Millo and devour Abimelech!"

²¹ And Jotham ran away and fled; and he went to Beer and dwelt there, for fear of Abimelech his brother.

2. Identifying and Marking Narrative Constituents

A

¹ Then **Abimelech** the son of Jerubbaal went to Shechem, to his mother's brothers, and spoke with them and with all the family of the house of his mother's father, ***saying***,

² "Please speak in the hearing of all the men of Shechem: 'Which is better for you, that all seventy of the sons of Jerubbaal reign over you, or that one reign over you?' Remember that I am your own flesh and bone."

B

³ And **his mother's brothers spoke** all these words concerning him in the hearing of all the men of Shechem; and their heart was inclined to follow Abimelech, for ***they said***, "He is our brother."

⁴ So ***they gave him*** seventy shekels of silver from the temple of Baal-Berith, with which Abimelech hired worthless and reckless men; and they followed him.

⁵ **Then he went** to his father's house at Ophrah and killed his brothers, the seventy sons of Jerubbaal, on one stone. But Jotham the youngest son of Jerubbaal was left, because he hid himself.
⁶ And **all the men of Shechem gathered together**, all of Beth Millo, and they went and made Abimelech king beside the terebinth tree at the pillar that was in Shechem.

A

⁷ Now when they told **Jotham**, he went and stood on top of Mount Gerizim, and lifted his voice and cried out. And **he said to them**: "Listen to me, you men of Shechem, That God may listen to you!
⁸ᵃ The trees once went forth to anoint a king over them.
⁸ᵇ And they [the trees] said to the olive tree, 'Reign over us!'
⁹ But the olive tree said to them, 'Should I cease giving my oil, With which they honor God and men, And go to sway over trees?'
¹⁰ Then the trees said to the fig tree, 'You come and reign over us!'
¹¹ But the fig tree said to them, 'Should I cease my sweetness and my good fruit, And go to sway over trees?'
¹² Then the trees said to the vine, 'You come and reign over us!'
¹³ But the vine said to them, 'Should I cease my new wine, Which cheers both God and men, And go to sway over trees?'
¹⁴ Then all the trees said to the bramble, 'You come and reign over us!'
¹⁵ And the bramble said to the trees, 'If in truth you anoint me as king over you, Then come and take shelter in my shade; But if not, let fire come out of the bramble And devour the cedars of Lebanon!'
¹⁶ Now therefore, if you have acted in truth and sincerity in making Abimelech king, and if you have dealt well with Jerubbaal and his house, and have done to him as he deserves—
¹⁷ for my father fought for you, risked his life, and delivered you out of the hand of Midian;
¹⁸ but you have risen up against my father's house this day, and killed his seventy sons on one stone, and made Abimelech, the son of his female servant, king over the men of Shechem, because he is your brother—
¹⁹ if then you have acted in truth and sincerity with Jerubbaal and with his house this day, then rejoice in Abimelech, and let him also rejoice in you.

²⁰ But if not, let fire come from Abimelech and devour the men of Shechem and Beth Millo; and let fire come from the men of Shechem and from Beth Millo and devour Abimelech!"

B

²¹ And *Jotham ran away and fled; and he went to Beer and dwelt there*, for fear of Abimelech his brother.

Note:
1. The narrative constituents are marked in **italics**.
2. The marking is based on a combination of *characters* and *speech*.
3. Straight narration might include reported speech, which is the case here in the second unit; it is different from direct speech.
4. There is two sets of matching units, vv1–2 (A) and vv7–20 (A) and vv3–6 (B) and v21 (B).

3. Structure

Parallel Structure

Avv1–2   direct speech

   Bvv3–6   straight narrative, including reported speech

Avv7–20   direct speech

   Bv21   straight narrative

~ JUDGES 11:12–27

1. Narrative Passage

> ¹² Now Jephthah sent messengers to the king of the people of Ammon, saying "What do you have against me that you have come to fight against men in my land?"
> ¹³ And the king of the people of Ammon answered the messengers of Jephthah, "Because Israel took away my land when they came up out of Egypt, from the Arnon as far as the Jabbok, and to the Jordan. Now therefore, restore those lands peaceably."
> ¹⁴ So Jephthah again sent messengers to the king of the people of Ammon,
> ¹⁵ and said to him, "Thus says Jephthah: 'Israel did not take away the land of Moab, nor the land of the people of Ammon;

The Process of Uncovering the Structure of a Narrative Text 39

[16] for when Israel came up from Egypt, they walked through the wilderness as far as the Red Sea and came to Kadesh.

[17] Then Israel sent messengers to the king of Edom, saying, 'Please let me pass through your land.' But the king of Edom would not heed. And in like manner they sent to the king of Moab, but he would not consent. So Israel remained in Kadesh.

[18] And they went along through the wilderness and bypassed the land of Edom and the land of Moab, came to the east side of the land of Moab, and encamped on the other side of the Arnon. But they did not enter the border of Moab, for the Arnon was the border of Moab.

[19] Then Israel sent messengers to Sihon king of the Amorites, king of Heshbon; and Israel said to him, 'Please let us pass through your land into our place.'

[20] But Sihon did not trust Israel to pass through his territory. So Sihon gathered all his people together, encamped in Jahaz, and fought against Israel.

[21] And the Lord God of Israel delivered Sihon and all his people into the hand of Israel, and they defeated them. Thus Israel gained possession of all the land of the Amorites, who inhabited that country.

[22] They took possession of all the territory of the Amorites, from the Arnon to the Jabbok and from the wilderness to the Jordan.

[23] And now the Lord God of Israel has dispossessed the Amorites from before His people Israel; should you then possess it?

[24] Will you not possess whatever Chemosh your god gives you to possess? So whatever the Lord our God takes possession of before us, we will possess.

[25] And now, are you any better than Balak the son of Zippor, king of Moab? Did he ever strive against Israel? Did he ever fight against them?

[26] While Israel dwelt in Heshbon and its villages, in Aroer and its villages, and in all the cities along the banks of the Arnon, for three hundred years, why did you not recover them within that time?

[27] Therefore I have not sinned against you, but you wronged me by fighting against me. May the Lord, the Judge, render judgment this day between the children of Israel and the people of Ammon.'"

2. Identifying and Marking the Narrative Constituents

A

¹² Now **Jephthah** sent messengers to the king of the people of Ammon, *saying* "What do you have against me that you have come to fight against men in my land?"

B

¹³ And **the king of** the people of **Ammon answered** the messengers of Jephthah, "Because Israel took away my land when they came up out of Egypt, from the Arnon as far as the Jabbok, and to the Jordan. Now therefore, restore those lands peaceably."

A

¹⁴ So **Jephthah** again sent messengers to the king of the people of Ammon, ¹⁵ and **said to him**, "Thus says Jephthah: 'Israel did not take away the land of Moab, nor the land of the people of Ammon;

¹⁶ for when Israel came up from Egypt, they walked through the wilderness as far as the Red Sea and came to Kadesh.

¹⁷ Then Israel sent messengers to the king of Edom, saying, 'Please let me pass through your land.' But the king of Edom would not heed. And in like manner they sent to the king of Moab, but he would not consent. So Israel remained in Kadesh.

¹⁸ And they went along through the wilderness and bypassed the land of Edom and the land of Moab, came to the east side of the land of Moab, and encamped on the other side of the Arnon. But they did not enter the border of Moab, for the Arnon was the border of Moab.

¹⁹ Then Israel sent messengers to Sihon king of the Amorites, king of Heshbon; and Israel said to him, 'Please let us pass through your land into our place.'

²⁰ But Sihon did not trust Israel to pass through his territory. So Sihon gathered all his people together, encamped in Jahaz, and fought against Israel.

²¹ And the Lord God of Israel delivered Sihon and all his people into the hand of Israel, and they defeated them. Thus Israel gained possession of all the land of the Amorites, who inhabited that country.

²² They took possession of all the territory of the Amorites, from the Arnon to the Jabbok and from the wilderness to the Jordan.

²³ And now the Lord God of Israel has dispossessed the Amorites from before His people Israel; should you then possess it?
²⁴ Will you not possess whatever Chemosh your god gives you to possess? So whatever the Lord our God takes possession of before us, we will possess.
²⁵ And now, are you any better than Balak the son of Zippor, king of Moab? Did he ever strive against Israel? Did he ever fight against them?
²⁶ While Israel dwelt in Heshbon and its villages, in Aroer and its villages, and in all the cities along the banks of the Arnon, for three hundred years, why did you not recover them within that time?
²⁷ Therefore I have not sinned against you, but you wronged me by fighting against me. May the Lord, the Judge, render judgment this day between the children of Israel and the people of Ammon.'"
²⁸ However, the king of the people of Ammon did not heed the words which Jephthah sent him.

Note:
1. The narrative constituents are marked in **italics**.
2. The marking is based on the combination of *characters* and *speech*.
3. There is one set of matching units, v12 (A) and vv14–27 (A).

3. Structure

Ring Structure

A v12   Jepthath's speech
   B v13   **King of Ammon's speech**
A vv14–27   Jepthath's speech

CONCLUSION

The work of Phyllis Trible is an excellent source for examples of marking texts.[5] The narrative constituents of character and speech are the basis for the narrative structures in these examples, but it does not follow that they are the only narrative constituents which are repeated in biblical narratives. The different narrative structures in chapter 4 have a variety of narrative constituents which affirms this point.

---

5. Trible, *Rhetorical Criticism*, 237–44.

Identifying Narrative Closure

The process of uncovering the structure of a narrative passage has been illustrated above. But even before this can be done there is a very important prerequisite, namely, identifying the closure of the narrative, narrative passage, or episode or narrative unit.

The first phase of a structured-repetition approach (as is the case with many other approaches) is identifying where the story or unit begins and where it ends. This is crucial and has serious consequences for narrative structure, exegesis, and interpretation and should therefore be done very carefully. The limit and the scope of the narrative text is determined in this phase. Erickson states, "for responsible exegesis, the crucial thing about pericopes is the proper, fair, and text sensitive identification of their boundaries, their delimitations, both their external and internal delineations. Where does a particular pericope legitimately begin and end?"[6] This holds true for narratives as well.

Establishing the beginning and ending, or the limit of the narrative, is not unique to historical narrative. It applies to all types of literature, including poetic, prophetic, and wisdom, and it is germane to the interpretation of a piece of writing. It helps uncover the narrative structure, episode, or scene of the story.

This process of finding out where the narrative unit begins and ends is known as closure. Dorsey (1999) has an extensive list of indicators that help establish the closure of the story.[7] He groups these under three headings: beginning markers, end markers, and markers indicating the limit of the narrative. Below is a summary of these indicators:

1. Beginning Markers

The writers of Old Testament stories use a variety of literary techniques to indicate to the reader the starting point of the story:

    a. Title or story announcement

    b. Introductory formula

    c. Common beginning words or phrases

    d. Rhetorical question

    e. Imperative (giving of a command/order)

---

6. Erickson, *Beginner's Guide*, 62.
7. Dorsey, *Literary Structure*, 21–22. See also Amit, *Reading*, 37–45.

f. Orientation (background information)
g. Abstract (the opening paragraph that summarizes the whole article in about 150 words)
h. First part of a concentric pattern
i. Shift in time (morning to evening; midday to midnight, first day to second day, thirteenth year to fiftieth year)
j. Shift in place
k. Shift in characters or speaker
l. Shift in theme or topic
m. Shift in genre (change from a travelogue to a genealogy)
n. Shift in speed of action (a new action take place or event happens)
o. Shift from prose to poetry or vice versa
p. Shift in tense, mood, or person of the verbs

2. End Markers

The writers of Old Testament stories use a variety of literary techniques to indicate to the reader the end point of the story:

a. A concluding formula
b. Poetic refrain
c. Summary
d. Conclusion of narrative/unit
e. Last part of inclusion or concentric pattern
f. Flashback
g. Link with the audience's own time
h. Formula: "Says Yahweh"[8]

3. Markers Indicating Narrative Limit

The writers of Old Testament stories use a variety of literary techniques to indicate to the reader the extent, scope, and length of the story:

a. Sameness of time

---

8. Dorsey, *Literary Structure*, 23–24.

- b. Sameness of place
- c. Sameness of participants / characters
- d. Sameness of topic or theme
- e. Sameness of genre
- f. Sameness of narrative technique
- g. Sameness of speed of action
- h. Sameness of literary form (prose, poetry)
- i. Sameness of grammatical / syntactic forms
- j. Concentric pattern
- k. Keyword
- l. Patterned repetition of information
- m. Recurring motif [9]

All of these techniques help the reader determine the closure of the narrative. Chapter 6 has examples of how the closure of the narrative is determined.

---

9. Ibid., 24–25.

3

Other Approaches to Narrative Analysis

INTRODUCTION

IN CHAPTER 2, THE link between narrative constituents and narrative structure was established. Building on this, chapter 3 describes, compares, and discusses a number of approaches used in the analysis of the biblical narrative.

1. Mathewson

Mathewson[1] uses the following steps for narrative analysis:

a. Analyze the *plot (a sequence of events)*, which means identifying the exposition, crisis, resolution, and denouement (conclusion) of the narrative, and also giving attention to literary devices present in the text, such as repetition, time, place, setting, point of view, etc.

b. Create an exegetical outline based on the plot analysis and the insights gathered from studying the literary devices referred to above.

c. Identify and classify the characters and the type of dialogue encountered in the story.

d. Find and formulate the exegetical idea in the story.

e. Develop the exegetical idea of the narrative. The exegetical idea is developed as it is explained, validated, or applied in the narrative. At this point, the actual crafting of the sermon can begin.[2]

---

1. Mathewson, *Art*, 44–90, 126.
2. Ibid., 93–157.

Evaluation: The classic plot refers to the events and actions of the story, which are ordered in a cause-effect relationship in the narrative text and which move from the initial situation of the story through the complication, transformation, and denouement to the final situation. *Action (event)* is the main narrative constituent that shapes and informs the narrative structure. Other narrative constituents (repetition, character, time, space, and place) do not have structuring significance.

2. Chisholm Jr.

Robert Chisholm Jr.[3] proposes an exegetical-literary method. It is described as "an interpretive method that is essentially *synchronic*, but that is also sensitive to the historical and cultural background of the text and respectful of the narrator's authority" (my emphasis).[4] It has the following phases:

a. "Place the text in its historical-cultural and broader literary contexts.

b. "Analyze the basic elements of a story (setting, characterization, plot, and determine how they contribute to its message).

c. "Identify the text's discourse structure, dramatic structure, and other structural features and explain how they contribute to the story's message and impact.

d. "Analyze the narrative's quotations and dialogues with respect to the discourse type and speech function.

e. "Avoid excesses when filling gaps, but do not be afraid to resolve ambiguity.

f. "Respect the authority of the narrator and attempt to identify his assessment of events and characters.

g. "Relate stories to their macro-plot and explain how the differences in a story contribute to its overall message.

h. "Be sensitive to matters of intertextuality and how they contribute to the message of the narrative.

---

3. Chisholm Jr., *Interpreting*, 184–86.
4. Ibid., 184.

i. "Summarize the theme(s) of the story and consider how it contributes to the theme(s) of the book as a whole.

j. "Consider how the story impacted the implied reader(s), given their time, place, and circumstances."

Evaluation: Three references are made to narrative structure, namely, plot, dramatic structure, and discourse structure, which are synonyms. Structure in Chisholm Jr.'s method means the classic-plot structure (see b and c above).

This type of structure has similarities to the approach described in this book, but differs in that it does not integrate the elements of structure, structural features, and the message and meaning of the story in a systematic manner.

3. Long

Thomas Long uses Greimas's actantiel model for the decomposition of biblical narratives, to analyze and interpret biblical narratives for sermon crafting based on narratives. Actantiel refers to a function, action, or role performed in a narrative. The functions are abstract elements, such as objects, helpers, subjects, opponents, etc. Long lists the following steps:

a. Determine the beginning and ending of the narrative unit.

b. Eliminate the elements of the narrative which do not contribute to the analysis of the plot and are therefore extraneous and make unclear elements explicit. "The goal of normalization is to focus the structure analysis upon the genuinely plot-related elements of the narrative and to place the narrative in a form congenial to the discovery of the actant or function relations."[5]

c. Compare the beginning of the narrative with the end of the narrative in order to determine the major transformation which occurs in the narrative.

d. Determine the *actants*.

e. Determine "how the reader is involved in the narrative structure depicted by the grammar"[6] of the narrative, which is through

---

5. Long, *Structure*, 195.
6. Ibid., 208.

identification with a character in the story. The preacher arranges for the text and the congregation to meet; the sermon becomes the meeting place of the text and "congregation in such a way that the 'perspective-changing, faith-producing' power of the text can be experienced at the most strategic points in the life of a specific congregation in quite particular circumstances."[7] Here the sermon is a meeting place. The manner in which this meeting takes place is through the "identification with character" by the congregation; with a narrative character, facilitated by the preacher; in this context a "character is a surface expression of an actantiel element which generates that character"[8] in contrast to the view that sees characters as "real historical people."

f. "Build a bridge between text and sermon. [This is done] by determining the most effective point of character identification for a particular text and congregation; [secondly,] enabling, encouraging and supporting that character identification in the sermon, [and thirdly] illuminating in the sermon the functional role of that character in the narrative . . . so that the way the narrative plot serves to define the character potentially can impact the process of identification."[9]

Evaluation: Long's definition of structure is that of plot-structure, that is, the relationship of the actantiel roles in the narrative text. The "plot is the way the content of the narrative is shaped and the situations of the characters are transformed, and, thus is deeper."[10] This concept of plot here is from the work of Greimas, which is a refinement of Vladimir Propp's idea that the plot of the story is made up of narrative functions. These functions are essential to bring about the transformation that is at the center of the narrative.[11] This is a concept of deep structure, lying below the surface level of the narrative text, as Marguerat and Bourquin remark, "now structuralism is interested in what governs the action in depth and takes place at the higher level of abstraction."[12] This deep-

7. Ibid., 210.
8. Ibid., 217.
9. Ibidl., 224–25.
10. Ibid., 59.
11. Marguerat and Bourquin, *How To*, 62.
12. Ibid., 63.

structure approach is in contrast to our surface-level approach, which focuses on narrative design. The structure analysis is based on the narrative constituents of action and character, which are referred to as actantiel roles. The application of narrative analysis to preaching is similar to the approach presented in this book.

4. Green and Pasquarello III

Green and Pasquarello III's approach[13] is informed primarily by the conviction that the reading of scriptures is not primarily the translation of the ancient meaning into a more contemporary meaning, but is rather the transformation of the readers of scripture, the community of faith, the people of God. Reading scripture is not about mastering the text but about being mastered by the text. One result of this conviction is that the focus of the method brought to the scripture is not of prime importance. The concern is ultimately with the validity of interpretation, which can be accomplished by the following procedure:

a. "Account for the text in its final form.

b. "Account for the text as a whole.

c. "Welcome the 'otherness' of the biblical text and its sociocultural world so that it is able to challenge attitudes and practices we have taken for granted for so long.

d. "Account for the canonical address of the text, particularly with reference to the location of particular biblical witnesses within an all-encompassing story.

e. "Account for the witness of scripture as seen in is effects within and among the community of God's people."

This approach is a critically engaged reading of scripture and it seeks to avoid what Green would regard as a "need to construct a 'technology' of biblical engagement."[14]

Evaluation: Green does not present a particular procedure in line with his belief that there is no need to construct a technology of biblical engagement. However, his definition of narrative suggests that his approach is based on the classic plot structure. He defines narrative as:

---

13. Green and Pasquarello, *Reading, Preaching*, 22–28.
14. Ibid., 25.

Narrative 1 "... a particular form of writing, notoriously difficult to define, but usually regarded as the recounting of one or more real or fictitious *events understood to share a causal relationship* in an array of forms: history writing, epics, novels, ballads, and so on" (my emphasis).[15]

Narrative 2 "... a theological claim about the coherence of the Genesis-Revelation story... which serves as a necessary theological context for interpretation... [which] find its nonnegotiable point of reference in *the purpose and action of God in creation (beginning), redemption (middle), and consummation (end)*" (my emphasis).[16] His aim is to provide a framework in which the New Testament genres can be read as narrative. Understanding narrative in terms of the second definition especially, provides such a framework.

The value of Green's approach lies in the concept of the grand narrative of scripture as the narrative within which each narrative scene, unit, and even "book" should be located. Each of these literary units should be approached hermeneutically with the question: how does each one contribute to and reflect the ways of the working of God in the cosmos; what is its place and role within the grand narrative of scripture?

5. Trible

Trible's[17] approach to narrative analysis is called "biblical rhetorical criticism." Rhetoric is defined as *the art of composition with a focus on structure*. In part two of Trible's book what is learnt about rhetorical criticism in part one, is applied. The book of Jonah is used to illustrate what a biblical rhetorical criticism method looks like. Practical guidelines[18] are given for using the method: "Attend closely to the following features of the text:

   a. "Beginning and ending.

   b. "Repetition of words, phrases, and sentences. As a basic phenomenon in biblical speech, repetition (verbatim or modified) provide the backbone for discerning structures and meaning.

   c. "Discern how narrated discourse and direct discourse interact.

---

15. Ibid., 30.
16. Ibid.
17. Trible, *Rhetorical Criticism*, 32–40, 101–6.
18. Ibid., 102–6.

d. "Design and structure. Much like a building, an individual text has an overall design and numerous sections . . . Describing the architecture is your task.

e. "Plot development. Trace the movement of narratives from their beginning to their ends. Observe how, when, where, and what changes happen: those that work for the movement, those that work against it, and those that seem to make no difference.

f. "Character portrayals. Observe the interaction (or lack thereof) among characters.

g. "Syntax. Note divergence from the usual order of Hebrew syntax. They may signal emphasis or contrast.

h. "Show structure by using the very words of the text in the order they occur.

i. "Devise a series of markers to indicate prominent features of the text, particularly repetition.

j. "[D]escribe in clear prose what the structure diagram shows and interpret both diagram and description.

k. "Correlate your discoveries. How do structural units relate to plot development? Does a particular unit interrupt the narrative flow to slow down action, build suspense, or distract readers? How do narrated introductions to direct discourse affect character portrayals?"

Evaluation: In the eleven features described above, *structure* is referred to three times and *repetition* is referred to three times, which reveals that they are dominant in this approach.

According to Trible, structure is the pattern that results from explicating the inter-connections and associations between words at the surface level of the narrative text. To determine this structure one uses ". . . a standard procedure in rhetorical criticism . . . [employing] a series of markings under words, phrases, and clauses to indicate various connections."[19] Trible clarifies this as follows ". . . *in rhetorical criticism structure presents the ipsissima verba of the text. It shows the patterns of*

---

19. Trible, *Rhetorical Criticism*, 34, 38, 104–5.

relationships residing in the very words, phrases, sentences, and larger units" (my emphasis).[20]

This understanding is very similar to the understanding of structure developed in chapter 1 and illustrated in chapter 2, with a small but important difference: Trible focuses on the ipsissima verba of the text in a general sense, and my focus is on the narrative constituent(s) represented by the ipsissima verba of the text. Structural analysis is understood as the decomposition of the stylistic arrangement of the surface level of the narrative text, and in this regard Trible and the approach presented in this book are similar.

7. Borden

Paul Borden's[21] approach has the following phases:

a. "Closure—determine where the story begins and ends.

b. "Determine the design of the story [see c and h below]; why is the story designed the way it is?

c. "Divide the story into scenes.

d. "List the characters.

e. "Note the action; track how the events unfold [see h below].

f. "Examine any dialogue or discourse present in the narrative to determine its role.

g. "List any narrative comments.

h. "Discover the plot, i.e., events that create disequilibrium, reversal, and resolution.

i. "Examine the tone of the story, that is, what is the world view that informs the story and that is being communicated by the story?

j. "Identify the rhetorical structure of the story [see b and c above].

k. "Gather data from the context, that is, the narratives that precede and follow the narrative being exegeted.

---

20. Ibid., 92.
21. Borden, *Big Idea?* 73–79.

l. "Write a single descriptive sentence for each of the scenes or paragraphs, then write a descriptive sentence for the entire narrative using the sentences of each of the scenes or paragraphs. This latter sentence should reflect the narrator's emphasis in the story.

m. "Identify the subject of the narrative.

n. "Determine what is being said about the subject of the narrative.

o. "Once the subject and the predicate are joined you have the exegetical idea of the narrative."

Evaluation: In Borden's approach, structure plays an important role (see b, c, e, h, and k above), and his approach has a lot in common with the approach presented in this book. There are differences though, the main ones being:

The process is reversed. The analysis is started at j. This decision is informed by communication theory, which maintains that every piece of communication wants to make one main point, or has one main idea and the writer structures the communication in such a way as to communicate this main idea. Each type of rhetorical structure has a focus point, which facilitates the location of the narrator's emphasis and the main point of the narrative, and the formulation of the exegetical idea of the story.

The approach presented in this book uses the information gathered from l to o and describes how to transition from an exegetical idea to the sermon outline. The approach takes Borden's approach a step further and applies it to sermon crafting.

CONCLUSION

This comparison demonstrates the close link between narrative structure and narrative constituents and confirms the theoretical observation derived from the analysis of Bar-Efrat (see chapters 1 and 2) that the story teller or narrator uses narrative constituents to structure the story and the key to the structure of the story is to identify how the story narrator uses the narrative constituents. In comparing these approaches to uncovering the structure of the narrative, it appears that they fall into two categories.

The first category is rooted in the classical model of narrative structure, which has its origin in the *theatre* and has the following elements: exposition—complication—climax or turning point—denouement—ending. In this approach, a story is defined by the fact *that change takes place*.

The second category includes approaches that are derived from communication theory and rhetorical criticism, and which are focused on the surface level of the narrative text. Its focus is the ear, even in written form. In this approach, a story is defined by *an idea, a message, meaning which is to be communicated*.[22]

Yet all the approaches have a number of things in common:

a. They are all based on narrative constituents time, plot, character, place, structure, speech, repetition, action (event), point of view, etc.[23]

b. Two narrative constituents are chosen as the basis of the method, either repetition and action (event), or repetition and character.

c. All the methods uncover structure.

d. All the methods determine the burden, message, and meaning of the narrative.

There are, however, differences between the approaches discussed above and the structured-repetition approach presented in this book:

a. In other approaches, structure is not placed on the foreground as the key to the meaning of the narrative text.

b. In other approaches, repetition does not function as dominantly for determining the structure of the narrative text.

c. In the structured-repetition approach, the presentation of the interaction between the parts of the narrative and the whole narrative in determining the message and meaning of the narrative is set out much more clearly.

The discussion above is presented in the diagram below:

---

22. Brink, *Vertelkunde*, 41.

23. See Amit, *Reading*, 62, who discusses different structural methods, which all demonstrate the interrelationship between narrative constituents and narrative structure.

OTHER APPROACHES

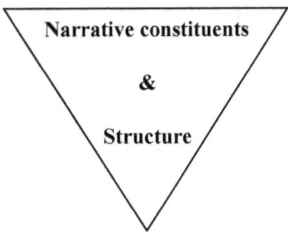

Meaning / Message

STRUCTURED-REPETITION APPROACH

Meaning / message

4

Describing and Illustrating the Five Basic Narrative Structures

INTRODUCTION

HEBREW WRITERS CREATE A variety of narrative structures by repeating narrative constituents. By marking these repetitions, the narrative can be divided into a number of units. The units are then labeled and matched according to the marked narrative constituents. Once the labeled units are linked, the narrative structure is unveiled.

Five basic types of narrative structural patterns are encountered in Old Testament narratives. These are illustrated below using narrative passages from different Old Testament books. The five basic types of narrative structures are:

1. Linear structure: None of the units that make up the narrative structure of the story can be linked or matched with each other. Each unit is independent of the others.

2. Concentric structure: More than one of the narrative units can be linked or matched with each other, and there is one unlinked or unmatched unit.

3. Chiastic structure: More than one of the narrative units can be linked or matched with each other, and there are no unlinked or unmatched units.

4. Parallel structure: There is an alternation of the narrative units that make up the story. Alternate narrative units are linked to or matched with each other.

Describing and Illustrating the Five Basic Narrative Structures

5. Ring structure: One of the narrative units can be linked or matched with one other narrative unit, and there is one unlinked or unmatched unit.

The five basic types of structures can be expanded in an unlimited way in the narrative material of the Old Testament.[1]

The examples that follow illustrate each of the five basic narrative structures.

Linear Structure

~ JOB 1:14–22

1. Marking the Narrative

A

¹⁴And *a messenger came to Job and said,* "The oxen were plowing and the donkeys feeding beside them,
¹⁵ and *the Sabeans attacked and took them.* They also slew the servants with the edge of the sword, and I alone have escaped to tell you."

B

¹⁶ While he was still speaking, *another also came and said, "The fire of God fell from heaven and burned up* the sheep and the servants and consumed them, and I alone have escaped to tell you."

C

¹⁷ While he was still speaking, *another also came and said, "The Chaldeans* formed three bands and *made a raid* on the camels and took them and slew the servants with the edge of the sword; and I alone have escaped to tell you."

D

¹⁸ While he was still speaking, *another also came and said*, "Your sons and your daughters were eating and drinking wine in their oldest brother's house,

---

1. Walsh, *Style and Structure.*

¹⁹ and behold, ***a great wind*** came from across the wilderness and ***struck*** the four corners of the house, and it fell on the young people and they died; and I alone have escaped to tell you."

E

²⁰ ***Then Job arose and tore his robe and shaved his head, and he fell to the ground and worshiped.***
²¹ And ***he said***, "Naked I came from my mother's womb, And naked I shall return there. The Lord gave and the Lord has taken away. Blessed be the name of the Lord."

F

²² Through all this Job did not sin nor did he blame God.

2. Comment

The narrative constituents identified and marked in this narrative are *character, speech, and action* (event).

3. Structure

The structure is based on the labeling of the narrative constituents character, speech, and action (event) as indicated by the bold italics:

A vv13–15	Messenger One: the Sabeans took the oxen and killed the servants	
B v16	Messenger Two: fire from heaven destroyed the sheep and the servants	
C v17	Messenger Three: the Chaldeans took the camels and killed the servants	
D vv18–19	Messenger Four: a great wind destroyed the house and the sons were killed	
E vv20–21	Response of Job: he mourned and worshipped	
F v22	***Narrator's comment: Job did not blame God***	

Describing and Illustrating the Five Basic Narrative Structures

∽ 2 Samuel 13: 1–22

1. Marking the Narrative

A

¹ Now it was after this that Absalom the son of David had a beautiful sister whose name was Tamar, and **Amnon** the son of David loved her.
² And **Amnon** was so frustrated because of his sister Tamar that he made himself ill, for she was a virgin, and it seemed hard to Amnon to do anything to her.
³ And **Amnon** had a friend whose name was Jonadab, the son of Shimeah, David's brother; and **Jonadab** was a very shrewd man.
⁴ And he said to him, "O son of the king, why are you so depressed morning after morning? Will you not tell me?" Then **Amnon** said to him, "I am in love with Tamar, the sister of my brother Absalom."
⁵ **Jonadab** then said to him, "Lie down on your bed and pretend to be ill; when your father comes to see you, say to him, 'Please let my sister Tamar come and give me *some* food to eat, and let her prepare the food in my sight, that I may see *it* and eat from her hand.'"
⁶ª So **Amnon** lay down and pretended to be ill.

B

⁶ᵇ When **the king** came to see him, **Amnon** said to the king, "Please let my sister Tamar come and make me a couple of cakes in my sight, that I may eat from her hand."
⁷ Then **David** sent to the house for Tamar, saying, *"Go now to your brother* **Amnon's house**, and prepare food for him."
⁸ª So Tamar *went to her brother* **Amnon's house**, and he was lying down.

C

⁸ᵇ And **she** took dough, kneaded *it*, made cakes in his sight, and baked the cakes.
⁹ And **she** took the pan and dished *them* out before him, but he refused to eat. And **Amnon** said, "Have everyone go out from me." So everyone went out from him.
¹⁰ Then **Amnon** said to **Tamar**, "Bring the food into the bedroom, that I may eat from your hand." So **Tamar** took the cakes which she had made and brought them into the bedroom to her brother **Amnon**.

¹¹ When **she brought them to him** to eat, **he** took hold of her and **said to her**, "Come, lie with me, my sister."
¹² But **she answered him**, "No, my brother, do not violate me, for such a thing is not done in Israel; do not do this disgraceful thing!
¹³ "As for me, where could I get rid of my reproach? And as for you, you will be like one of the fools in Israel. Now therefore, please speak to the king, for he will not withhold me from you."
¹⁴ However, **he would not listen to her**; since he was stronger than she, **he violated her** and lay with her.
¹⁵ Then **Amnon hated her** with a very great hatred; for the hatred with which he hated her was greater than the love with which he had loved her. And **Amnon said to her**, "Get up, go away!"
¹⁶ But **she said to him**, "No, because this wrong in sending me away is greater than the other that you have done to me!" Yet he would not listen to her.
¹⁷ Then **he** called his young man who attended him and **said**, "Now throw this woman out of my *presence*, and lock the door behind her."

D

⁸ Now **she** had on a long-sleeved garment; for in this manner the virgin daughters of the king dressed themselves in robes. Then his attendant took her out and locked the door behind her.
¹⁹ And **Tamar** put ashes on her head, and tore her long-sleeved garment which *was* on her; and she put her hand on her head and went away, crying aloud as she went.
²⁰ Then **Absalom** her brother said to her, "Has Amnon your brother been with you? But now keep silent, my sister, he is your brother; do not take this matter to heart." So **Tamar** remained and was desolate in her brother Absalom's house.
²¹ Now when King David heard of all these matters, he was very angry.
²² But **Absalom** did not speak to Amnon either good or bad; for Absalom hated Amnon because he had violated his sister **Tamar**.

2. Comment

The narrative constituent identified and marked in this narrative is *character*.

Describing and Illustrating the Five Basic Narrative Structures

3. Structure

The structure is based on the labeling of the narrative constituent character:

A vv1–6a   Meeting One: Amnon—Jonadab
B vv6b–8a   Meeting Two: Amnon—David
C vv8b–17   Meeting Three: Amnon—Tamar
D vv18-22   **Meeting Four: Absalom—Tamar**

JUDGES 9:7–21

1. Marking the Narrative

A

⁷ Now when they told **Jotham**, he went and stood on the top of Mount Gerizim, and lifted his voice and called out. Thus **he said to them**, "Listen to me, O men of Shechem, that God may listen to you.
⁸ Once **the trees** went forth to anoint a king over them, and they **said to the olive tree**, 'Reign over us!'
⁹ But the olive tree said unto them, 'Should I leave my fatness with which God and men are honored and go to wave over the trees?'

B

¹⁰ Then **the trees said to the fig tree** 'You come and reign over us!'
¹¹ But the fig tree said unto them, 'Should I forsake my sweetness, and my good fruit, and go to be promoted over the trees?'

C

¹² Then said **the trees unto the vine**, 'Come thou, *and* reign over us.'
¹³ And the vine said unto them, 'Should I leave my wine, which cheereth God and man, and go to be promoted over the trees?'

D

¹⁴ Then said **all the trees unto the bramble**, 'Come thou, *and* reign over us.'
¹⁵ And **the bramble said unto the trees**, 'If in truth ye anoint me king over you, *then* come *and* put your trust in my shadow: and if not, let fire come out of the bramble, and devour the cedars of Lebanon.'

E

¹⁶ *[Jotham continued]* Now therefore, if you have dealt in truth and integrity in making Abimelech king, and if you have dealt well with Jerubbaal and his house, and have dealt with him as he deserved—

¹⁷ for my father fought for you and risked his life and delivered you from the hand of Midian;

¹⁸ but you have risen against my father's house today and have killed his sons, seventy men, on one stone, and have made Abimelech, the son of his maidservant, king over the men of Shechem, because he is your relative—

¹⁹ if then you have dealt in truth and integrity with Jerubbaal and his house this day, rejoice in Abimelech, and let him also rejoice in you.

²⁰ But if not, let fire come out from Abimelech and consume the men of Shechem and Beth-Millo; and let fire come out from the men of Shechem and from Beth-Millo, and consume Abimelech."

²¹ Then **Jotham** escaped and fled, and went to Beer and remained there because of Abimelech his brother.

2. Comment

The narrative constituents identified and marked in this narrative are *character and dialogue*.

3. The structure is based on the labeling of the narrative constituents character and dialogue:

A vv7–9		Attempt one unsuccessful: the olive tree refused
B vv10–11		Attempt two unsuccessful: the fig tree refused
C vv12–13		Attempt three unsuccessful: the vine refused
D vv14–15		Attempt four successful: the bramble accepted
E vv16–21		***Jotham's speech: a warning***

Chiastic Structure

∽ GENESIS 24:1–67

1. Marking the Narrative

A

¹ Now Abraham was old, advanced in age; and the Lord had blessed Abraham in every way.

Describing and Illustrating the Five Basic Narrative Structures

²And **Abraham said to his servant**, the oldest of his household, who had charge of all that he owned, "Please place your hand under my thigh,
³and I will make you swear by the Lord, the God of heaven and the God of earth, that you shall not take a wife for my son from the daughters of the Canaanites, among whom I live,
⁴but you shall go to my country and to my relatives, and take a wife for my son Isaac."
⁵And **the servant said to him**, "Suppose the woman will not be willing to follow me to this land; should I take your son back to the land from where you came?"
⁶Then **Abraham said to him**, "Beware lest you take my son back there!
⁷The Lord, the God of heaven, who took me from my father's house and from the land of my birth, and who spoke to me, and who swore to me, saying, 'To your descendants I will give this land,' He will send His angel before you, and you will take a wife for my son from there.
⁸But if the woman is not willing to follow you, then you will be free from this my oath; only do not take my son back there."
⁹So the **servant** placed his hand under the thigh of Abraham his master, and swore to him concerning this matter.
¹⁰Then **the servant** took ten camels from the camels of his master, and set out with a variety of good things of his master's in his hand.

B

¹⁰ᵇand he arose, and went to **Mesopotamia, to the city of Nahor**.
¹¹And he made the camels kneel down outside **the city [of Nahor] by the well of water** at evening time, the time when women go out to draw water.
¹²And **he said**, "O Lord, the God of my master Abraham, please grant me success today, and show loving kindness to my master Abraham.
¹³Behold, I am standing by the spring, and the daughters of the men of the city are coming out to draw water;
¹⁴now may it be that the girl to whom I say, 'Please let down your jar so that I may drink,' and who answers, 'Drink, and I will water your camels also';—*may* she *be the one* whom Thou hast appointed for Thy servant Isaac; and by this I shall know that Thou hast shown lovingkindness to my master."

¹⁵ And it came about before he had finished speaking, that behold, **Rebekah** who was born to Bethuel the son of Milcah, the wife of **Abraham's brother Nahor**, came out with her jar on her shoulder.

¹⁶ And the girl was very beautiful, a virgin, and no man had had relations with her; and she went down to the spring and filled her jar, and came up.

¹⁷ Then the servant ran to meet her, and said, "Please let me drink a little water from your jar."

¹⁸ And *she said*, "Drink, my lord"; and she quickly lowered her jar to her hand, and gave him a drink.

¹⁹ Now when she had finished giving him a drink, she said, "I will draw also for your camels until they have finished drinking."

²⁰ So she quickly emptied her jar into the trough, and ran back to the well to draw, and she drew for all his camels.

²¹ Meanwhile, the man was gazing at her in silence, to know whether the Lord had made his journey successful or not.

²² Then it came about, when the camels had finished drinking, that the man took a gold ring weighing a half-shekel and two bracelets for her wrists weighing ten shekels in gold,

²³ *and said*, "Whose daughter are you? Please tell me, is there room for us to lodge in your father's house?"

²⁴ And *she said to him*, "I am the daughter of Bethuel, the son of Milcah, whom she bore to Nahor."

²⁵ *Again she said to him*, "We have plenty of both straw and feed, and room to lodge in."

²⁶ Then the man bowed low and worshiped the Lord.

²⁷ *And he said*, "Blessed be the Lord, the God of my master Abraham, who has not forsaken His loving kindness and His truth toward my master; as for me, the Lord has guided me in the way to **the house of my master's brothers**."

²⁸ Then the girl ran and told **her mother's household** about these things.

²⁹ Now **Rebekah** had a brother whose name was **Laban**; and Laban ran outside to the man **at the spring**.

³⁰ And it came about that when he saw the ring, and the bracelets on his sister's wrists, and when he heard the words of Rebekah his sister, saying, "This is what the man said to me," he went to the man; and behold, he was standing by the camels **at the spring**.

³¹ And **he said**, "Come in, blessed of the Lord! Why do you stand outside since I have prepared the house, and a place for the camels?"

B

³² So **the man** entered **the house**. Then **Laban** unloaded the camels, and he gave straw and feed to the camels, and water to wash his feet and the feet of the men who were with him.

³³ But when *food* was set before him to eat, **he said**, "I will not eat until I have told my business." And **he said**, "Speak on."

³⁴ So he said, "I am Abraham's servant.

³⁵ And the Lord has greatly blessed my master, so that he has become rich; and He has given him flocks and herds, and silver and gold, and servants and maids, and camels and donkeys.

³⁶ Now Sarah my master's wife bore a son to my master in her old age; and he has given him all that he has.

³⁷ And my master made me swear, saying, 'You shall not take a wife for my son from the daughters of the Canaanites, in whose land I live;

³⁸ but you shall go to my father's house, and to my relatives, and take a wife for my son.'

³⁹ And I said to my master, 'Suppose the woman does not follow me.'

⁴⁰ And he said to me, 'The Lord, before whom I have walked, will send His angel with you to make your journey successful, and you will take a wife for my son from my relatives, and from my father's house;

⁴¹ then you will be free from my oath, when you come to my relatives; and if they do not give her to you, you will be free from my oath.'

⁴² So I came today to the spring, and said, 'O Lord, the God of my master Abraham, if now Thou wilt make my journey on which I go successful;

⁴³ behold, I am standing by the spring, and may it be that the maiden who comes out to draw, and to whom I say, "Please let me drink a little water from your jar";

⁴⁴ and she will say to me, "You drink, and I will draw for your camels also"; let her be the woman whom the Lord has appointed for my master's son.'

⁴⁵ Before I had finished speaking in my heart, behold, Rebekah came out with her jar on her shoulder, and went down to the spring and drew; and I said to her, 'Please let me drink.'

⁴⁶ And she quickly lowered her jar from her *shoulder*, and said, 'Drink, and I will water your camels also'; so I drank, and she watered the camels also.

⁴⁷ Then I asked her, and said, 'Whose daughter are you?' And she said, 'The daughter of Bethuel, Nahor's son, whom Milcah bore to him'; and I put the ring on her nose, and the bracelets on her wrists.

⁴⁸ And I bowed low and worshiped the Lord, and blessed the Lord, the God of my master Abraham, who had guided me in the right way to take the daughter of my master's kinsman for his son.

⁴⁹ "So now if you are going to deal kindly and truly with my master, tell me; and if not, let me know, that I may turn to the right hand or the left."

⁵⁰ Then **Laban and Bethuel answered and said**, "The matter comes from the Lord; *so* we cannot speak to you bad or good.

⁵¹ Behold, Rebekah is before you, take *her* and go, and let her be the wife of your master's son, as the Lord has spoken."

⁵² And it came about when Abraham's servant heard their words, that he bowed himself to the ground before the Lord.

⁵³ And **the servant** brought out articles of silver and articles of gold, and garments, and gave them to Rebekah; he also gave precious things to her brother and to her mother.

⁵⁴ Then **he and the men** who were with him ate and drank and spent the night. When they arose in the morning, **he said**, "Send me away to my master."

⁵⁵ But **her brother and her mother said**, "Let the girl stay with us *a few days, say ten*; afterward she may go."

⁵⁶ And **he said to them**, "Do not delay me, since the Lord has prospered my way. Send me away that I may go to my master."

⁵⁷ And **they said**, "We will call the girl and consult her wishes."

⁵⁸ Then **they** called Rebekah and **said to her**, "Will you go with this man?" And she said, "I will go."

⁵⁹ Thus they sent away their sister Rebekah and her nurse with **Abraham's servant and his men**.

⁶⁰ And **they** blessed Rebekah and **said to her**, "May you, our sister, Become thousands of ten thousands, And may your descendants possess The gate of those who hate them."

⁶¹ Then Rebekah arose with her maids, and they mounted the camels and followed the man. So the servant took Rebekah and departed *[from the city of Nahor]*.

Describing and Illustrating the Five Basic Narrative Structures

A

⁶² Now **Isaac** had come from going to **Beer-lahai-roi**; for he was living in **the Negev**.

⁶³ And **Isaac** went out to meditate in the field toward evening; and he lifted up his eyes and looked, and behold, camels were coming.

⁶⁴ And Rebekah lifted up her eyes, and when she saw Isaac she dismounted from the camel.

⁶⁵ And **she said to the servant**, "Who is that man walking in the field to meet us?" And **the servant said**, "He is my master." Then she took her veil and covered herself.

⁶⁶ And **the servant** told **Isaac** all the things that he had done.

⁶⁷ Then **Isaac** brought her into his mother Sarah's tent, and he took **Rebekah**, and she became his wife; and he loved her; thus Isaac was comforted after his mother's death.

2. Comment

The narrative constituents identified and marked are *geography (place), character, and speech*.

3. The structure is based on the labeling of the narrative constituents geography (place), character, and speech:

A vv1–10		*Canaan—covenant between Abraham and his servant*
	B vv11–31	Mesopotamia—the servant met Abraham's relatives
	B vv32–61	Mesopotamia—the servant got a wife from Abraham's relatives
A vv62–67		*Canaan—the servant returned with a wife for Abraham's son*

∽ GENESIS 38:1–30

1. Marking the Narrative

A

¹ **And it came about at that time**, that Judah departed from his brothers, and visited a certain Adullamite, whose name was Hirah.

² And **Judah saw** there a daughter of a certain Canaanite whose name was **Shua**; and **he took her and went in to her**.

³ So **she conceived and bore a son** and he named him **Er**.

⁴ Then **she conceived again and bore a son** and named him **Onan**.
⁵ And **she bore still another son** and named him **Shelah**; and it was at Chezib that she bore him.
⁶ Now **Judah took a wife for Er** his first-born, and her name *was* Tamar.
⁷ But Er, Judah's first-born, was evil in the sight of the Lord, *so the Lord took his life.*
⁸ **Then Judah said to Onan**, "Go in to your brother's wife, and perform your duty as a brother-in-law to her, and raise up offspring for your brother."
⁹ And **Onan** knew that the offspring would not be his; so it came about that when he went in to his brother's wife, he **wasted his seed on the ground**, in order not to give offspring to his brother.
¹⁰ But what he did was displeasing in the sight of *the Lord*; so He **took his life also**.
¹¹ Then Judah said to his daughter-in-law Tamar, "Remain a widow in your father's house until my son Shelah grows up"; for he thought, "*I am afraid* that he too may die like his brothers." So Tamar went and lived in her father's house.

B

¹² **Now after a considerable time** Shua's daughter, **the wife of Judah, died**; and **when the time of mourning was ended, Judah went up to** his sheep-shearers at **Timnah**, he and his friend Hirah the Adullamite.
¹³ And it was told to **Tamar**, "Behold, your father-in-law is going up to Timnah to shear his sheep."
¹⁴ So **she removed her widow's garments and covered herself with a veil**, and wrapped herself, and **sat in the gateway of Enaim**, which is on the road to Timnah; for she saw that Shelah had grown up, and she had not been given to him as a wife.
¹⁵ When **Judah** saw her, he thought she was a harlot, for she had covered her face.
¹⁶ So he **turned aside to her by the road**, and said, "Here now, let me come in to you"; for he did not know that she was his daughter-in-law. And she said, "What will you give me, that you may come in to me?"
¹⁷ He said, therefore, "I will send you a kid from the flock." She said, moreover, "Will you give a pledge until you send it?"

¹⁸ And he said, "What pledge shall I give you?" And she said, "Your seal and your cord, and your staff that is in your hand." So he **gave them to her, and went in to her, and she conceived by him.**
¹⁹ **Then she arose and departed**, and removed her veil and put on her widow's garments.
²⁰ **When Judah sent the kid** by his friend the Adullamite, **to receive the pledge** from the woman's hand, **he did not find her.**
²¹ And he asked the men of her place, saying, "Where is the temple prostitute who was by the road at Enaim?" But they said, "There has been no temple prostitute here."
²² So he returned to Judah, and said, "I did not find her; and furthermore, the men of the place said, 'There has been no temple prostitute here.'"
²³ Then Judah said, "Let her keep them, lest we become a laughingstock. After all, I sent this kid, but you did not find her."

B

²⁴ **Now it was about three months later** that Judah was informed, "Your daughter-in-law Tamar has played the harlot, and behold, she is also with child by harlotry." Then Judah said, "Bring her out and let her be burned!"
²⁵ It was **while she was being brought out** that she sent to her father-in-law, saying, "I am with child by the man to whom these things belong." And she said, "Please examine and see, whose signet ring and cords and staff are these?"
²⁶ And Judah recognized *them*, and said, "She is more righteous than I, inasmuch as I did not give her to my son Shelah." And he did not have relations with her again.

A

²⁷ **And it came about at the time** she was giving birth, that behold, there were twins in her womb.
²⁸ Moreover, **it took place while she was giving birth**, one put out a hand, and the midwife took and tied a scarlet *thread* on his hand, saying, "This one came out first."
²⁹ But **it came about as he drew back** his hand, that behold, his brother came out. Then she said, "What a breach you have made for yourself!" **So he was named Perez.**

³⁰ And ***afterward his brother came out*** who had the scarlet *thread* on his hand; and ***he was named Zerah***.

2. Comment

The narrative constituents identified and marked are *character, time, and action*.

3. The structure is based on the labeling of the narrative constituents character, time, and action:

A vv1-11 *Compressed time—the death of Judah's sons*
 B vv12-23 Expanded time—the actions of Tamar
 B vv24-26 Expanded time—the action of the community and Judah
A vv27-30 *Compressed time—the birth of the twins*

2 Kings 17:25-28

1. Marking the Narrative

A

²⁵ ***And it came about*** at the beginning of their living there, ***that they did not fear the Lord***; therefore the Lord sent lions among them which killed some of them;

B

²⁶ So ***they spoke to the king of Assyria, saying***, "The nations whom you have carried away into exile in the cities of Samaria do not know the custom of the god of the land; so he has sent lions among them, and behold, they kill them because they do not know the custom of the god of the land."

B

²⁷ Then ***the king of Assyria commanded, saying***, "Take there one of the priests whom you carried away into exile, and let him go and live there; and let him teach them the custom of the god of the land."

A

²⁸ So ***one of the priests*** whom they had carried away into exile from Samaria ***came and lived at Bethel***, and taught them how they should fear the Lord.

2. Comment

The narrative constituents identified and marked are straight narrative and speech.

3. The structure is based on the labeling of the narrative constituents straight narrative and speech:

A v25		***The Lord sent lions among the people which killed some of them***
	B v26	The killings are reported to the king of Assyria
	B v27	The king instructed that a priest be sent to the people to teach them
A v28		***Priests went to live among the people and taught them the fear of God***

Ring Structure

~ 2 SAMUEL 11:1–27

1. Marking the Narrative

A

¹ Then it happened in the spring, at the time when kings go out *to battle*, that **David sent Joab** and his servants with him and all Israel, and they destroyed the sons of Ammon and besieged Rabbah. **But David stayed at Jerusalem.**

² Now when evening came **David arose from his bed and walked** around on the roof of the king's house, and from the roof **he saw a woman** bathing; and *the woman was very beautiful in appearance*.

³ So **David sent and inquired** about the woman. And **one said**, "Is this not Bathsheba, the daughter of Eliam, *the wife of Uriah the Hittite*?"

⁴ And **David sent messengers and took her**, and when **she came to him, he lay with her**; and when she had purified herself from her uncleanness, **she returned to her house.**

⁵ And **the woman conceived**; and she sent and **told David**, and said, "**I am pregnant.**"

B

⁶ **Then David sent to Joab, saying,** "Send me Uriah the Hittite." **So Joab sent Uriah to David.**
⁷ When **Uriah came to him**, David asked concerning the welfare of Joab and the people and the state of the war.
⁸ Then **David said to Uriah**, "Go down to your house, and wash your feet." And Uriah went out of the king's house, and a present from the king was sent out after him.
⁹ But **Uriah slept at the door of the king's house** with all the servants of his lord, and did not go down to his house.
¹⁰ Now when they told David, saying, "Uriah did not go down to his house," **David said to Uriah**, "Have you not come from a journey? Why did you not go down to your house?"
¹¹ And **Uriah said to David**, "The ark and Israel and Judah are staying in temporary shelters, and my lord Joab and the servants of my lord are camping in the open field. Shall I then go to my house to eat and to drink and to lie with my wife? By your life and the life of your soul, I will not do this thing."
¹² Then **David said to Uriah**, "Stay here today also, and tomorrow I will let you go." So **Uriah remained in Jerusalem** that day and the next.
¹³ Now **David called him**, and **he ate and drank before him**, and he made him drunk; and in the evening he went out to lie on his bed with his lord's servants, but **he did not go down to his house.**
¹⁴ Now it came about in the morning that **David wrote a letter to Joab**, and sent *it* by the hand of Uriah.
¹⁵ And he had written in the letter, **saying**, "Place Uriah in the front line of the fiercest battle and withdraw from him, so that he may be struck down and die."
¹⁶ So it was as **Joab** kept watch on the city, that he **put Uriah at the place where he knew there were valiant men.**
¹⁷ And **the men of the city** went out and **fought against Joab, and some of the people among David's servants fell; and Uriah the Hittite also died.**
¹⁸ Then **Joab sent and reported to David** all the events of the war.
¹⁹ And he charged the messenger, **saying**, "When you have finished telling all the events of the war to the king,

Describing and Illustrating the Five Basic Narrative Structures

[20] and if it happens that the king's wrath rises and he says to you, 'Why did you go so near to the city to fight? Did you not know that they would shoot from the wall? [21] Who struck down Abimelech the son of Jerubbesheth? Did not a woman throw an upper millstone on him from the wall so that he died at Thebez? Why did you go so near the wall?'—then you shall say, 'Your servant Uriah the Hittite is dead also.'"

[22] *So the messenger departed and came and reported to David all that Joab had sent him to tell.*

[23] And *the messenger said to David,* "The men prevailed against us and came out against us in the field, but we pressed them as far as the entrance of the gate. [24] Moreover, the archers shot at your servants from the wall; so some of the king's servants are dead, and your servant Uriah the Hittite is also dead."

[25] *Then David said to the messenger,* "Thus you shall say to Joab, 'Do not let this thing displease you, for the sword devours one as well as another; make your battle against the city stronger and overthrow it'; and *so* encourage him."

C

[26] Now when *the wife of Uriah* heard that Uriah her husband was dead, *she mourned for her husband.*

[27] When the *time of* mourning was over, *David sent and brought her to his house and she became his wife*;

[27b] *then she bore him a son.*

[27c] But the thing that David had done was evil in the sight of the Lord.

2. Comment

The narrative constituents identified and marked are *character, speech, and action*.

3. The structure is based on the labeling of the narrative constituents character, speech, and action:

A vv1–5   Bathsheba—impregnated by David
  B vv6–25   Uriah—killed by David to cover up what he did
    B1v6–
      B2vv7–24
    B1v25
A vv26–27   Bathsheba—married by David to cover up what he did

Note: an interesting observation here is that there is a ring structure (Bv1, Bvv7–24, Bv25) within a ring structure.

Judges 1:1–2:5

1. Marking the Narrative

A

¹ Now it came about after the death of Joshua that **the sons of Israel inquired of the Lord, saying**, "Who shall go up first for us against the Canaanites, to fight against them?"
² And **the Lord said**, "Judah shall go up; behold, I have given the land into his hand."

B

³ Then **Judah said to Simeon his brother**, "Come up with me into the territory allotted me, that we may fight against the Canaanites; and I in turn will go with you into the territory allotted you." So Simeon went with him.
⁴ And **Judah went up**, and the Lord gave the Canaanites and the Perizzites into their hands; and **they defeated** ten thousand men at Bezek.
⁵ And **they found Adoni-bezek in Bezek and fought against him** and they defeated the Canaanites and the Perizzites.
⁶ But **Adoni-bezek fled**; and they pursued him and caught him and cut off his thumbs and big toes.
⁷ And **Adoni-bezek said**, "Seventy kings with their thumbs and their big toes cut off used to gather up *scraps* under my table; as I have done, so God has repaid me." So they brought him to Jerusalem and he died there.
⁸ Then **the sons of Judah fought against Jerusalem** and captured it and struck it with the edge of the sword and set the city on fire.
⁹ And **afterward the sons of Judah went down to fight against the Canaanites** living in the hill country and in the Negev and in the lowland.

¹⁰ **So Judah went against the Canaanites** who lived in Hebron (now the name of Hebron formerly *was* Kiriath-arba); and they struck Sheshai and Ahiman and Talmai.

¹¹ Then from there **he went against the inhabitants of Debir** (now the name of Debir formerly *was* Kiriath-sepher).

¹² And **Caleb said**, "The one who attacks Kiriath-sepher and captures it, I will even give him my daughter Achsah for a wife."

¹³ And **Othniel** the son of Kenaz, Caleb's younger brother, **captured it**; so he gave him his daughter Achsah for a wife.

¹⁴ Then it came about when she came *to him*, that she persuaded him to ask her father for a field. Then she alighted from her donkey, and **Caleb said to her**, "What do you want?"

¹⁵ And **she said to him**, "Give me a blessing, since you have given me the land of the Negev, give me also springs of water." So **Caleb gave her the upper springs and the lower springs**.

¹⁶ And **the descendants of the Kenite**, Moses' father-in-law, **went up** from the city of palms with the sons of Judah, to the wilderness of Judah which is in the south of Arad; and they went **and lived with the people**.

¹⁷ Then **Judah went with Simeon** his brother, and **they struck the Canaanites living in Zephath**.

¹⁸ And **Judah took Gaza** with its territory and **Ashkelon** with its territory and **Ekron** with its territory.

¹⁹ Now the Lord was with Judah, and they took possession of the hill country; but they could not drive out the inhabitants of the valley because they had iron chariots.

²⁰ Then **they gave Hebron to Caleb**, as Moses had promised; and he drove out from there the three sons of Anak.

²¹ But **the sons of Benjamin did not drive out** the Jebusites who lived in Jerusalem; so the Jebusites have lived with the sons of Benjamin in Jerusalem to this day.

²² Likewise **the house of Joseph went up against Bethel**, and the Lord was with them.

²³ And the house of Joseph spied out Bethel (now the name of the city was formerly Luz).

²⁴ And the spies saw a man coming out of the city, and they said to him, "Please show us the entrance to the city and we will treat you kindly."

²⁵ So he showed them the entrance to the city, and **they struck the city with the edge of the sword, but they let the man and all his family go free.**

²⁶ And the man went into the land of the Hittites and built a city and called it Luz, which is its name to this day.

²⁷ But **Manasseh did not take possession** of Beth-shean and its villages, or Taanach and its villages, or the inhabitants of Dor and its villages, or the inhabitants of Ibleam and its villages, or the inhabitants of Megiddo and its villages; so the Canaanites persisted in living in that land.

²⁸ And it came about when **Israel** became strong, that they put the Canaanites to forced labor, but they *did not drive them out completely*.

²⁹ **Neither did Ephraim drive out** the Canaanites who were living in Gezer; so the Canaanites lived in Gezer among them.

³⁰ **Zebulun did not drive out** the inhabitants of Kitron, or the inhabitants of Nahalol; so the Canaanites lived among them and became subject to forced labor.

³¹ **Asher did not drive out** the inhabitants of Acco, or the inhabitants of Sidon, or of Ahlab, or of Achzib, or of Helbah, or of Aphik, or of Rehob.

³² So the Asherites lived among the Canaanites, the inhabitants of the land; for they did not drive them out.

³³ **Naphtali did not drive** out the inhabitants of Beth-shemesh, or the inhabitants of Beth-anath, but lived among the Canaanites, the inhabitants of the land; and the inhabitants of Beth-shemesh and Beth-anath became forced labor for them.

³⁴ Then **the Amorites forced the sons of Dan into the hill country**, for they did not allow them to come down to the valley;

³⁵ **yet the Amorites** persisted in living in Mount Heres, in Aijalon and in Shaalbim; but when the power of the house of Joseph grew strong, they **became forced labor**.

³⁶ And the border of the Amorites ran from the ascent of Akrabbim, from Sela and upward.

A

¹ **Now the angel of the Lord came up** from Gilgal to Bochim. **And he said**, "I brought you up out of Egypt and led you into the land which I have sworn to your fathers; and I said, 'I will never break My covenant with you,

² and as for you, you shall make no covenant with the inhabitants of this land; you shall tear down their altars.' But you have not obeyed Me; what is this you have done?

Describing and Illustrating the Five Basic Narrative Structures 77

³ ***Therefore I also said***, 'I will not drive them out before you; but they shall become *as thorns* in your sides, and their gods shall be a snare to you.'"
⁴ And it came about when the angel of the Lord spoke these words to all **the sons of Israel**, that the people **lifted up their voices and wept**.
⁵ So **they named that place Bochim; and there they sacrificed to the Lord**.

2. Comment

The narrative constituents identified and marked are *character, speech, and action*.

3. The structure is based on the labeling of the narrative constituents character, speech, and action:

A vv1–2   God told the people that Judah must lead the settlement of Canaan
   B vv3–36   *The result of the settlement of Canaan by the rest of the tribes*
A vv1–5   God rebuked the people and told them why they failed to take the land

Concentric Structure

~ 2 Kings 21:21–22

1. Marking the Narrative

A

²¹ For ***he walked*** in all the way that his father had walked,

B

²¹ᵇ and ***served the idols*** that his father had served

C

²¹ᶜ and ***worshiped them***.

B

²² So ***he forsook the Lord***, the God of his fathers,

A

²²ᵇ and **did not walk** in the way of the Lord.

2. Comment

The narrative constituents identified and marked are *character and action*.

3. The structure is based on the labeling of the narrative constituents character and action:

A v21		Manasseh behaved like his father
	B v21b	He committed idolatry like his father
		C v21c **He swore loyalty to the idol**
	B v22a	He turned his back on his forefather's God
A v22b		He did not behave the way his forefathers behaved

∽ Genesis 7: 10—8:10

Marking narrative constituents content and time:

1. Marking the Text

A

¹⁰ And it came about after the **seven days**, that the water of the flood came upon the earth.
¹¹ In the six hundredth year of Noah's life, in the second month, on the seventeenth day of the month, on the same day all the fountains of the great deep burst open, and the floodgates of the sky were opened.

B

¹² And the rain fell upon the earth for **forty days and forty nights**.
¹³ On the very same day Noah and Shem and Ham and Japheth, the sons of Noah, and Noah's wife and the three wives of his sons with them, entered the ark,
¹⁴ they and every beast after its kind, and all the cattle after their kind, and every creeping thing that creeps on the earth after its kind, and every bird after its kind, all sorts of birds.
¹⁵ So they went into the ark to Noah, by twos of all flesh in which was the breath of life.

Describing and Illustrating the Five Basic Narrative Structures 79

¹⁶ And those that entered, male and female of all flesh, entered as God had commanded him; and the Lord closed *it* behind him.

¹⁷ Then the flood came upon the earth for ***forty days***; and the water increased and lifted up the ark, so that it rose above the earth.

¹⁸ And the water prevailed and increased greatly upon the earth; and the ark floated on the surface of the water.

¹⁹ And the water prevailed more and more upon the earth, so that all the high mountains everywhere under the heavens were covered.

²⁰ The water prevailed fifteen cubits higher, and the mountains were covered.

²¹ And all flesh that moved on the earth perished, birds and cattle and beasts and every swarming thing that swarms upon the earth, and all mankind;

²² of all that was on the dry land, all in whose nostrils was the breath of the spirit of life, died.

²³ Thus He blotted out every living thing that was upon the face of the land, from man to animals to creeping things and to birds of the sky, and they were blotted out from the earth; and only Noah was left, together with those that were with him in the ark.

C

²⁴ And the water prevailed upon the earth ***one hundred and fifty days***.

¹ But God remembered Noah and all the beasts and all the cattle that were with him in the ark; and God caused a wind to pass over the earth, and the water subsided.

² Also the fountains of the deep and the floodgates of the sky were closed, and the rain from the sky was restrained;

³ and the water receded steadily from the earth, and at the end of ***one hundred and fifty days*** the water decreased.

⁴ And in the seventh month, on the seventeenth day of the month, the ark rested upon the mountains of Ararat.

⁵ And the water decreased steadily until the tenth month; in the tenth month, on the first day of the month, the tops of the mountains became visible.

B

⁶ Then it came about at the end of ***forty days***, that Noah opened the window of the ark which he had made;

⁷ and he sent out a raven, and it flew here and there until the water was dried up from the earth.
⁸ Then he sent out a dove from him, to see if the water was abated from the face of the land;
⁹ but the dove found no resting place for the sole of her foot, so she returned to him into the ark; for the water was on the surface of all the earth. Then he put out his hand and took her, and brought her into the ark to himself.

A

¹⁰ So he waited yet another **seven days**; and again he sent out the dove from the ark.

2. Comment

The narrative constituents identified and marked are *content and time*.

3. The structure is based on the labeling of the narrative constituents content and time:

A vv10–11	seven days
B vv12–23	forty days
C vv24–5	*one hundred and fifty days*
B vv6–9	forty days
A v10	seven days

∾ Genesis 25:20–26

1. Marking the Narrative

A

²⁰ And ***Isaac was forty years old when he took Rebekah***, the daughter of Bethuel the Aramean of Paddan-aram, the sister of Laban the Aramean, ***to be his wife.***

B

²¹ And ***Isaac prayed*** to the Lord on behalf of his wife, because she was barren; and ***the Lord answered*** him and ***Rebekah his wife conceived.***

Describing and Illustrating the Five Basic Narrative Structures

C

²² But ***the children struggled*** together within her; and she said, "If it is so, why then am I *this way*?" So ***she went to inquire of the Lord***.
²³ And ***the Lord said to her***, "Two nations are in your womb; And two peoples shall be separated from your body; And one people shall be stronger than the other; And the older shall serve the younger."

B

²⁴ ***When her days to be delivered were fulfilled***, behold, there were twins in her womb.
²⁵ Now ***the first came forth red***, all over like a hairy garment; and they named him Esau.
²⁶ And ***afterward his brother came forth*** with his hand holding on to Esau's heel, so his name was called Jacob;

A

²⁶ᵇ and ***Isaac was sixty years old*** when she gave birth to them.

2. Comment

The narrative constituents identified and marked are *character, time, and narration*.

3. The structure is based on the labeling of the narrative constituents character, time, and narration:

A v20		Jacob married Rebekah
	B v21	God removed Rebekah's barrenness
		C vv22–23 ***God answered Rebekah's concern about her pregnancy***
	B vv24–26a	Twins were born—one hairy red, one holding the other's heel
A v26b		Rebekah gave birth when Isaac was sixty years old

1 Kings 5:3–6

1. Marking the Narrative

A

³ "You know that **David my father** was unable to build a house for the name of the Lord his God because of the wars which surrounded him, until the Lord put them under the soles of his feet.

B

⁴ But now **the Lord my God has given me rest** on every side; there is neither adversary nor misfortune.

C

⁵ Behold, **I intend to build a house for the name of the Lord my God**, as the Lord spoke to David my father, saying, 'Your son, whom I will set on your throne in your place, he will build the house for My name.'

B

⁶ Now therefore, **command that they cut for me** cedars from Lebanon, and my servants will be with your servants;

A

⁶ᵇ and **I will give you wages for your servants** according to all that you say, for you know that there is no one among us who knows how to cut timber like the Sidonians."

2. Comment

The narrative constituent identified and marked is *speech and character*.

3. The structure is based on the labeling of the narrative constituent speech:

A v3		War prevented David from building a house for God
	B v4	God gave the land rest from war
		C v5 ***Solomon expressed his intention to build a house for God***
	B v6a	Solomon asked for a supply of cedar trees

A v6b   Solomon made a commitment to pay for the expertise and the cedar

2 KINGS 2:1–25

1. Marking the Narrative

A

¹ ***And it came about when the Lord was about to take up Elijah*** by a whirlwind to heaven, that Elijah went with Elisha ***from Gilgal***.

B

² And ***Elijah said to Elisha***, "Stay here please, for the Lord has sent me as far as ***Bethel***." ***But Elisha said***, "As the Lord lives and as you yourself live, I will not leave you." ***So they went down to Bethel***.
³ Then ***the sons of the prophets who were at Bethel*** came out to Elisha and ***said to him***, "Do you know that the Lord will take away your master from over you today?" And he said, "Yes, I know; be still."

C

⁴ And ***Elijah said to him***, "Elisha, please stay here, for the Lord has sent me to ***Jericho***." ***But he said***, "As the Lord lives, and as you yourself live, I will not leave you." ***So they came to Jericho.***
⁵ And ***the sons of the prophets who were at Jericho*** approached Elisha and ***said to him***, "Do you know that the Lord will take away your master from over you today?" And ***he answered***, "Yes, I know; be still."

D

⁶ Then ***Elijah said to him***, "Please stay here, for the Lord has sent me to **the Jordan**." And ***he said***, "As the Lord lives, and as you yourself live, I will not leave you." ***So the two of them went on.***
⁷ Now fifty men of **the sons of the prophets went and stood opposite them** at a distance, while **the two of them stood by the Jordan**.

E

⁸ And ***Elijah took his mantle and folded it together and struck the waters***, and they were divided here and there, so that **the two of them crossed over [the Jordan] on dry ground**.

F

⁹ **Now it came about when they had crossed over**, that **Elijah said to Elisha**, "Ask what I shall do for you before I am taken from you." And Elisha said, "Please, let a double portion of your spirit be upon me."
¹⁰ And **he said**, "You have asked a hard thing. **Nevertheless**, if you see me when I am taken from you, it shall be so for you; but if not, it shall not be *so*."
¹¹ Then **it came about as they were going along and talking**, that behold, **there appeared a chariot of fire** and horses of fire which separated the two of them. **And Elijah went up by a whirlwind to heaven.**
¹² And **Elisha** saw *it* and **cried out**, "My father, my father, the chariots of Israel and its horsemen!" And **he saw him no more. Then he took hold of his own clothes and tore them in two pieces.**
¹³ **He also took up the mantle of Elijah** that fell from him, and returned **and stood by the bank of the Jordan.**

E

¹⁴ And **he took the mantle of Elijah** that fell from him, and **struck the waters and said**, "Where is the Lord, the God of Elijah?" And when he also had struck **the waters they were divided here and there; and Elisha** *crossed over [the Jordan]*.

D

¹⁵ Now when **the sons of the prophets who were at Jericho [by the Jordan]** opposite him saw him, **they said**, "The spirit of Elijah rests on Elisha." And **they came to meet him and bowed themselves to the ground before him.**
¹⁶ And **they said to him**, "Behold now, there are with your servants fifty strong men, Please let them go and search for your master; perhaps the Spirit of the Lord has taken him up and cast him on some mountain or into some valley." And he said, "You shall not send."
¹⁷ But when they urged him until he was ashamed, **he said**, "Send." **They sent therefore fifty men; and they searched three days, but did not find him.**
¹⁸ And **they returned to him while he was staying at Jericho [by the Jordan]; and he said to them**, "Did I not say to you, 'Do not go'?"

C

¹⁹ Then **the men of the city [Jericho] said to Elisha**, "Behold now, the situation of this city is pleasant, as my lord sees; but the water is bad, and the land is unfruitful."
²⁰ And **he said**, "Bring me a new jar, and put salt in it." So they brought *it* to him.
²¹ And **he** went out to the spring of water, and **threw salt in it and said**, "Thus says the Lord, 'I have purified these waters; there shall not be from there death or unfruitfulness any longer.'"
²² *So the waters have been purified to this day, according to the word of Elisha which he spoke.*

B

²³ *Then he went up from there to Bethel*; and as he was going up by the way, *young lads came out from the city and mocked him and said* to him, "Go up, you bald head, go up, you bald head."
²⁴ When **he looked behind him and saw them, he cursed them** in the name of the Lord. Then *two female bears came out of the woods and tore up forty-two lads of their number.*

A

²⁵ And he went from there **to Mount Carmel**, and from there he returned **to Samaria**.

2. Comment

The narrative constituents identified and marked are *geography, narration, and speech*.

3. The structure is based on the labeling of the narrative constituents geography, narration and speech:

A v1		Elijah went with Elisha from Gigal
	B vv2–3	Elijah and Elisha then went to Bethel
	C vv4–5	From there they went to Jericho
	D vv6–7	Next they went to the Jordan
	E v8	They crossed over the Jordan
	F vv9–13	*Elijah was taken up by chariot and his mantle fell on Elisha*

E v14	Elisha crossed over the Jordon alone
D vv15–18	Elisha was acknowledged as Elijah's successor
C vv19–22	Elisha purified the water of Jericho
B vv23–24	Elisha went to Bethel and on the way the children mocking him were killed
A v25	Elisha arrived back at Samaria

～ Jonah 1:4–15

1. Marking the Narrative

A

⁴ And **the Lord hurled a great wind** on the sea and **there was a great storm on the sea** so that the ship was about to break up.

B

⁵ Then **the sailors became afraid, and every man cried to his god, and they threw the cargo** which was in the ship **into the sea** to lighten *it* for them.

C

⁵ᵇ But **Jonah had gone below** into the hold of the ship, lain down, **and fallen sound asleep.**
⁶ So **the captain** approached him and **said**, "How is it that you are sleeping? Get up, call on your god. Perhaps *your* god will be concerned about us so that we will not perish."

D

⁷ And **each man said** to his mate, "Come, let us cast lots so we may learn on whose account this calamity *has struck* us."
⁷ᵇ So they cast lots and **the lot fell on Jonah.**

E

⁸ **Then they said to him**, "Tell us, now! On whose account *has* this calamity *struck* us? What is your occupation? And where do you come from? What is your country? From what people are you?"
⁹ And **he said to them**, "I am a Hebrew, and I fear the Lord God of heaven who made the sea and the dry land."

Describing and Illustrating the Five Basic Narrative Structures

¹⁰ Then **the men** became extremely frightened and they **said to him**, "How could you do this?"
¹⁰ᵇ For *the men knew that he was fleeing from the presence of the Lord*, because he had told them.

D

¹¹ So **they said to him**, "What should we do to you that the sea may become calm for us?"—for the sea was becoming increasingly stormy.

C

¹² And **he said to them**, "Pick me up and throw me into the sea. Then the sea will become calm for you, for I know that on account of me this great storm *has come* upon you."
¹³ However, *the men rowed desperately to return to land but they could not*, for the sea was becoming *even* stormier against them.

B

¹⁴ Then **they called on the Lord and said**, "We earnestly pray, O Lord, do not let us perish on account of this man's life and do not put innocent blood on us; for Thou, O Lord, hast done as Thou hast pleased."

A

¹⁵ So **they picked up Jonah, threw him into the sea, and the sea stopped** its raging.

2. Comment

The narrative constituents identified and marked are *character, narration, and speech*.

3. The structure is based on the labeling of the narrative constituents character, narration, and speech:

A v4		The Lord made the sea stormy and the ship was about to sink
	B v5a	The sailors prayed and dumped cargo to make it lighter
	C vv5b–6	The captain confronted Jonah who was sleeping
	D v7	Lots were cast and the lot fell on Jonah
	E vv8–10	*Jonah was questioned*

	D v11	They asked Jonah what they must do
	C vv12–13	He told them but they did the opposite
	B v14	They prayed not to be held accountable for Jonah's death
A v15		Jonah was thrown overboard and the storm ended

～ 2 Chronicles 25:1–28

1. Marking the Narrative

A

¹ **Amaziah was twenty-five years old when he became king**, and he reigned twenty-nine years in Jerusalem. And **his mother's name was Jehoaddan of Jerusalem.**
² And **he did right in the sight of the Lord, yet not with a whole heart.**
³ Now it came about **as soon as the kingdom was firmly in his grasp, that he killed his servants** who had slain his father the king.
⁴ However, **he did not put their children to death**, but did as it is written in the law in the book of Moses, which the Lord commanded, saying, "Fathers shall not be put to death for sons, nor sons be put to death for fathers, but each shall be put to death for his own sin."

B

⁵ Moreover, **Amaziah assembled Judah** and appointed them according to *their* fathers' households under commanders of thousands and commanders of hundreds throughout Judah and Benjamin; **and he took a census of those from twenty years old and upward**, and found them to be 300,000 choice men, *able* to go to war *and* handle spear and shield.
⁶ He **hired also 100,000 valiant warriors** out of Israel for one hundred talents of silver.
⁷ But **a man of God came to him saying**, "O king, do not let the army of Israel go with you, for the Lord is not with Israel *nor with* any of the sons of Ephraim.
⁸ But if you do go, do *it*, be strong for the battle; *yet* God will bring you down before the enemy, for God has power to help and to bring down."
⁹ And **Amaziah said to the man of God**, "But what *shall* we do for the hundred talents which I have given to the troops of Israel?" And **the man of God answered**, "The Lord has much more to give you than this."

¹⁰ **Then Amaziah dismissed them**, the troops which came to him from Ephraim, to go home; so their anger burned against Judah and they returned home in fierce anger.
¹¹ Now **Amaziah strengthened himself, and led his people forth**, and went to the Valley of Salt, **and struck down 10,000** of the sons of Seir.
¹² The sons of Judah **also captured 10,000 alive** and brought them to the top of the cliff, and threw them down from the top of the cliff so that **they were all dashed to pieces.**
¹³ But **the troops whom Amaziah sent back** from going with him to battle, raided the cities of Judah, from Samaria to Beth-horon, and **struck down 3,000 of them, and plundered much spoil.**

C

¹⁴ **Now it came about after Amaziah came from slaughtering the Edomites that he brought the gods of the sons of Seir, set them up as his gods**, bowed down before them, and burned incense to them.
¹⁵ Then **the anger of the Lord burned against Amaziah, and He sent him a prophet who said to him**, "Why have you sought the gods of the people who have not delivered their own people from your hand?"
¹⁶ And it came about as he was talking with him that **the king said to him**, "Have we appointed you a royal counselor? Stop! Why should you be struck down?" Then **the prophet stopped and said**, "I know that God has planned to destroy you, because you have done this, and have not listened to my counsel."

B

¹⁷ Then **Amaziah** king of Judah took counsel and **sent to Joash** the son of Jehoahaz the son of Jehu, the king of Israel, **saying**, "Come, let us face each other."
¹⁸ And **Joash** the king of Israel sent to Amaziah king of Judah, **saying**, "The thorn bush which was in Lebanon sent to the cedar which was in Lebanon, saying, 'Give your daughter to my son in marriage.' But there passed by a wild beast that was in Lebanon, and trampled the thorn bush.
¹⁹ You said, 'Behold, you have defeated Edom.' And your heart has become proud in boasting. Now stay at home; for why should you provoke trouble that you, even you, should fall and Judah with you?"

²⁰ But **Amaziah would not listen, for it was from God**, that He might deliver them into the hand *of Joash because they had sought the gods of Edom.*

²¹ So Joash king of Israel went up, and he and **Amaziah king of Judah faced each other at Beth-shemesh**, which belonged to Judah.

²² And **Judah was defeated by Israel**, and they fled each to his tent.

²³ Then **Joash king of Israel captured Amaziah** king of Judah, the son of Joash the son of Jehoahaz, at Beth-shemesh, and brought him to Jerusalem, and **tore down the wall of Jerusalem** from the Gate of Ephraim to the Corner Gate, 400 cubits.

²⁴ And **he took all the gold and silver, and all the utensils which were found in the house of God** with Obed-edom, and **the treasures of the king's house, the hostages also**, and returned to Samaria.

A

²⁵ And **Amaziah**, the son of Joash king of Judah, **lived fifteen years after the death of Joash**, son of Jehoahaz, king of Israel.

²⁶ Now the rest of the acts of Amaziah, from first to last, behold, are they not written in the Book of the Kings of Judah and Israel?

²⁷ And from the time that Amaziah turned away from following the Lord **they conspired against him in Jerusalem, and he fled to Lachish; but they** sent after him to Lachish and **killed him there**.

²⁸ Then **they brought him on horses and buried him with his fathers** in the city of Judah.

2. Comment

The narrative constituents identified and marked are character, speech, and narration.

3. The structure is based on the labeling of the narrative constituents character, speech and narration:

A vv1–4		Amaziah did not serve God wholeheartedly
	B vv5–13	Amaziah listened to the prophet, sent the Israelite troops home and has victory
		Cvv14–16 *Amaziah turned to idolatry and the prophet predicted his death*

  B vv17–24 Amaziah went to war against Israel and was utterly defeated and captured
A vv25–28 Amaziah was murdered like his father before him

∽ RUTH 4:1–10

1. Marking the Narrative

A

¹ Now ***Boaz went up to the gate and sat down there***; and behold, *the close relative* of whom Boaz had spoken came by. ***So Boaz said***, "Come aside, friend, sit down here."

B

¹ᶜ So ***he came aside and sat down.***

C

² And **he took** ten men of the elders of the city, ***and said***, "Sit down here." So they sat down.
³ Then **he said to the close relative**, "Naomi, who has come back from the country of Moab, sold the piece of land which *belonged* to our brother Elimelech.
⁴ And I thought to inform you, saying, 'Buy *it* back in the presence of the inhabitants and the elders of my people. If you will redeem *it*, redeem *it*; but if you will not redeem *it, then* tell me, that I may know; for *there is* no one but you to redeem *it,* and I *am* next after you.'

D

⁴ᵇ And ***he said***, "I will redeem *it*."

C

⁵ ***Then Boaz said***, "On the day you buy the field from the hand of Naomi, you must also buy *it* from Ruth the Moabitess, the wife of the dead, to perpetuate the name of the dead through his inheritance."

B

⁶ And ***the close relative said***, "I cannot redeem it for myself, lest I ruin my own inheritance. You redeem my right of redemption for yourself, for I cannot redeem *it*."

⁷ Now this was the custom in former times in Israel concerning redeeming and exchanging, to confirm anything: one man took off his sandal and gave it to the other, and this was a confirmation in Israel.
⁸ Therefore **the close relative said to Boaz**, "Buy it for yourself." So he took off his sandal.

A

⁹ And **Boaz said** to the elders and all the people, "You *are* witnesses this day that I have bought all that was Elimelech's, and all that *was* Chilion's and Mahlon's, from the hand of Naomi.
¹⁰ "Moreover, Ruth the Moabitess, the widow of Mahlon, I have acquired as my wife, to perpetuate the name of the dead through his inheritance, that the name of the dead may not be cut off from among his brethren and from his position at the gate. You *are* witnesses this day."

2. Comment

The narrative constituents identified and marked are *character, speech, and action*.

3. The structure is based on the labeling of the narrative constituents character, speech, and action:

A v1ab		*Boaz:* he invited the close relative to sit down
	B v1c	*So + So:* he sat down at the gate
		C vv2–4a *Boaz:* he set up a court and informed the close relative about the land
		D v4b **So + So: decided to redeem the land**
		C v5 *Boaz:* informed the close relative about the condition for redemption
	B vv6–8	*So + So:* declined and Boaz redeemed the land
A vv9–10		*Boaz:* he sealed the redemption before the elders at the gate

∽ Genesis 25:19–34

1. Marking the Narrative

A

¹⁹ Now **these are the records of the generations of Isaac**, Abraham's son: Abraham became the father of Isaac;

Describing and Illustrating the Five Basic Narrative Structures 93

²⁰ and ***Isaac was forty years old when he took Rebekah***, the daughter of Bethuel the Aramean of Paddan-aram, the sister of Laban the Aramean, to be his wife.

²¹ And ***Isaac prayed to the Lord*** on behalf of his wife, because she was barren; and ***the Lord answered him and Rebekah his wife conceived***.

B

²² But the children struggled together within her; ***and she said***, "If it is so, why then am I *this way*?" So she went to inquire of the Lord.

²³ And ***the Lord said to her***, "Two nations are in your womb; And two peoples shall be separated from your body; And one people shall be stronger than the other; And the older shall serve the younger."

C

²⁴ ***When her days to be delivered were fulfilled***, behold, there were ***twins in her womb***.

²⁵ Now ***the first came forth red***, all over like a hairy garment; and they ***named him Esau***.

²⁶ And ***afterward his brother came forth with his hand holding on to Esau's heel***, so his name was ***called Jacob***; and Isaac was sixty years old when she gave birth to them.

²⁷ When the boys grew up, ***Esau became a skillful hunter***, a man of the field; but ***Jacob was*** a peaceful man, ***living in tents***.

²⁸ Now ***Isaac loved Esau***, because he had a taste for game; but ***Rebekah loved Jacob***.

²⁹ And when ***Jacob had cooked stew, Esau*** came in from the field and he ***was famished***;

B

³⁰ and ***Esau said to Jacob***, "Please let me have a swallow of that red stuff there, for I am famished." Therefore his name was called Edom.

³¹ But ***Jacob said***, "First sell me your birthright."

³² And ***Esau said***, "Behold, I am about to die; so of what *use* then is the birthright to me?" And Jacob said, "First swear to me."

A

³³ᵇ so he swore to him and sold his birthright to Jacob

³⁴ Then ***Jacob gave Esau bread and lentil stew***; and he ate and drank, and rose and went on his way. ***Thus Esau despised his birthright***.

2. Comment

The narrative constituents identified and marked are *character, narration, and speech*.

3. The structure is based on the labeling of the narrative constituents character, speech, and action:

A vv19–21	Narration
B vv22–23	Discourse
C vv24–29	***Narration***
B vv30–33a	Discourse
A vv33b–34	Narration

Parallel Structure

∽ GENESIS 1:3—2:4

1. Marking the Narrative

A

³ Then God said, "Let there be **light**"; and there was **light**.
⁴ And God saw that the **light** was good; and God separated the **light** from the darkness.
⁵ And God called the **light day**, and the **darkness** He called **night**. And there was **evening** and there was **morning, one day.**

B

⁶ Then God said, "Let there be an **expanse in the midst of the waters**, and let it separate the waters from the waters."
⁷ And God made **the expanse**, and separated the waters which were below the expanse from the waters which were above the expanse; and it was so.
⁸ And God **called the expanse heaven**. And there was evening and there was morning, **a second day**.

C

⁹ Then God said, "Let the waters below the heavens be gathered into one place, and let **the dry land** appear"; and it was so.

Describing and Illustrating the Five Basic Narrative Structures 95

¹⁰ And God **called the dry land earth**, and the gathering of **the waters He called seas**; and God saw that it was good.

¹¹ Then God said, "Let the **earth sprout vegetation, plants yielding seed, and fruit trees bearing fruit** after their kind, with seed in them, on the earth"; and it was so.

¹² And the earth brought forth vegetation, plants yielding seed after their kind, and trees bearing fruit, with seed in them, after their kind; and God saw that it was good.

¹³ And there was evening and there was morning, **a third day**.

A

¹⁴ Then God said, "Let there be **lights in the expanse** of the heavens to separate the day from the night, and let them be for signs, and for seasons, and for days and years;

¹⁵ and let them be for **lights in the expanse of the heavens** to give light on the earth"; and it was so.

¹⁶ And God made the **two great lights**, the greater light to govern the day, and the lesser light to govern the night; **He made the stars** also.

¹⁷ And God placed them **in the expanse of the heavens** to give light on the earth,

¹⁸ and to govern the day and the night, and to separate the light from the darkness; and God saw that it was good.

¹⁹ And there was evening and there was morning, **a fourth day**.

B

²⁰ Then God said, "Let the **waters teem with swarms of living creatures**, and let **birds fly above the earth** in the open expanse of the heavens."

²¹ And **God created the great sea monsters**, and **every living creature that moves**, with which the waters swarmed after their kind, and every winged bird after its kind; and God saw that it was good.

²² And God blessed them, saying, "Be fruitful and multiply, and fill the waters in the seas, and let birds multiply on the earth."

²³ And there was evening and there was morning, **a fifth day**.

C

²⁴ Then God said, "Let **the earth bring forth living creatures** after their kind: cattle and creeping things and beasts of the earth after their kind"; and it was so.

²⁵ And God made **the beasts of the earth** after their kind, and the *cattle* after their kind, and **everything that creeps on the ground** after its kind; and God saw that it was good.

²⁶ Then God said, "**Let Us make man** in Our image, according to Our likeness; and let them rule over the fish of the sea and over the birds of the sky and over the cattle and over all the earth, and over every creeping thing that creeps on the earth."

²⁷ And **God created man** in His own image, in the image of God He created him; **male and female He created them**.

²⁸ And God blessed *them*; and God said to them, "Be fruitful and multiply, and fill the earth, and subdue it; and rule over the fish of the sea and over the birds of the sky, and over every living thing that moves on the earth."

²⁹ Then God said, "Behold, I have given you **every plant yielding seed** that is on the surface of all the earth, and **every tree which has fruit yielding seed; it shall be food for you**;

³⁰ and to **every beast** of the earth and to **every bird** of the sky and to **every thing that moves** on the earth which has life, **I have given every green plant for food**"; and it was so.

³¹ And God saw all that He had made, and behold, it was very good. And there was evening and there was morning, **the sixth day**.

2. Comment

2.1 The narrative constituent identified and marked is *content*.

2.2 In a parallel structure, the focus point is the last units of the structure which stands in a contrasting relationship to the other units.

3. The structure is based on the labeling of the narrative constituent content:

```
A vv3–5         light
   B vv6–8      sea and sky
      C vv9–13  dry land and vegetation
A vv14–19       lights
   B vv20–23    fish and birds
      C vv24–31 dry land, animals, and humans
```

Describing and Illustrating the Five Basic Narrative Structures

~ 2 KINGS 21:23–24

1. Marking the Narrative

A

²³ And **the servants of Amon conspired** against him

A

²³ᵇ and *[the servants of Amon] killed the king* in his own house.

B

²⁴ Then **the people of the land** killed all those who had conspired against King Amon,

B

²⁴ᵇ and **the people of the land** made Josiah his son king in his place.

2. Comment

The narrative constituents identified and marked are *character and action.*

3. The structure is based on the labeling of the narrative constituents character and action:

A v23a the servants of Amon conspired against him
A 23b the [servants of Amon] killed him in his own house.
 B v24a *the people killed all those who had conspired against King Amon*
 B v24b *the people of the land made Josiah his son king*

~ 2 SAMUEL 13:1–22

1. Marking the Narrative

A

¹ **Now it was after this** that **Absalom** the son of **David** had a beautiful sister whose name was **Tamar, and Amnon** the son of David loved her.
² And **Amnon was so frustrated because of his sister Tamar** that he made himself ill, for she was a virgin, and it seemed hard to Amnon to do anything to her.

³ But **Amnon had a friend** whose name was **Jonadab**, the son of Shimeah, David's brother; and Jonadab was a very shrewd man.
⁴ And **he said to him**, "O son of the king, why are you so depressed morning after morning? Will you not tell me?" Then **Amnon said to him**, "I am in love with Tamar, the sister of my brother Absalom."
⁵ **Jonadab then said to him**, "Lie down on your bed and pretend to be ill; when your father comes to see you, say to him, 'Please let my sister Tamar come and give me *some* food to eat, and let her prepare the food in my sight, that I may see *it* and eat from her hand.'"

B

⁶ᵃ ***So Amnon lay down and pretended to be ill***;
⁶ᵇ when the king came to see him, **Amnon said to the king**, "Please let my sister Tamar come and make me a couple of cakes in my sight, that I may eat from her hand."

C

⁷ Then **David sent to the house for Tamar, saying**, "Go now to your brother Amnon's house, and prepare food for him."
⁸ᵃ **So Tamar went** to her brother Amnon's house, and he was lying down.

A

⁸ᵇ And **she took dough**, kneaded *it*, made cakes in his sight, and **baked the cakes**.
⁹ And **she took the pan and dished them out before him,** but he refused to eat. And **Amnon said**, "Have everyone go out from me." So everyone went out from him.
¹⁰ **Then Amnon said to Tamar**, "Bring the food into the bedroom, that I may eat from your hand." So **Tamar took the cakes** which she had made and brought them **into the bedroom** to her brother Amnon.
¹¹ When she brought *them* to him to eat, **he took hold of her and said** to her, "Come, lie with me, my sister."
¹² **But she answered him**, "No, my brother, do not violate me, for such a thing is not done in Israel; do not do this disgraceful thing!
¹³ As for me, where could I get rid of my reproach? And as for you, you will be like one of the fools in Israel. Now therefore, please speak to the king, for he will not withhold me from you."

Describing and Illustrating the Five Basic Narrative Structures 99

[14] However, ***he would not listen to her***; since he was stronger than she, ***he violated her and lay with her***.

B

[15] Then ***Amnon hated her with a very great hatred***; for the hatred with which he hated her was greater than the love with which he had loved her. And ***Amnon said to her***, "Get up, go away!"
[16] But ***she said to him***, "No, because this wrong in sending me away is greater than the other that you have done to me!" Yet he would not listen to her.
[17] Then ***he called his young man who attended him and said***, "Now throw this woman out of my *presence*, and lock the door behind her."
[18] Now she had on a long-sleeved garment; for in this manner the virgin daughters of the king dressed themselves in robes. Then ***his attendant took her out and locked the door behind her***.

C

[19] And ***Tamar put ashes on her head***, and ***tore her long-sleeved garment*** which *was* on her; and she ***put her hand on her head and went away, crying aloud as she went***.
[20] Then ***Absalom*** her brother ***said to her***, "Has Amnon your brother been with you? But now keep silent, my sister, he is your brother; do not take this matter to heart." So ***Tamar remained and was desolate in her brother Absalom's house***.
[21] Now when ***King David*** heard of all these matters, he ***was very angry***.
[22] But ***Absalom did not speak to Amnon*** either good or bad; for ***Absalom hated Amnon because he had violated his sister Tamar***.

2. Comment

The narrative constituents identified and marked are *narration, character, and speech*.

3. The structure is based on the labeling of the narrative constituents narration, character, and speech:

```
A vv1–5      Amnon-Tamar-Jonadab
   B v6      Amnon-David
      C vv7–8a   David-Tamar
A vv8b–14  Tamar-Amnon
```

> **B vv15–18**   *Amnon-Tamar*
> **C vv19–22** *David-Absalom*

The five types of narrative structure illustrated above are basic. There are a variety of narrative structural types found in Hebrew narrative, which are combinations of the ones presented here.

5

Exegesis and Interpretation of the Narrative Structure

INTRODUCTION

THE ATTEMPT TO UNDERSTAND the message and meaning of the Old Testament narratives is motivated by the nature of the Scriptures. First, the Bible is rooted in a particular historical and cultural milieu, resulting in a gap between the modern reader and the Scriptures. Therefore, there is a need to establish the message and meaning of the narrative. Second, this historically and culturally conditioned Scripture[1] is the Word of God to the Church and the world. To make this Word of God accessible, finding out the message and meaning of the narratives is necessary and important.

In chapters 3 and 4, two important matters were dealt with in preparation for this task of exegeting and interpreting narrative structure. Uncovering or establishing the structure of a narrative was described and illustrated in detail in chapter 3, and chapter 4 gave extensive examples of the five basic types of narrative structures in the Old Testament. This was preparation for the important task of finding out the message and meaning of the narrative by exegeting and interpreting the structure of the narrative.

Narrative exegesis, as it will be practiced in this chapter, is based on the idea that structure is fundamental and indispensible for meaning in communication. It is for this reason that we focus on the exegesis and interpretation of the structure of the narrative. In this regard, Parunak[2] writes "our motive thus far has been to defend the study of

---

1. Botha, *Semeion*, 25, 28, 48; see also Ska, *Our Fathers*, 94.
2. Parunak, "Axioms," 9.

literary architecture as an exegetical technique." This defense is based on three axioms, which Parunak[3] states as follows, "biblical literature is essentially aural . . . Biblical writers could recognize two passages as similar or dissimilar . . . Biblical writers wrote in paragraphs."

Exegeting and interpreting the narrative involves the description of the structure, and the explanation and clarification of the meaning of the units of the narrative. This process is concerned with the meaning of the narrative structure as uncovered in the narrative text. It is concerned with the meaning of the narrative as a whole, because the structure of the narrative encompasses the whole narrative, thus enabling us to establish the message and the meaning of the whole narrative text.[4] It is part science[5] and part art. The art aspect implies that a measure of subjectivity is involved in the process, which is evident particularly when identifying the dominant narrative constituent of a narrative unit (see chapter 2). The science is evident in the controlled manner in which the exegesis and interpretation are done—the focus is specifically on the narrative text. The common exegetical tools used provide a controlled interpretative and exegetical process to determine the meaning of the narrative.

Ryken[6] describes the goal of determining the meaning of the narrative and its units well: "storytellers intend to communicate meaning," not just establishing the meaning of the narrative. Thus the whole exegetical and interpretation process aims to communicate the content and meaning of the narrative and to lay the foundation for *sermon crafting*. There are two important concepts that facilitate this link between establishing the meaning of the narrative text, communication of the meaning of the narrative text, and sermon crafting:

Focus point: The part of the narrative that has the position of prominence in the structure of the story. The focus point is emphasized by the narrator, and it is more important than the other narrative units because it plays a key role in determining the meaning of the parts and the whole of the narrative.

---

3. Ibid., 2–5.

4. Bar-Efrat, "Observations," 172; Erickson, *Beginner's Guide*, 69, 71; Amit, *Reading*, 57, 126–30; Trible, *Rhetorical Criticism*, 97, 228; Achtemeier, *Preaching*, 39–54; Dorsey, *Literary Structure*, 36; Botha, *Semeion*, 25.

5. Parunak, "Axioms," 9.

6. Ryken, *Words*, 81–83.

Exegesis and Interpretation of the Narrative Structure

Main Point(s): A synthesis in two to three sentences of the exegesis of the narrative unit(s) of the structure. The main point expresses the *main idea* of a narrative unit. It is written at the end of the narrative unit after the exegesis has been completed. It is formulated and written in the language of the text and based on the exegesis and interpretation of the narrative units.

The remainder of this chapter illustrates the exegesis and interpretation of narrative structure, which establishes both the focus point and the main points.

EXAMPLE 1

Genesis 25:20–26

The chiastic structure of this narrative unit is based on the narrative constituents of time and action (event):

- A   v20 Isaac married Rebekah at age forty
  - B   v21a Isaac prayed because Rebekah was barren
    - C   vv21b–22a God answered and Rebekah conceived but there was a struggle in her womb
      - **D   vv22b–23 Rebekah consulted God and he explained what was going on**
    - C   v24 Rebekah carried the pregnancy to full term
  - B   vv25–26a Two sons were born and named
- A   v26b Isaac was sixty years old when Rebekah gave birth to the twins

Description of the Structure

The concentric structure has seven narrative units. It has three matching units with a pivotal unit, D vv22b–23, and gives God a central role in the story. Each unit involves one of the characters in the story. The narrative describes the events in the lives of Isaac and Rebekah from the time Isaac married her until the time she gave birth to the twins; a period of twenty years.

Focus point

D vv22b–23

Rebekah had a strange experience, which she concluded was a struggle in her womb between the twins. Worried that this might result in the premature termination of the pregnancy, she went to enquire of God, who gave her the gift of life. She could have done this for two reasons: 1) culturally, oracles were consulted to explain strange experiences; 2) she was aware that her pregnancy was the answer to Isaac's prayer, and if that was the case, how could God allow something to happen which would undo the answer? So she went to enquire of God.

The oracle of v23 is God's answer to Rebekah's question in v22a: "if it is so, why then am I this way?" literally, "if thus, why this I am? This is a very difficult phrase to translate, but there are at least two possibilities: 1) if the pregnancy is going to terminate prematurely, what was the point in me becoming pregnant in the first place?; 2) if there is this struggle and I stand to lose the babies, what is the point of living, why don't I just die? (see Gen 29:1–4).

Whichever way the question is translated, God made it clear to Rebekah that she need not fear a premature termination of her pregnancy. The assurance is given to her by explaining the meaning of what was happening inside her womb, partial though it was (v23a):

> Two nations are in your womb;
> Two peoples will be separated from your body
> And one shall be stronger than the other
> And the older shall serve the younger.

Rebekah's experience here is similar to that of Mary in Luke 2:29–35.

This oracle of God implies that neither her pregnancy nor the way things will turn out for Esau and Jacob is the arbitrary result of circumstances, or a fluke of history. What she was experiencing was part of something bigger, the meaning of which can only be understood partially.

Rebekah's experience represents what the sons will experience in future (their conflict and struggle) as God works out his purpose and intention.

Main point: Rebekah, concerned that her pregnancy would be prematurely terminated, enquired of God who explained to her what was going on in her womb.

A v20

The narrative unit is much more than just an indication of the age at which Isaac married. The chronological phrase "Isaac was forty years when he married Rebekah," affirms the events of chapter 24, namely, that Abraham's servant carried out his covenant obligations, 24:2–49, and that Abraham's confidence in God was rewarded, 24:7–8. It further underlines that God honored his promissory covenant with Abraham, 24:5–7. The emphasis on the significance of the "land" is important here. Isaac married Rebekah in the land of promise in fulfillment of God's promise to Abraham, which portrays God as the promise- and covenant-keeping God.

Main point: Isaac married Rebekah when he was forty years old which affirmed the faithfulness of the servant, that Abraham was rewarded for his faith, and emphasized that God kept his promise.

B v21a

Rebekah is barren. It is stated as a fact with no explanation given. The barrenness of Rebekah casts a shadow over the picture of God we just saw in v20. It would appear that v20 and its significance is now undone; in fact, an important element of the promissory-covenant (24:7) is now under threat. A descendant of Abraham was in the land, so that part of the promise was realized; however, the promise that Abraham's descendants would continue to inherit the land was now under threat due to Rebekah's barrenness.

Main point: Rebekah's barrenness threatened the Abrahamic promissory-covenant.

C vv21b–22a

God answered the prayers of Isaac and the threat was removed. But the threat of not carrying the pregnancy full-term (v22a) soon followed. Rebekah perceived the "struggle" to mean that she would lose the babies. But not only that, she stood to lose more: "if it is thus, why do/should I live?" This literally reads, "if thus, why this I am?" This could mean: a) if there is this possibility of losing the children, what is the point of being pregnant? If I am to lose the children why did I get pregnant in the first place? b) if there is this struggle and I stand to lose the babies, what is the point of living? (See Gen 29:1–4). The threat has now widened; not only is the promissory-covenant under threat, but it potentially has socio-cultural consequences for Rebekah's dignity, as her position in the community was also under threat.

Main point: *The answer to Isaac's prayers was under threat, as was Rebekah's future, due to the possibility of an early termination of the pregnancy.*

C v24

Rebekah's concern was that she would not carry the pregnancy to full-term (25:22b). The words of the narrator "when *her days* to be delivered *were fulfilled*" (my emphasis), meant the threat had been removed and she did carry the pregnancy to full-term. When she was giving birth, it was found that she indeed had twins. It was in the actual act of giving birth that something of the meaning of the oracle became evident, for the text says "there were twins in her womb," which she did not know in v22. If she had known she had twins and her uncomfortable feeling was a result of their movement, it would not have been necessary for her to do what she did in v22b. Verse 22a makes it clear that she was perplexed about what was happening to her.

Main point: *Rebekah partially understood the significance of what she had experienced at the time she actually gave birth.*

B vv25–26a

This unit describes the birth and the naming of the twins, which sees half of the oracle of v23 fulfilled. The founding fathers of the two nations are born. The naming of the founding fathers symbolized the continuation of the struggle: ". . . the first came forth red . . . they named him Esau . . . his brother came forth with his hand holding on to Esau's heel." The second half of the oracle starts at this point; the struggle continues outside the womb.

Main point: *The manner in which the twins were born signaled the continuation of the struggle outside the womb.*

A v26b

A second time reference is given in the text when the events in the narrative come to end: "Isaac was sixty years old." A period of twenty years had passed between the marriage of Isaac to Rebekah and the birth of his sons. During this time, the realization of the promissory-covenant seemed in doubt (cf. 25:21a, v22a), but it was reaffirmed with the birth of the twins. The repetition of the time reference in the narrative unit makes the point that the length of time it took God to keep his word is not important; it is the timing that matters.

Main point: Twins were born to Isaac when he was sixty years old, signaling that God is still at work to fulfill his promise to Abraham.

SUMMARY

Isaac married and twenty years later sons were born to him. But before the birth, the pregnancy was under threat by the struggle of the twins in her womb, which symbolized the future struggle and conflict between the sons. However, the oracle of God explained the struggle, although Rebekah did not have a full understanding of the significance of v23b. After a wait of twenty years, sons are born to Isaac, signaling that God is keeping his promise to Abraham.

EXAMPLE 2

Genesis 24:1–67

The concentric structure based is on the narrative constituents of character and action (events):

- A *vv1–9 Abraham made his servant swear an oath*
    - B vv10–31 The servant was guided by God to the house of Nahor
    - B vv32–61 The servant convinced the family that his mission was from God and departed with Rebekah for Canaan
- A *vv62–67 The servant fulfilled the oath he swore*

DESCRIPTION OF THE STRUCTURE

This is a concentric structure, and as such the outer matching units are the point of focus.

In the first unit in A vv1–9, Abraham made a covenant with his servant. The last unit A (vv62–67) describes the fulfillment of vv1–9; the fulfillment of the oath sworn by the servant. The servant's journey now completed, meant that the task was also completed. God made the journey successful; God had "sent his angel before you" (v40, v7). The focus point of the story is the oath sworn by the servant and his success in carrying out the oath, aided by God. At a second level, it is about God continuing to keep his promise to the descendants of Abraham.

FOCUS POINT

A vv1–9 and A vv62–67

The two units are exegeted together. This is because in a concentric structure, the focus point and thus the key to the meaning of the structure are the beginning and end units of the structure. Verses 1–9 describes the steps Abraham took as he did his final duty as a father; find a wife for Isaac his heir, and so ensure posterity. Even though v1 says "the Lord had blessed him *in every way*" (my emphasis), there was still something missing: assurance of descendants, for Isaac who was not married. The idea that he could die without seeing his seed through Isaac, or at least have the promise of seed through Isaac's marriage, motivated Abraham to take action. He made his chief servant swear an oath that he would find a wife for Isaac from Haran and not from Canaan.

Abraham told his servant "put your hand under my thigh" (v2b). The oath-swearing ceremony is detailed in vv2–4. Since the hand is under the thigh and therefore near the genitals, some commentators understand the placing of the hand under the thigh, near the genitals, as making the vow in the presence of the seed; but this seems unlikely. On the other hand, since Abraham's seed is the continuation of his *life*, putting the hand near the genitals or grasping the genitals means that if Abraham's *life* comes to end as a result of the servant's doing, the life of the servant will also come to an end (v5+v8). If he cuts off the seed of Abraham, his life will be cut off.

The oath is taken in the name of "the Lord, the God of heaven and the God of earth" (v3). "The Lord" describes God as the covenantal God, while "the God of heaven and the God of earth" describes him as the creator.

The servant raised a concern (v5) that Rebekah may refuse to come with him, even though vv50–51 suggests that she had no say in the matter, although she is consulted in vv57–59. These verses are better understood as one of Laban's schemes to keep Rebekah at Haran, given vv54b–56 (see also v30). Laban will try this again later (29:25–27). Rebekah's refusal is a *possible* complication, but custom and convention suggests it is not a *real* one (vv50–51, 29:15–30). Abraham, however, treats it as a real possibility and did two things: he agreed that if the girl refused, the servant would be free from the consequences of not fulfilling the oath, and in this way the fear of the servant is dealt with (v8a). By making a way out for the servant, Abraham put his trust in God, hoping that God will do what Abraham says in v7. So in effect, the story became a "test" for God and not really a test for the servant. In a sense, the situations were reversed in terms of Genesis 22. But although the story was a "test" of God, it was also a testimony of Abraham's matured faith. And to indicate that the Abraham here is the one of whom God said "now I know that you fear God" (22:12), the narrator records Abraham's expression of absolute and bold confidence that his God who covenanted with him will ensure the success of the servant (vv6–7). The ceremony is concluded in v9. Everything is now ready for the return journey to begin, which indicates that the oath has been performed, that God had passed the "test," and that Abraham's confidence in God was rewarded and his faith had matured.

Verses 62–67 bring the story full circle. The servant returned with a wife for Isaac from Abraham's clan, as Abraham had instructed. Moreover, Isaac was still in the Promised Land, something Abraham was adamant about (v3b–4, 6, 8b). Ending the story as described in vv62–67 adds another dimension to v1, "and the Lord blessed Abraham in every way." The implication is that Abraham finally got everything he wanted. But according to v1, "Abraham was old and advanced in age," and he might not see grand children from Isaac. Thus the "blessed Abraham in every way" of v1 includes the hope that the potential of v7 would be realized. The most important thing Abraham received was the assurance that God would honor the covenant (24:7). This is the significance of vv62–67: they affirm Abraham's confidence in God as expressed in the words of v7, as well as the realization of Abraham's hope that the servant will bring back a wife for Isaac from his clan. Therefore, even though Abraham is not referred to in the unit, and we are not told whether

Rachel met Abraham, the unit is still all about him. Although the focus seems to be on the servant who accomplished what he swore he would do, it is really not about him. After all, the servant had "an escape clause" in the oath (v8). So it is really not about the servant, it is about God passing the "test" set by Abraham (v7). Abraham can now get on with putting "his house in order" (25:1–11) before he died, which is what he did in chapter 25.

Against this background, the outer matching units A and A, which describe how a wife was found for Isaac, are really a symbol of the fulfillment of the covenant; and a pointer to the covenant faithfulness of God. The message is that the fulfillment of the covenant was still on track, which sets the direction for the episodes to follow. So the arrival of the servant back in Canaan with a wife for Isaac not only meant he had fulfilled his oath but also that God had passed the "test" and that the promise would still be fulfilled.

Main point: *The servant, having sworn an oath, arrived back with the right wife for Isaac, affirming Abraham's trust in God and proving that God had passed the "test."*

B vv10–31 and B vv32–61

Apparently the servant did not have difficulty in finding a wife for Isaac from the clan of Abraham. His problem was her willingness to go with him to Canaan, or rather, the willingness of her family to let her go with him.

In these narrative units there are recorded incidences on the journey to Haran that would give the servant enough to share with the family that would convince them that his mission was divinely ordained and that the girl should go with him. The incidences are not for the benefit of the servant, but for the girl's family.

The servant nearly exactly repeats the details of the journey and the different incidences:

1. His request to God and God's fulfillment of it.

2. Abraham's instructions to him and how this worked out. The details stress that what happened in B and B was miraculous and supernatural, so that Laban came to the conclusion he did in v50 (see also v51, v52). Moreover, the inner units B and B

Exegesis and Interpretation of the Narrative Structure   111

also describe *how* God demonstrated his covenant faithfulness (see vv62–67).

In vv10–31 the servant prayed for God's guidance to find the house of Nahor. His prayer was answered as vv10–21 shows. The servant prayed (vv12–14), and he had hardly ended his prayer when the answer came (vv15–20). Verse 21 is interesting, because in vv12–14 he prayed and everything for which he prayed happened and yet we are told that "he gazed at her in silence to learn." Was the servant dumbstruck? I don't think so. In addition, one would have thought that there was nothing more to learn for the answer to his prayer was happening right before his eyes. But vv22–27 clarifies what he was seeking to learn: whether she was from the clan of Abraham. He was not taking the first signs of answered prayer as conclusive evidence that she was the girl. He wanted firmer evidence and received this in v24. It was at this point that he gave her the gifts (v10, v30, v47). The fact that he was certain beyond a shadow of a doubt reverberates from the prayer in vv26–27. There are two prayers: one to make a request, the second to give thanks.

In vv28–49 there is a near verbal repetition of everything that had happened on his journey. Why does he do this? It was repeated for the benefit of Rebekah, who heard his story and agreed to go with him (v5, vv57–58). So, one function of the near verbatim repetition was to persuade Rebekah to go with him, as his mission was clearly from God (vv32–61).

But Rebekah was not the only one that had to be persuaded that this was a divine mission. Rebekah's mother, Laban and her father also had to be persuaded of this. The process of persuasion is now described in vv50–61. The verbatim and detailed account by the servant of how God brought him to their house, resulted in the men in the family, her brother Laban and her father Bethuel, agreeing to let her go with him. They were convinced that what had happened to the servant was God's work (vv50–51). Now that he had their agreement, his mission was accomplished. He "bow[ed] to the Lord" v52; in this way he acknowledged and affirmed the role of God in all that had happened. At the same time his "bow to the Lord" affirmed the conclusion of Laban and Bethuel (vv50–51): the servant's request had the blessing of God. Next, as was the custom, he gave gifts (v53), which affirmed his declaration in v35.

After this, they settled down to have a meal, which celebrated and sealed the agreement reached in vv50–51.

The next morning, when the servant wanted to return home, the family tried to delay him, vv54b–55. The mother's reluctance and request seemed genuine, but Laban's request was questionable (v30). The servant overcame the reluctance of Laban and Rebekah's mother in v56b: "do not delay me since the Lord has prospered my way," in other words, do not stand in the way of God, for you yourself admitted that my mission was God ordained (vv51–52); do not work against what God is busy doing by delaying me. In this way the servant appealed to the decision the family arrived at earlier, that everything that had happened up to that point was the work of God.

Verses 57–58a did not unnerve the servant, because he was convinced that God would make Rebekah agreeable, even though her willingness to go with him appeared to be his biggest concern. Rebekah was consulted and she agreed to go. So the family blessed Rebekah, and sent the caravan on its way to Canaan v59–61. "So the servant took Rebekah and departed" (v61).

Main point: *The servant persuaded Rebekah and her family to let her go to Canaan with him by demonstrating that his mission was ordained of God.*

EXAMPLE 3

Judges 1:1–2:5

The ring structure is based on the narrative constituent of event (action):

- A vv1–2 God said Judah must lead the war to take the land and assured them of victory
    - **B vv3–36 *The successes and failures of the tribes in taking the land***
- A vv1–5 Failure to take the land was blamed on the people's covenant unfaithfulness

DESCRIPTION OF THE STRUCTURE

This ring structure (or inclusion) deals with the war effort, led by Judah, to take the land allotted to the various tribes. The experience of Judah

Exegesis and Interpretation of the Narrative Structure 113

served as an example of what was required to have success. The point of focus is unit B, vv3–36. The unit alternates between success and failure. When unit B is examined, the reason for the failure seems to be that there is a natural explanation for the failures (v27b and 29): the adoption of the wrong battle tactics, or the wrong equipment for war, or the fact that the people were too strong and determined not to be removed from their land.

The narrative units A and A explain the mixed results of the focus point. It was not the natural explanation evident from vv3–36; the problem was deeper. The units A and A attribute the mixed results to a fundamental failure of Judah's covenant loyalty. God had already given the land to Judah (v2), but their covenant unfaithfulness by intermingling with the people of the land resulted in their failure. And the same was true of the rest of tribes who were guilty of different types of covenant unfaithfulness.

Focus Point

B vv3–36

In vv3–7, the defeat of the Canaanites and the Perizzites, and especially Adoni-Bezek, is discussed. In vv 3–4, the campaign is generally described. The unit is framed by the narrative device technique; the narrator used speech and narration in v3, v7, and vv4–6 to describe what happened to the town of Bezek and its king, Adoni-Bezek:

> v3 *Speech and narration—Judah*
>
> v4a "the Lord gave *the Canaanite and the Perizzites* into their hands" (see v2b) and
> v4b "they defeated ten thousand of them at Bezek"
> v5a "They came upon Adoni-Bezek at Bezek"
> v5b "and defeated *the Canaanites and the Perizzites*" (my emphasis)
>
> v6a "Adoni-Bezek fled"
> v6b "but they pursued him"
> v6c "and caught him"
> v6d "and cut off his thumbs and his great toes"
>
> v7 *Speech and narration—Adoni-Bezek*

"Canaanites and Perizzites" (v4a) is the term used to describe the population of Palestine (cf. v4, 5, 9, 10). Verses 4–5 describe the defeat of the city Bezek and confirm what God said in v2b, "I have given the land into his hand." The defeat of Bezek and Adoni-Bezek represented the defeat of the Canaanites and the Perizzites, and also represented the realization of v2b.

In vv6–7a, the punishment meted out to Adoni-Bezek, the king of the city, is retributive judgment. He was punished for what he did to seventy other kings (v7), in terms of the lex talionis principle (an eye for an eye), as Adoni-Bezek confirms "as I have done, so God had requited me" (v7). Judah's action is understood by the narrator as God's act of retributive justice; Judah is the instrument for bringing about justice. This could signify God's expectation of the role of Israel in the new land about to be occupied; Israel was to be God's instrument of ensuring justice.

Verse 7c reports that Judah brought Adoni-Bezek to Jerusalem where he died. Sparing the life of Adoni-Bezek was in contrast to vv8–10 and vv16–17. The actions in the latter verses are more in keeping with the strategy of the campaign under Joshua. Therefore it would appear that the death of Adoni-Bezek is reported here as a flashback to a past event to make the point that the first phase of the campaign was a success. But the success was only partial, because the king of Bezek was still alive. The fact that he was still alive was evidence that the campaign was not a complete success and symbolic of Judah's covenant unfaithfulness because he did not follow the campaign strategy under Joshua. The allusion to the Joshua campaign in vv8–10 and vv16–17 links up with the double reference to Caleb in vv11–15 and v20. It also supports the idea that the reference to Caleb is a flashback to the Joshua campaign and not a report of an actual battle at the time of the Judah campaign, which in turn strengthens the idea that vv11–15 and v20 are example stories. They symbolize what was required for success.

Main point: *Judah had both success and failure in its campaign against the Canaanites and Perizzites.*

Verse 8 describes the defeat and complete destruction of Jerusalem. This battle was the second phase of the campaign. Given what is said in v7c, it would appear that Jerusalem already belonged to Judah, or at least to a group on friendly terms with Judah, because in v7c Judah left

Exegesis and Interpretation of the Narrative Structure 115

Adoni-Bezek in Jerusalem, where he died. The destruction of Jerusalem described in v8 must have happened some time after vv3–7, otherwise it would not have been possible for Judah to bring Adoni-Bezek to Jerusalem to die there.

Alternative explanations for the reference to Jerusalem in v7c and v8 are: the Jerusalem referred to in v7c is not the same place, and the place called Jerusalem in v8 had a different name before; or the Jerusalem in v8 refers to Salem (Gen 14) at the southern tip of the Dead Sea (see Josh 15:3). If this is the case, then the geographical movement would make more sense: Bezek (vv3–7), to Salem (v8), to Hebron (vv9–10), to Diber (vv11–15), to Hormah (16–17), to Gaza, Ashkelon, and Ekron (vv18).

The town is utterly destroyed. It is possible that Adoni-Bezek died when the town was set on fire (v7c). Thus the defeat and destruction of Jerusalem reflected the successful second phase of the campaign. This success maintained the momentum of progress and the partial success achieved in the first campaign (vv3–7, for some background see Joshua 10). The account in Judges was the second time war was made against Jerusalem. The first war was against Adoni-*Zedek*, as recorded in Joshua (10:20b), and here it is against Adoni-*Bezek*.

Main point: *The town of Jerusalem was utterly destroyed and Adoni-Bezek was killed in the process.*

Verses 9–10 focus on the third phase of the campaign, indicated by the expression "afterward" (v9); taking place *after* the events of v8. The campaign moved further south into the Negev and in particular: the hill country (mountainous regions of the Negev); the lowland (foothills of the Negev); then the campaign moved north-west to Hebron. The sons of Anak, Sheshai, Ahiman, and Talmai were defeated (cf. Josh 15:13–14), and the city burnt down. It was a repeat of what happened at Jerusalem (v8) and very similar to what happened under Joshua's campaign, which was characterized by the implementation of the ban (haram). This flashback to the success of the previous generation may have been an example of what the current tribes should have done as they moved into the country.

Main point: *The regions of the Negev were utterly destroyed.*

The unit vv11–15 does not describe a battle during the campaign of the tribe of Judah. It recalls a previous event: the defeat of Debir/Kiriath-sepher by Caleb and Othniel. Debir was defeated during the campaign of Joshua (15:14–19; 14:6–15) and it is mentioned again in v20. The narrator deemed it important to refer twice to this historical event while narrating Judah's campaign, using this past event as an ideal, a standard of what was required of the tribes if they were to be successful in occupying their allotted territories. This was the narrator's point of view. Caleb possessed a trait which is described in Joshua 14:6–9, and which is now held up by the narrator as the ideal to be imitated for complete success.

In Joshua 14:6–9, Caleb's trait is found in the expressions "I brought word back to him as it was in my heart . . . but I followed the Lord my God fully . . . you have followed the Lord my God fully." Caleb was wholeheartedly committed to God, and it was this trait that the narrator held up as a requirement for success. Chapter 3:1–5 indicates that they did not have this quality. So this unit does not describe a battle of the current campaign, but is a flashback to a previous event to point out what was required for complete success in the present campaign.

Main point: Caleb's wholehearted commitment to God was held up as an example of what was required for complete success in taking the land.

The Kenites, vv16–18, who were relatives of Moses, now joined Judah and Simeon in the campaign to take the land allotted to Simeon (v16; see v3b). This was the fourth phase of the campaign, moving to the mountainous areas (hill country) on the west towards the Mediterranean Sea, which bordered on Philistine territory. The addition of the Kenites strengthened the fighting force, and they successfully captured the territory allotted to Simeon.

Main point: Simeon occupied his allotted territory successfully with the help of Judah and the Kenites.

Verses 9–20 are similar to vv11–15; they do not describe an event of the campaign, no battle is fought and no area is settled. It is a summary of the campaign of Judah: "he took possession of the hill country." The hill country refers to all the territory taken by Judah.

Verse 19a states "and the Lord was with Judah and he took possession of the hill country." This sentence goes back to v2b, "I have given the land into his hand." It summarizes the campaign of the tribe of Judah in response to v1, which suggests that the whole campaign was a complete success. But then in v19b it says: "but he could not drive out the inhabitants of the plain, because they had chariots of iron." It is clear from this half-verse that the war effort was not a *complete* success. This half-verse was the Achilles heel; the weakness in an otherwise successful campaign.

But how is this sentence to be understood given v2b, where we are told that the Lord had given the land into Judah's hand? It is clear that there was a portion of the land that had not been given into Judah's hand. Does this mean the Lord could not overcome the chariots of iron? The answer to these questions is found in v20. It recalls the success of Caleb in taking the portion of land allotted to him, vv11–15, which is an allusion to Joshua 14 and 15. The two campaigns are compared: Judah failed, Caleb succeeded. Verse 19b is contrasted with v20. The failure might be considered fairly insignificant, but when compared to Caleb's campaign, it becomes significant. It violated a fundamental principle illustrated by Caleb; a principle which was necessary for the successful occupation of allotted territory.

When Debir was taken, and the giants (Anakim) who lived in Kiriath-sepher (Debir) were defeated, Caleb/Othniel had a very small fighting force. But Judah, with his huge fighting force, could not take the valley, because of "chariots of iron." Caleb's lack of resources is reinforced in Joshua 14:11–12, and yet he had complete success.

Chapter 14:12b of Joshua reads "perhaps the Lord will be with me." This counters the confident speech of Caleb in vv11–12a. This could be an expression of doubt and uncertainty, in contrast to v12b which reads, "and I will them drive out as the Lord has spoken." Two points will help clarify this matter. We must separate what the Lord said from what the Lord did not say. According to Caleb, the Lord said that the land would be his and that of his children as an inheritance (v12a, Josh 14:10). The Lord did not say that he was going to be with Caleb on the day when he actually takes the land, even though this was Caleb's expectation. The following translation of the half-verse might help to clarify this point: "the Lord will be with me, *perhaps*" (my emphasis). He made the statement and then realized that he was *presuming too much*, stopped, and rectified himself by adding "perhaps." So the "perhaps" was rather an expression of the fact that he was not presumptuous, rather than doubt or uncertainty. Moreover, "perhaps" (Hebrew *'ula*) can also mean hope, so Caleb's expression could be a statement of what he had hoped for, with no guarantee. Caleb was careful to do as the Lord spoke (Josh 14:8b, 9b, 14b) and expected from the Lord only what he had spoken; for the rest he could only hope, as it was up to the Lord. This implies that even now, Caleb had to follow the Lord wholeheartedly, as he did previously. This was the type of person Caleb was, in contrast to the tribe of Judah.

The failure of Judah is stated by Wong[7] as follows, "Judah's failure to live up to its full potential . . . [the narrator draws attention to] their [incorrect] perception of reality." This is in direct contrast to Caleb (see Josh 14:11–12; 6–12).

Verse 20 recalls the success of Caleb in taking the portion of land allotted to him, (see vv11–15, of which v20 is a summary). On the basis of this recall, there is an internal concentric pattern:

A vv11–15   ***Caleb's success***
B v16–18–19a   Judah (and Simeon's) success: Judah is the dominant person
B v19b   Judah's failure
A v20   ***Caleb's success***

The fact that Caleb's success features so prominently suggests a contrast on a broader level. Caleb is part of the group that took the land under Joshua; that generation had complete success under Joshua and God. Caleb now appears in a campaign by the next generation, in which each tribe must settle the land allotted to them. And to do that they must drive out whoever still occupied their portion of the land. The contrast between the complete success of Caleb's generation and the partial success of the current generation is the narrator's way of announcing the theme for the book of Judges already seen in the prologue, namely, the *inability to realize God's purpose and follow His will was to be a main characteristic of the next generation.*

This specific inability to follow God is also brought out with this contrast. In the campaign to settle Judah's allotted territory, the tribes of Judah and Simeon are joined by the Kenites. In contrast, Caleb was alone when he took his allotted territory, v20 (cf. Othniel at Debir, vv11–15).

---

7. Wong, *Strategy*, 49.

Caleb and Othniel had fewer people to fight the enemy and yet they were successful, whereas Judah with all his people only achieved partial success. Success is not dependent upon numbers, it is dependent on other factors as illustrated in the life of Caleb.

In summary, the tribes of Judah and Simeon set out to settle in the territory allotted to them. This alliance was led by Judah. It had almost complete success except for a small strip of land, the area in the valley on the south-west, which it failed to settle. The first attempt to possess an allotted tribal territory was characterized by success mixed with failure. The allusion to Caleb's successful settlement in vv11–15 and v20 is in contrast to this failure. The Judah alliance may have had the resources and the fighting force, but what they lacked was the character of the previous generation under Joshua, represented by Caleb: to follow the Lord wholeheartedly.

Main point: *The Judah alliance only had partial success in possessing their allotted territory because they lacked the character trait of wholehearted commitment to God, as shown by Caleb.*

Verse 21 records the attempt of the tribe of Benjamin to take its allotted territory. The attempt is described as follows, the "sons of Benjamin did not drive out." The outcome is then stated in v21b: "the Jebusites lived with the sons of Benjamin." This remained the situation "to this day," that is, to the point at which the story was recorded.

The first thing to note in this verse is the phrase "did not drive out," which is then affirmed in v21b "lived with." The tribe of Benjamin failed.

Further, the words "the Jebusites lived with" give the impression that the tribe of Benjamin was in control and that they allowed the local people to live among them. But Judges 19 shows that the Jebusites had a devastating influence on the social life of Benjamin. The Benjamites took over the practices of the people of the town of Gibeah. It appears that the locals were in control, rather than the Benjamites.

Main point: *The tribe of Benjamin failed to take its allotted territory.*

The house of Joseph was the next tribe that attempted to occupy its allotted land (vv 22–29). The tribe consisted of the two half tribes of Manasseh and Ephraim, and therefore the attempts by both tribes of the house of Joseph are dealt with as one attempt.

Verses 22–26 describe the attempt of the house of Joseph as one unit. There are a number of subtle links, via *allusions,* between this story and the Rahab story in Joshua chapters 2 and 6. The following similarities are observed in this story and the Rahab story:

1. An offer is made: "we will treat you with kindness and faithfulness."
2. The man and his family are sent away. Rahab and her family are brought out to safety.
3. Both endings are qualified in the same way, "until this day." Both stories are recorded after the fact and have an enduring significance.

But there are significant differences. Rahab and her family were integrated into the Israelite community, probably living in the community until they died. The man and his family went and rebuilt the destroyed city, so that Luz lived on. The continued existence of Luz as Bethel symbolized the failure of the house of Joseph, whereas in the account in Joshua, the spies were successful and Jericho was conquered.

But why this difference? In both stories a promise was made. But the circumstances under which the promises were made were different:

a. In the Rahab story: she asked to be shown kindness (*hesed*). This request was based on her profession of faith in Yahweh, which is informed by Yahweh's demonstration of his supremacy and invincibility (Josh 2:9–11). This was not just a simple offer in exchange for Rahab's cooperation; it was based on a relationship rooted in Rahab's profession of faith in Yahweh. *Hesed* is normally used in covenants, which establishes a relationship (Josh 2:12; see also chapter 9).

b. In the Judges story: the spies made the offer of kindness (*hesed*) in exchange for help and assistance from the man. Put differently, the offer of *hesed* was not preceded by a confession of faith or an acknowledgement of Yahweh on the part of the man. This led to their failure. The promise of *hesed* was inappropriate, because the conditions for the promise did not exist. The condition is not a prerequisite for the promise of *hesed*, it is the warrant for *hesed*. And by promising *hesed*, they entered into a covenant with the man, which as 2:1–5 will show was an act of disobedience to God. Boling comments that this type of covenant-making in v22 ". . . seems to have served to the final editor as an example of the covenant-making that had been outlawed by Yahweh according to the indictment of Israel in [Judges] 2:2."[8]

The idea that there was no basis for showing mercy to the man follows from the meaning of Luz: "to turn aside, to depart, with devious connotations." The man of Luz was a deceptive person.

Furthermore, Jericho was taken without human help, whereas in 1:22–26, the house of Joseph depended on human help. But was Rahab's help not that of a human person? Yes, but it was God working through Rahab, who professed her faith in Yahweh based on the reports she heard. In this sense, God had prepared her long in advance to be his help to his people, so that the outcome of the incident is ascribed to God and his doing. This is what was different from the events in vv22–26. *The house of Joseph gained a military victory not based on the instructions of God, but based on presumptuous deal making.*

There was also the statement "that God was with them." If this was so, then they had all the help they needed to enter and take the city. They did not need the help of the man. In addition, they were presumptuous and careless in relying on Joshua's strategy, and omitted an important element of that strategy, the ban (*haram*), which led to their failure. The man re-established the city of Bethel under the name Luz.

Verses 27–28 describe the attempt by the tribe of Manasseh. The unit is framed by two phrases:

> v27a "And not had taken possession of Manasseh"
> v28b " . . . Israel . . . did not drive them out completely"

Manasseh also failed to take possession of his territory. The "and" is translated variously; for example the New American Standard reads "so," and Revised Standard Version "but." It is affixed in Hebrew to the verb *y'l*, with the root meaning "to be intent on, to resolve." Given this, the Hebrew conjunction "and" should be translated as causative. So v27b would read "because the Canaanites resolved to live in that land" (see 1 Chr 17:27, Gen 18:27, 31; Job 6:9; Exod 2:21, Judg 1:35, 19:6). The Canaanites were not going to move. This implies that when the tribes of Manasseh attacked, they experienced strong resistance from Beth-

---

8. Boling, *Judges*, 65.

shean, Tanaach, Dor, Ibleam, Megiddo, and their villages. The tribe of Manasseh capitulated and allowed the Canaanites to live among them. In other words, they accepted that these cities and their villages were unconquerable, despite the fact that "God was with them" (v22b). They failed because they accepted the resolve and stubbornness of the Canaanites; they resigned themselves to the idea that these cities and villages could not be taken.

Verse 28 begins "and it came to pass," indicating some time had elapsed when the event described here had taken place. "Israel" in this immediate context could be a reference to Manasseh, and not to the nation Israel. Further, all the verbs in vv27–28 are *hiphil* verbs, which join the two verses into one unit. The verbs are also causative in general, suggesting that the tribe of Manasseh had ability and capacity; they were able to cause the land to be dispossessed. So they did not lack ability, but self-belief, God-belief, and determination.

After some time, Manasseh (Israel) became strong and "they put the Canaanites to forced labor." Instead of using their strength to dispossess the Canaanites, the tribe of Manasseh extracted tribute from them. They used their strength to meet their immediate economic and social needs rather than achieving the intention of the covenant: dispossess the inhabitants. They used their strength in the wrong way; achieving short-term goals instead of the divine covenantal goal. So "Israel did not drive out the nations."

The issue here was not one of inability or capacity; they had it. They used their strength, capacity, and ability to break covenant rather than obey the covenant. They used their strength to do what was right in their eyes; extract an economic benefit from the Canaanites rather than using their strength to do what was right in the eyes of Yahweh.

In addition, by not using their strength, capacity, and ability to obey the covenant, they indirectly used their strength to help accomplish the Canaanites' objective to continue to live in the land (v27b).

Verse 29 records the attempt of Ephraim to dispossess those occupying his allotted territory. The house of Joseph consists of the two tribes Ephraim and Manasseh, the sons of Joseph (Gen 48), and vv22–29 forms one unit based on this genealogical link. In dealing with Ephraim's attempt, the refrain "Ephraim did not drive out" returns once more. No reason is given for this failure, but because Ephraim is part of the house of Joseph, it is reasonable to attribute the failure in v27 to the belief that

Exegesis and Interpretation of the Narrative Structure 123

the inhabitants were invincible even though God was with the house of Joseph, and therefore with Ephraim.

Main point: The house of Joseph failed because it covenanted inappropriately, lacked self-belief, and settled for short-term socio-economic gains.

Verse 30: The next tribe to attempt dispossessing the inhabitants was Zebulun. And once again, "Zebulun did not drive out." The inhabitants became *lāmass*; from the root *mass* meaning "a tax, or tribute." The inhabitants became a source of income (a tax) for the tribe of Zebulun. This suggests that Zebulun had the power to dispossess the inhabitants, but decided to use them as forced labor (tributary). As seen before, economic advantage is chosen over the command of God to possess the land he promised to their forefathers.

Main point: Zebulun failed because they chose to use the inhabitants as a source of income rather than achieving God's purpose.

The description of the fortunes of the tribe of Asher, vv31–32 is bracketed by the now familiar refrain:

> v31 "And Asher did not drive out the inhabitants"
> v32 "for they lived among the Canaanite inhabitants . . ."

This passage reverses the trend. Until this point, inhabitants live among the other tribes, but here "the Asherites lived among the Canaanites" (v32a). This implies that the Asherites were assimilated by the Canaanites (see 1:33 and 3:5–6 below). This action risked their identity; they were under the control of the inhabitants of the land and subjected to the influences of the society, and at risk of losing their status as the people of Yahweh.

Main point: Asher was assimilated by the Canaanites and stood to lose their identity.

Naphtali (v33), like Asher, lived among the Canaanites. There was a difference though; the Canaanites became a *tributary* to Naphtali, unlike Asher which merely allowed themselves to be assimilated into the Canaanite society and culture. Naphtali took this action despite the fact that they had the power to dispossess the locals: "Naphtali did not dispossess" and the inhabitants became tributary, a means of economic gain. Naphtali's position was not the result of inability but one of choice; he decided not to dispossess the inhabitants and settled for less.

Dispossessing the inhabitants meant war, and it appears that Naphtali was not willing to do this. So he settled for receiving tributary from the inhabitants instead of possessing the land itself.

The text seems to suggest that they developed a lack of enthusiasm for Yahweh's purpose to make them his people, a people distinct and different from the nations around them. By living in the midst of the Canaanites, they would, over time, become indistinguishable from the locals and stood to lose their identity as a covenant people of Yahweh.

Main point: *Naphtali failed, by choice, to take possession of the land allotted to him.*

The tribe of Dan is discussed in vv34–36. The refrain "and . . . did not drive out the inhabitants" is missing from this discussion. The inhabitants are the Amorites, and they dominated the Danites, and "pressed the sons of Dan into the hill country." The Amorites forced the Danites into the hill country and kept them out of the valley, so that they could live in the valley themselves (v34b–35a). The Danites made several attempts to take the valley, but were pressed back every time. Although the text does not explicitly say that the Danites did not drive out the Amorites, it is clear that this is what happened.

Even though the Amorites were able to force Dan out of the valley, they could not do the same with the house of Joseph (v35b). The "house of Joseph" refers to the tribe of Ephraim located to the north of the Amorites. The Amorites were a source of forced labor to the house of Joseph (Ephraim). Ephraim, who was in a position to help his brother Dan, appeared to be more interested in his own economic prosperity. Against this background, Dan seems to be a victim both of a greedy brother and his own lack of determination. He did not demonstrate the determination needed to fight for his inheritance until it was achieved.

Verse 36 gives a detailed description of the southern border of the Amorites, demonstrating that they maintained the integrity of their land. They lost nothing; the tribe of Dan failed to dispose of the inhabitants of its allotted land.

Main point: Dan failed for two reasons: a lack of determination, and not receiving help from the greedy house of Joseph.

Summary, vv3–36: After the death of Joshua, all the tribes failed to take complete possession of their allotted territory primarily because they lacked the *strength of character* characteristic of the previous generation.

A vv1–2 and A vv1–5

In contrast to the B unit, the A and A units give a further reason for the failures (see 2:2b). However, the apparent reason in this narrative unit is not the real reason for the failure of the tribes to conquer and occupy their allotted territory.

In v1, the tribes who had not yet dispossessed the inhabitants were ready to take possession of the land allotted to them by Joshua. The reference in 1:1a to "after the death of Joshua" indicates that what follows took place after the period of the conquest under Joshua. A major difference is that there seemed to be no leader. Joshua did not appoint someone to succeed him, nor did God. Yet the people were not leaderless (v1b): "the sons of Israel enquired of Yahweh." The fact that they went to God suggests that Yahweh was their leader.

So the question asked by the "sons of Israel (of Jacob)," now the nation Israel is "who shall go for us against the Canaanites first?" This is a question of leadership. God did not appoint a leader because he was their leader. He said that one of the tribes would be the first to go up and fight.

The answer to the question of v1 is found in v2: "behold *I have given* the land into his hand" (my emphasis). God has already *completed* the dispossession; they just had to go in and appropriate it. The idea of the land as already conquered either refers to the allotment by Joshua or a decision God made, which renders the land theirs. All they had to do was to go and take it.

Main point: God told the tribes he was their leader, and that the land was already conquered, they just had to go in and take it.

In Judges 1:1, the tribes approached God after the death of Joshua. This meeting with God must have happened when they met together as a tribal-group. Here in 2:1, they are together once again in such a meeting and "the Angel of the Lord" appeared to them.

The verses 1–5 have the following pattern:

A v1a Narration: The Angel of the Lord goes to *Bochim*
B vv1b–3 Speech: *The speech of the Angel of the Lord*
A vv4–5 Narration: The people weep and the place is named *Bochim*

Verse 1a and vv4–5 frame the unit based on the repetition of the place-name Bochim. The pivot of 2:1–5 is the speech by the Angel of Yahweh (vv1b–3). The speech points out the consequence of the irrevocable covenant God made with the fathers of that generation. The consequence was loyalty to Yahweh by *positively* breaking down and destroying the idols and altars of the Canaanites (see Judg 6:25–28) and *negatively* not making covenants with them, as is illustrated by 3:5–6 and the oft-repeated phrases in 1:21–36, "they made the Canaanites pay tribute," "the Canaanites lived among them," and "they lived among the Canaanites, the inhabitants of the land."

The speech's main point is in v3: "I shall not cast them out before you," which links back to 1:2b–36. Further, 2:3 finds its fulfillment in 2:20–23 and 3:5–6, which supports the link between 1:1—2:5 and 2:20—3:6. Amit[9] says the following regarding the link between 1:1–36 and 2:1–5: "the linking of the etiological tradition of Bochim with recounting the acts of non-taking possession lends this tradition the status of a summary of the results of the non-possession and its conclusions. It points towards the beginning of *the cultural assimilation* [my emphasis] that follows of necessity from the dwelling together of the inhabitants of the land and the Israelites" (cf. Josh 23:12).[10]

Verse 1b "I will never break my covenant with you" (cf. 1:2, 19) summarizes v1a; God remained true to his solemn promise and covenantal obligations to "you," that is, to the generations past (patriarchs), the people who came from Egypt, the Joshua generation, and the present generation. Because God had not and would not break his covenant, they had to deal with the *consequence* of this faithfulness on the part of God, namely, obey him; meet their covenantal obligations, as expressed in v2a-b: "you shall not make a covenant with the people of this land, you shall break down their altars" (cf. 3:5–6).

---

9. Amit, *Book of Judges*, 153.
10. Ibid., 157.

Exegesis and Interpretation of the Narrative Structure 127

In verse 2c, God charges the tribes: "yet you have not listened to my voice." They had failed to meet the demands of the covenant and had broken their promise. Note the play on "break" in 2:1a and 2b. The question that is raised by the charge of God is: how did the tribes fail in their covenant obligation? Judges 1:3–36 demonstrates their failure to keep their solemn promise. In 1:2b, "behold I have given [completed action] the land into his hand"; this statement was true not only for Judah, but all the tribes. What follows from 1:3–36 is characterized by the oft-repeated refrain "and . . . did not drive out the inhabitants." This is the way in which they broke covenant.

Verse 3 is the result of their failure to keep covenant. Now God will not give them victory over the inhabitants of the land, an echo of the refrain of 1:2b–36; verse 3b is alluded to in 2:17b, 21–23.

Main point: God declared that the inhabitants will continue to be a snare, because they failed to meet their covenant obligation to possess the allotted territory.

EXAMPLE 4

Job 1:13–22

The structure is based on the narrative constituents of character and action (event):

A vv13–15 Messenger One: the Sabeans took the oxen and the donkeys and killed the servants
B v16   Messenger Two: the fire of God burnt up the sheep and the servants
C v17   Messenger Three: the Chaldeans took the camels and killed the servants
D vv18–19 Messenger Four: a great wind destroyed the house and killed the children
E v20   Response of Job: he mourned and he worshipped
F v22   Narrator's comment; Job did not blame God

DESCRIPTION OF THE STRUCTURE

This is a linear structure with an introduction (v13), which is included in unit A and a conclusion (v22), which is narrative commentary, unit F. Each of the six narrative units concerns an *event*, an action that happened to Job. The focus point is narrative unit F (v22), which focuses on how Job dealt with the events that befell him. He demonstrated his faith and trust in God as seen in his worship of God in the midst of mourning. He did not blame God nor sought an explanation or reason for the events, but expressed his trust in God in an act of worship. Job responded to tragedy by worshipping God and in the worship of God found the strength needed to be sustained in the midst of his pain and suffering.

Focus Point

F v22

This unit is the narrator's perspective of how Job dealt with the events of vv13–20. It also gives insight into the origin of the events. Their origin was both human and natural, and this contributes to our understanding of Job's response to them. The narrator evaluates Job and comes to specific conclusions about him:

1. "Job did not sin"; the source of what happened to Job is not to be found in Job himself. Job was blameless; nothing he said, did, did not say, or did not do was the reason for what happened, as vv14–19 makes clear.

2. "And not did he attribute unseemliness (*tiplâ*) to God." Job did not believe God was the source of the events. Job did not "give to God"; he did not ascribe to God that which is "insipid, empty, unsteady."[11] Job had a particular view and understanding of God, which was not changed as a result of the events that happened to him.

Job held on to his understanding of God; it remained unaffected by the vicissitudes of life. His theology remained unshakable and his self understanding unalterable. He articulates this view of God in vv20–21.

Main point: Job was struck by tragedy but remained unshakable in his self understanding and his understanding of God.

---

11. Holladay, *Lexicon*, 394.

A vv13–15 Messenger One

The first of Job's servants arrived, brining extremely bad news. His children were having a meal or a celebration "eating and drinking" at their oldest brother's house (v13). The setting of joy and celebration sets the stage for the impact of what is to follow. It contrasts with the rest of the narrative, pointing to the vulnerability and uncertainty of life. One moment there was joy and celebration, the next tragedy and pain.

Immediately following the festive scene, the first servant gives his the report. The Sabeans attacked and took *the oxen and the donkeys* and killed the servants working the fields. He was the only one who escaped.

B vv16 Messenger Two

Next is a report that *the sheep* were destroyed by "the fire of God," probably lighting. The herdsman and the shepherds were killed as well. Ascribing what happened to the "fire of God" could produce a potential crisis of faith, specifically regarding Job's understanding of God. Job's view of God was different from that of his wife (2:9–10) and his contemporaries in the rest of the book, but it is being tested here.

C vv17 Messenger Three

Another servant came to report that the Chaldeans attacked and carried off *his camels*, killing the camel drivers.

D vv18–19 Messenger Four

Finally, there was the report that his children were having a meal or a celebration "eating and drinking" at their oldest brother's house. A violent wind-storm from the wilderness blew down the house and his sons were killed, but his daughters were still alive.

Wealth in the ancient Near East included oxen, donkeys, sheep, camels, and sons. Job was thus a rich man. His wealth was destroyed, in the words of v21 "the Lord has taken away." He was left destitute and without a future, as his sons were dead. His present was destroyed (oxen, donkeys, sheep, camels) as was his future (only his daughters survived).

There is a symmetry in this unit through the repetition in v13 and v18 of the expression *"your sons and your daughters were eating and drinking wine in the house of their elder brother,"* giving the unit coherence. In addition, there is the alternation between *human causes* of the disasters (v14 and v17) and *natural (of nature) causes* (v16 and v19). Since Job understood that the causes were human and natural, the narrator could say "Job did not sin" (v22a). How? Job did not blame God for the events that brought such pain and suffering into his life.

E vv20–21 Response of Job

The response of Job to these events is depicted in three ways:

a. He mourned (v21). The actions of Job are acts of mourning: the tearing of clothes and shaving of head were the normal acts mourning (see Gen 37:29; 1 Sam 4:12; 2 Sam 1:11–12, 13:19; Esth 4:1). Job's response was a normal human response, which gives a reality to the tragedy, pain, and suffering he experienced. Job was not stoic in the midst of his tragedy.

b. He worshipped. The act of prostration before God recognizes his status and position of honor and reflects the person's humility. Job's actions made the statement: God is higher than I am (v22b). His actions were an atypical human response to tragedy: worship. Human beings do not typically worship as a response to pain and suffering, Job did.

c. He made a confession: "I came naked out of my mother's womb, and naked I shall return there." The reference to "naked" is of course to the things he lost—oxen, donkeys, sheep, camels, and even the sons. Job did not bring these with him when he came into the world, and he was not going to take them with him when he left this world. The expression "return there," that is, to the womb is a metaphor for death.

"The Lord gave and the Lord has taken away" means that all the things he lost were gifts received from the Lord. They belonged to him and therefore he had the right to take them away. This understanding was not limited to the wealth—it included his very life. Life was given by God and life could therefore be taken away by God. "[B]lessed be the name of the Lord." Job worshipped God with this statement; it is a praise-statement. In other words, Job exclaimed, "the Lord be blessed." In fact he declares: ascribe to the Lord blessing and honor not blame (*tiplâ*), see v22. It was not just a confession; it was also an invitation from

Job to the reader to join him in blessing the name of the Lord. It was a call to agree with him that even in his situation, it is right to bless the name of the Lord.

Main point: Job worshipped God even though he lost all, because he understood the significance of life and wealth. It is a gift of God and not a reward for how good we are.

EXAMPLE 5

Judges 9:7–21

The structure is based on the narrative constituent action (event):

A vv7–9   Attempt one unsuccessful: the olive tree refused to reign over the trees

B vv10–11   Attempt two unsuccessful: the fig tree refused to reign over the trees

C vv12–13   Attempt three unsuccessful: the vine refused to reign over the trees

D vv14–15   Attempt four successful: the bramble bush agreed to reign over the trees

E vv16–21   Jotham's speech: he challenged the integrity of the Shechemites' actions

Description of the Structure

The narrative has a linear structure. The trees make three unsuccessful attempts to appoint a king to rule over them, but succeeded with the fourth attempt. The focus point is Jotham's speech in vv16–21, which is in the form of a parable. The parable is a warning to the Shechemites that failure to act truthfully, sincerely, and with integrity was self-destructive, as the rest of the narrative shows.

Focus Point

vv16–21

In the focus point, the parable is applied to the actual situation in which the leaders (v19) (*ḳol-baʿalēy*) of the town of Shechem participated in the murders of the sons of Gideon by giving Abimelech the seventy pieces of silver needed to pay the worthless men who killed Gideon's sons. The leaders appointed Abimelech king because he was a kinsman (relative), a fellow Shechemite.

The application of the parable to the actions of the leaders has the following elements: (it is formed syntactically as a conditional sentence, and it has a parallel structure as seen below)

A v16a-c   "if you ... if you ... if you ..."
B vv17–18 [then you would not have risen up against my father's house]
A v19a   "if in truth ..."
B v19b   [then] "rejoice in Abimelech, and he shall rejoice, even he and you"
A v20a   "if not" points back to vv16–19a.
B v20b   [then] "let fire come ..."

All the "if you ..." clauses are the protasis clauses; these clauses set out the conditions for the resulting state of affairs expressed in the apodosis (then clauses) in vv17–18, v19b, and v20b. The conditions are as follows:

1. Acted in truth and sincerity.
2. Have done well with Jerubbaal and his household.
3. Have done to him as his hands did to you.
4. Acted in truth and sincerity toward Jerubbaal and his house.
5. On condition that all the conditions were met.

The resulting state is expressed by the apodosis in vv17–18 and v19b. Verses 17–18 has as its apodosis: "then you would not have participated in the killing of my father's sons." Verse 19b has as its apodosis: "then rejoice"; celebrate as you are now doing, after the anointing of Abimelech. Jotham's statement implies that celebration and joy was only appropriate if the actions causing the celebration were moral.

If the actions were not moral, the "if not" (v20a), then the celebrations taking place were in fact misplaced, warned Jotham. The warning was realized in chapter 6:22–57, when destruction fell upon the Shechemites. Jotham's speech said that the celebrations at "the oak of the camp which is in Shechem" (v6) was premature, because it was based on dishonesty, insincerity, and a lack of integrity.

Exegesis and Interpretation of the Narrative Structure 133

This is the context for interpreting v7b "and God will listen to you"; God will be pleased with what you have done; God will bless it; God will approve of it, (see 6:22). So the main issue in this narrative is about what God would approve of, allow, and find acceptable.

In v18, Jotham points out that the conditions of vv16–18 and v19a were not met and therefore, in his words, "fire shall come out from Abimelech and devour the leaders of Shechem and the house of Millo and fire shall come out from the leaders of Shechem and the house of Millo and devour Abimelech" (v20). Complete destruction of the tribe of Shechem was predicted by Jotham, which was fulfilled in 6:57.

Jotham's charge was that the Shechemites did not act truthfully and sincerely. Their behavior was motivated by narrow family interest "because he is your brother" (v18c). It was not guided by what was good for the clan and the tribe and they put family before truth and sincerity. The Shechemites deliberately and conveniently changed customs and looked for a king from the mother's clan instead of the father's clan. They acted dishonorably and would pay for it.

Verse 21 brings the first part of the narrative to a close. Jotham departed for Beer, moving off the scene, which allows the predictive element of his parable to take place (6:22–57). His departure is a repetition of what happened previously to Abimelech, who was chased away even though he was part of the family.

Main point: Jotham warned the Shechemites through a parable that destruction will befall them because they acted dishonorably and insincerely towards the memory of Gideon (Jerubbaal).

A vv7–9—Attempt one unsuccessful

The unit consists of the speech of Jotham, thus a monologue dominates the passage.

Verse 7

Jotham was the sole survivor of Jerubbaal, the only one of the seventy sons of Jerubbaal left. He was told that the Shechemites were going to appoint Abimelech leader of the tribe of Shechem. Verse 7b has a very interesting phrase: "listen to me, that God may listen to you." The LXX translates this phrase as follows, "and God shall hear/listen to you," and the Hebrew literally reads "and shall listen to God." The Hebrew and

LXX readings suggest a conditional link; God will hear you on condition that you listen to me. But if you do not listen to me, God will not listen to you; *wᵉyišmaʾ*, is the conjunction "and" plus the verb *qal* third-person masculine future from *yišmaʾ* (to hear), meaning: "and he shall hear." The difference in translation between the LXX and the Hebrew and the modern translations is the interpretation of the "conjunction" (*vav*). The question is whether the *vav* is conjunctive or causal. The Hebrew and LXX see it as conjunctive, while the other modern translations see it as causal. But within the context of the narrative, the conjunctive *vav* fits better. The expression "and will hear you/listen to you God" would mean "has the approval, agreement, support, blessing and acceptance of God."

Verses 8–9

The parable of the trees electing a king begins at this point. The first tree approached was the olive. Its main function is described as "my fatness with which God and men are honored." Olive trees provided the olive oil used to anoint kings. The meaning expanded from the anointing of kings to the figurative sense of "weighty, noteworthy, or impressive." Common translations of the root are "honorable, honored, glorious, and glorified." Figuratively, the emphasis falls on the reputation or worth of the person. It describes a person of high social standing who was also wealthy. Such a person was automatically regarded as an honored or weighty person in the society. Occupying such a position accompanied by its riches and long life was regard as the reward for living a righteous life (1 Chr 29:28).

The other way in which a person became an honored person was by means of heroic acts of courage and fidelity. David's mighty men were honored in this way (1 Kgs 11:21) They were men who made a name for themselves. God is also to be honored; God's name is glorious in righteousness, faithfulness, judgment, and salvation (Ps 66:2; Ps 79:9; Isa 40:5).[12] Given the role played by the fruit of the olive tree, it would naturally see the trees' invitation to be of less worth than the honor its current role afforded it. Therefore, the olive tree felt that to accept the invitation was merely "to hold sway over." The root meaning of *nûaʾ* is "a back and forth swaying movement over a small geographic area." However, it is used comparatively here in Judges 9:9. The comparison is between "to hold sway over" and "to reign over." The olive tree and the

---

12. Holladay, *Lexicon*, 150–51.

trees have a different perspective on the olive tree's role. The trees see this as reigning, but the olive tree sees this merely as "holding sway over."

There is also a comparison between what the olive tree was doing with what it was asked to do. In this comparison, *nûa'* means "that which is insignificant, of far less weight and worth than what it is currently doing." It was being used to anoint kings, a far greater role with far wider influence than standing and swaying over a small number of trees. For the olive tree, therefore, just standing and swaying over trees was not worth it and it refused the invitation.

The olive tree and its oil were used in the worship of the gods and ritualistic ceremonies. It was also used for food, medicine, soap, and carpentry. It is unsurprising that the olive tree rejected the lowly invitation.

Main point: The olive tree rejected the invitation of the trees as of far less value and worth than its normal role, symbolizing God's disapproval of what the Shechemites had done.

B vv10–11 Attempt two unsuccessful

Verse 10

The fig tree was invited next. The sentence is made up of a series of commands: "you come, reign over us." "Reign" is a *qal* imperative feminine singular verb from the root *mālak*. The two imperatives: "you reign" and "you come" conveys a sense of anxiety and urgency on the part of the trees, as if they were starting to become desperate.

Verse 11

The fig tree refused, giving the following reason: "should I cease from my sweetness and good fruit." Fig trees were plentiful in Palestine and were found in a huge variety, some good, some bad. The early crop ripens between March and May, which is less useful. Some trees lose all of their figs, while other retains some, which ripen in June. The second crop, which ripens in August, was the best. Figs were dried and pressed to make fig cakes.

Figs were part of the daily diet of the people. They were known for their delicate flavor and taste and were "esteemed a delicacy" (Jer 24:2; Hos 9:10; Mic 7:1).[13] They were also used for medicinal purposes, for

---

13. Fausset, *Dictionary*.

example, the healing of Hezekiah's boil (Isa 38:21, 2 Kgs 20:7). The fig has a diverse character and it produces diverse fruit.

The fig tree turned down the invitation because it saw acceptance as a step down from what it already had. In comparison with the olive, however, the position of the fig tree is lower because the olive served divinity and not just humans.

Main point: *The fig tree refused the invitation, as it played a much more worthy role already, symbolizing God's disapproval of what the Shechemites had done.*

C vv12–13 Attempt three unsuccessful

The vine was the next candidate approached by the trees. The invitation was formulated in exactly the same way as in v10—"you come, reign over us." The vine gave the same reason for refusing the invitation; the vine served gods and men; it "makes both gods and men glad." The verb is a *piel* participle masculine plural from *ṣāmaḥ*, translated "it causes them to rejoice." This was a far higher and important position and task compare to swaying over the trees. The vine produces "new wine" (*tîrôšî*); this is an old Hebrew word for wine and it is usually found in ritual and poetic texts. It suggests wine used in the performance of religious rituals, as implied by the reference to "gods" here.

There is a ring pattern in the unit vv7–13, which describes the invitation to the olive, fig, and vine:

A   *Reign over us . . .* by me they honor *gods and men* v8b+9b
B   Come you, reign over us . . . my sweetness and my fruit is good v10b+11b
A   *Come reign over us . . .* makes glad *gods and men* v12b+13b

The pivotal point B is the invitation to the fig tree. The fruit of the fig tree was not as uniform as the other trees. Figs were harvested at different times of the year and the quality of the figs were variable, unpredictable, and of mixed value. It is this mixed, variable nature of the fig tree that is the focal point of this unit and which is it's the link with the last unit. The fig tree's characteristics foreshadowed the character of the tree in the final unit (vv14–15), which was also variable and mixed. Thus the pivotal unit was a prediction of what was to come in the last unit, as well as the rest of the narrative.

Main point: The vine refused the invitation of the trees because of its superior role of serving gods and men, once again symbolizing God's disapproval of what the Shechemites had done.

D vv14–15 Attempt four successful

The "bramble-bush" is the last tree to be asked. The formula of the invitation is the same as before: "come you, reign over us." The bramble-bush's reply is different from the other trees. All of the other trees pointed to an existing position, role, and function they already performed and which they regarded as of more importance and value than reigning over the trees. The bramble-bush implicitly accepts the invitation, but warns that any attempt by the trees use it for their own purposes will be met with total destruction (cf. 6:22–57).

Verse 15a—"if you truly." This is the protasis part of the conditional sentence of v15. The bramble-bush lays down a condition that he, the son the Jerubbaal's concubine, must be made king of the Shechemites. The anointing and appointing must be real; a true and genuine appointment to kingship.

Verse 15b, "come seek refuge in my shade." This is the main clause of v15. It expresses the demand of the bramble-bush; the other trees must be willing to relinquish their independence and hand over total control. The bramble-bush wanted complete power. And their willingness to do this would signal the genuineness of their intentions, proving that they really wanted a king to rule over them and that they were not just looking for someone to help them and whom they could control. So the bramble-bush's challenge was, Are you really honest and sincere in what you are asking? The bramble-bush's desire for total control and power had an inherent warning. The fact that it was the *bramble-bush* that accepted the invitation conveys the implicit warning: you are going to regret and pay dearly for appointing the thorn bush as king; it will be a real thorn in your flesh.

Verse 15c, "and if not . . ."—and if the condition is not met, if my appointment was not genuine, there will be serious consequences. "[Let] fire come out of the bramble-bush and destroy the cedars of Lebanon." The main clause of the second half of the conditional sentence spells out the consequence: the trees would suffer destruction. Put differently, their dishonesty would destroy them. The bramble-bush's threat revealed something of its character: it displayed dictatorial, despotic, and authoritarian tendencies, which held nothing good in store for the trees.

Main point: The bramble-bush accepted the invitation but warned that should the trees act dishonestly and without integrity they would be destroyed.

Summary

There is a downward progression from best to worst: from the olive tree, symbolizing honor and worth, character traits of Gideon (Jerubbaal), to the bramble-bush, symbolizing Abimelech. The trees ended up with the worst leader because they were not truthful.

The refusal of the olive, fig, and vine trees and the acceptance by the bramble-bush, implied that there was something wrong with the trees. Similarly, the acceptance by the leaders of Shechem of Abimelech and the fact that they gave him seventy pieces of silver signaled that there was something very wrong with the leaders of Shechem.

Furthermore, each of the trees had something important, originating from the way God created them and benefiting the people. Three of the trees believed their current roles were too important to leave in order to reign over the rest of the trees. This indicates that whoever agreed to be leader of Shechem did not have God's approval and would not be good for the people.

The main idea of the narrative is clear from the oft repeated words "truth and integrity." The parable is about the lack of integrity and truthfulness of the Shechemites in their dealings with the house of Gideon (Jerubbaal), appointing Abimelech king instead of one of the sons of Gideon.

EXAMPLE 6

2 Kings 2:1–25

The structure is based on the narrative constituent of space (geography):

    A   v1 Gilgal
       B   vv2–3 Bethel
          C   vv4–5 Jericho
             D   vv6–7 Jordan
                E   v8 Parting the waters of the Jordan

```
              F    vv9–13 Elijah departed and his mantle and
                   ministry passed over to Elisha
           E    v14 Parting the waters of the Jordan
        D    vv15–18 Jericho
     C    vv19–22 Purifying the waters of Jericho
  B    vv23–24 Bethel
A    v25 Samaria
```

Description of the Structure

The narrative pattern is a symmetrical, chiastic structure. This narrative links the prophetic ministries of Elijah and Elisha, which emphasizes the continuity between the two prophets. This continuity sends the message to the people and the king of Israel that Elisha's ministry will be similar to Elijah's. It is illustrated through Elijah's antagonism towards King Ahaziah of Israel (2 Kgs 1), and Elisha's antagonism in 2 Kings 3 towards King Jehoram of Israel. So even though a change in prophetic ministry had taken place, the prophetic message remains the same. This is demonstrated by the journey from Gilgal and back to Gilgal; and then from Gilgal to Samaria.

In addition, the narrative is in the form of a travelogue. Elisha repeats on his own, the exact travel route he took with Elijah. He also repeated the acts of Elijah.

Focus Point

F vv9–13

Elijah departs and his mantle and ministry passes on to Elisha. The unit is the pivotal point of the structure. It describes how Elisha becomes Elijah's successor as prophet to the nation of Israel. There is no formal ceremony for this transition; God is not directly active in this passing on of the prophetic role.

Verses 9–10

The unit is introduced by the traditional formula "and it came to pass," indicating a new event is about to happen. A discussion took place between Elijah and Elisha, in which Elijah first affirmed his departure to Elisha and invited him to request anything he wanted. Elisha responded: "let there now be a double portion of your spirit on me." What was

Elisha asking for? To do what Elijah did, or to do more than what Elijah did? The expression points out that Elisha saw a difference in Elijah's prophetic ministry when compared to the traditional school of the prophets, and he wanted this difference, and that was what he got in v14.

Elijah said the request was a "hard thing," because the spirit that was in him was a gift and it was not his to give away. It was something that God alone could impart: "if you shall see me taken from you . . ." (v10). These words take the fulfillment of the request out of the hands of Elijah. Whether Elisha gets what he asked for was now dependent on God, who was about to take Elijah to heaven (see v1, 9). This interaction took place as they were crossing the Jordan.

Verse 11

The verse begins with a phrase that indicates new events: "and it came to pass." As they were crossing the Jordan, another "crossing over" took place. Elijah was taken to heaven, in a supernatural way. A chariot and horses of fire came and took Elijah away. Elisha was with Elijah at the time, and so the condition set out by Elijah in v10b is met. Elisha will now be able to get a double portion of the spirit that was on Elijah. In addition, all this happened in the presence of the fifty "sons of the prophets" of Jericho, who "stood across, afar off" (v7).

Verse 12

Elisha's response is interesting:

 a. He watched as Elijah is taken away.
 b. He cried out.
 c. He tore his clothes in two.

Elisha's response here is very different to his reaction when Elijah said in v9 that he would be taken from him. There he showed no emotion; what happened here is in direct contrast. There are two possible reasons. He mourns (cries out, tears his clothes in two) the departure of his master. But he might also be crying out because with the departure of Elijah, his future as a prophet was under threat; he no longer had a master to learn from and follow.

Verse 13

The opening sentence of this verse makes it clear that Elijah's mantle fell down as he went up. Elisha picked up the mantle. At this point, v13a, the crossing of the Jordan had been completed and Elisha is standing on the east bank of the Jordan opposite Jericho. He turned back and went to the bank of the Jordan. He had the mantle of Elijah in his hand and did not know if he had received his request for "a double portion" (v9b). He had the mantle, which meant he was a prophet like Elijah, that is, not prepared in a school of the prophets but appointed by God. But he did not know if he had the spirit of Elijah and there was only one way to find out.

Main point: *The prophetic ministry transitioned from Elijah to Elisha as they crossed the Jordan in the presence of the sons of the prophets, implying that prophets are not usually trained, but anointed, and appointed.*

A v1 Introduction (Gilgal)

"And it came to pass" (*wayühî*), the usual introductory formula indicates the beginning of a new phase in the narrative. Together with v25, which records Elisha's arrival in Samaria and brings the episode to an end, they form the closure for this narrative unit. The formula marks the beginning and end of the narrative unit.

Verse 1 sets the scene for the events that follow. God was about to take Elijah to heaven, bringing his prophetic ministry to an end in Israel (cf. Gen 5:21–24).

Main point: *A new phase in the prophetic ministry within Israel was about to begin.*

B vv2–3 The journey to Bethel

The unit is characterized by a dialogue between Elijah and Elisha. In v2a, Elijah tells Elisha to remain in Samaria, indicating that the events in the story begin in the capital city of Israel, Samaria. He was going to Bethel as instructed by God. Elisha, who is a "son of the prophet" Elijah, a student of Elijah, responded as a student of a prophet should respond: "I will not leave you." He did so by using an oath (covenant) formula: "As Jehovah lives, and your soul lives, I will not leave you." This reply suggests a covenant relationship between Elijah and Elisha; for him to stay behind would be disloyal, a breaking of the covenant. Elisha was faithful and committed to Elijah.

In v3, the sons of the prophets tell Elisha that Elijah was to be taken away from him that day. Elisha's response is significant: he replied "yes, I know." How did Elisha know this? And was this the reason for his insistence on accompanying Elisha? The story later indicates that Elisha had been told this by the sons of another prophet.

The expression "take your lord *from over your head*" (my emphasis), is translated by the New Jerusalem Bible "take your lord and *master away*" (my emphasis). "From over your head" is equivalent to "master away"; your master is over your head, above you. This is a helpful way to clarify the meaning of the phrase. Elisha was told that his master and teacher would be taken away from him.

It seems Elisha did not want to be reminded that Elijah was about to leave him. He was told this twice, and his reaction was "keep silent." It appears he was disturbed by this; he was irritated and yet showed no visible emotion. His irritation could be that as the "son of a prophet" he would be status-less and lose his ministry as a potential prophet if he lost Elijah. If this is correct, then the issue addressed by the narrative was the question of what made a prophet. Is it about being trained by a teacher? Or perhaps there was a new way of becoming a prophet, beginning with this story.

The other sons of the prophets were looking down on Elisha. They still had a master, but soon he would not have a master which would make his prophetic ministry of less value and questionable; so he might have thought.

Main point: Elisha demonstrated the true character of a "son of the prophet" in his commitment to Elijah, but had a concern about his future ministry as a prophet.

C vv4–5 Jericho

The second dialogue and the second leg of the journey are recorded here, which is a word-for-word repetition of vv2–3; the difference is the location: Jericho instead of Bethel. In each case the "sons of the prophets" informed Elisha of Elijah's imminent departure. The departure of Elijah appeared to be common knowledge (perhaps revelatory knowledge?) among the "sons of the prophets."

Exegesis and Interpretation of the Narrative Structure

Main point: The future ministry of Elisha as a prophet was under threat, so he thought, with the imminent departure of Elijah his master.

D vv6–7 Jordan

Verse 6 is a repetition of v2 and v4. In v7, the "sons of the prophet," instead of speaking to Elisha, positioned themselves "across from them [Elisha and Elijah]," which suggests that they were expecting something to happen. So they positioned themselves opposite Elijah and Elisha *on the banks of the Jordan River*. In this unit, the prophets faced a flowing Jordan River, with the challenge of getting across it.

Main point: Elijah and Elisha stood on the banks of the Jordan River opposite the sons of the prophets, faced with the challenge of crossing the Jordan River in full flow.

E v8 Parting the waters of the Jordan [proof 1]

Verse 8 describes Elisha and Elijah crossing the Jordan. Elijah divided the waters of the Jordan by striking the river with his mantle. A path appeared in the river and they crossed over on dry ground. Their crossing symbolized their togetherness; although Elijah may depart, they would still be together somehow.

This event was witnessed by the fifty sons of the prophets from Jericho. The crossing of the Jordon River at Jericho confirmed that Elijah and Elisha were traveling from the capital of Samaria.

Main point: Elijah and Elisha crossed the Jordan River together was confirmation that Elisha would indeed have a future prophetic ministry.

E v14 Parted the waters of the Jordan [proof 2]

Elisha parted the waters in exactly the same way Elijah did previously. The parting of the waters seals the prophetic ministry of Elisha; it confirmed that he was a prophet in the spirit of Elijah and the spirit that was in Elijah was also in him.

> [14] And he took the mantle of Elijah that fell from him
> **and struck the waters and said,**
> "*Where is the Lord, the God of Elijah?*"
> **And when he also had struck the waters,**
> They were divided here and there; and Elisha crossed over.

This last sentence answers the question: "where is the Lord, the God of Elijah?" He was with Elisha. God had appointed Elisha in the same way he appointed Elijah. This was demonstrated when Elisha parted the waters as Elijah had.

Main point: Elisha parted the waters of the Jordon just like Elijah did, which confirmed that the God who was with Elijah was now also with Elisha.

D vv15–18 Jericho [proof 3]

There is further proof that the spirit of Elijah was on Elisha. Two incidents validated the prophetic ministry of Elisha (v15). The sons of the prophets saw Elisha cross the Jordan and when he came to them they bowed before him, acknowledging that he was a prophet like Elijah. They had witnessed the transition of prophetic ministry as the mantle fell and Elisha took it up. And although Elisha did not have a master, it did not invalidate his prophetic ministry because the "the Lord, the God of Elijah" was Elisha's God, his master.

In vv16–18, the sons of the prophets insisted on searching for the body of Elijah. All they saw was the whirlwind that took Elijah out of their sight, and they wanted to see if he had physically left the earth (see v5, v7). They wanted to see if there was no master "over your [Elisha's] head." Elisha told them that they should not search, because they would not find the body (see v10, 11b, 12a*a*, b*b*). After a three-day search, they returned home empty handed just as Elisha said they would, validating him as a prophet in the spirit of Elijah. What Elisha told them and predicted came to pass.

Main point: The sons of the prophets acknowledged that Elisha was indeed a prophet like Elijah, after they returned home empty handed from their search for Elijah's body.

C vv19–22 Healing the waters of Jericho [proof 4]

Elisha healed the "water [which was] bad"; water that made the land barren (v19). He asked for a new bowl with salt, threw that into the source point of the water (v20–21) and the water was healed. It no longer made the land barren, "according to the word of Elisha that he spoke." Once again, Elisha was validated as a prophet of Yahweh (v22). The expression "to this day" indicates that the incident did not happen in the time of the narrator. What stood out for those who remembered the story was that the barrenness caused by the water was reversed on the word of Elisha; what he declared happened, a sign that he was true prophet.

Main point: The removal of the barrenness caused by the water at Jericho proved that Elisha was a prophet in the spirit of Elijah.

B vv23-24 Bethel—The killing of forty boys [proof 5]

A significant difference between this event and the ones at the Jordan and Jericho is that here Elisha does not speak a word. He looked at the boys and cursed them "silently," as it is not recorded that Elisha spoke, v24. One translation says, "he declared them vile in the name of Jehovah."[14] But this declaration was not vocal.

The story reports that "little boys came from the city" (v23b), presumably Jericho city, and "two bears came from the forest" (v24b). The translation "little boys" for *ûn^e'ârîm q^{e}tannîm* is misleading, as the phrase referred to young men.

The young men is said to have *wayyitqall^{e}sû-bô*, and they scoffed him." The expression *yitqall^{e}sû* (they scoffed) derives from the root *qallēs*, meaning "to mock, to scorn" (2 Kgs 2:33; Ezek 16:31, 22:5; Hab 1:10). The root denotes a scornful belittling which arises from an attitude that regards as valueless that which is of real value. It can be compared to "make a fool of," "to scornfully mimic."[15]

The nature of the mocking is expressed by the phrase "go up bald (*qērēah*) head." The taunt hurled at Elisha (2 Kgs 2:23) was particularly serious because it showed complete disrespect for the prophet of God, and as a consequence for God himself. Such disrespect was punishable by death according to Leviticus 20:9.

We are told that Elisha "cursed them" (v24b). W*a-y^{e}qallēm*, "cursed them," is a verb, *piel qal* (future tense), third-person masculine "sing" plus a suffix third-person masculine plural derived from *qll*. The root meaning of *qll* is "be small, be lightly esteemed, despised, of little account"[16] In the *piel* form the stem is *qilēl*, which means "declared cursed, or declare someone cursed," and it is done "*b^e šēm yhwh*" (in the name of Yahweh).

14. Green Sr., *Bible*, 975.
15. Holladay, *Lexicon*, 318–19.
16. Ibid., 319.

By cursing them in the name of God, Elisha was handing them over to God (this is the significance of "in the name of God") for he would then deal with them for blaspheming.

In a culture dominated by honor and shame and in terms of the law of the Old Testament (Lev 20:9; Ex 21:17; Lev 24:11–23), what the young men did was a serious offense. They dishonored an elderly person, who was a prophet of God. The dishonoring of the prophet of God implied the dishonoring of God, which carried a punishment of death. Two bears suddenly appeared from the forest and killed the young men. The sudden appearance of the bears seems miraculous, something Elisha himself could not have orchestrated, and so the boys' death was an act of divine judgment. The incident happened as Elisha was leaving Jericho on his way to Bethel. Because it happened "on the highway," it took place in a public space where some people were probably traveling the highway. It was thus a public demonstration of the fact that Elisha was a prophet in the spirit of Elijah. There would now be public recognition that the spirit of Elijah was indeed upon Elisha.

Main point: *The divine judgment of God upon the young men who mocked Elisha and thus blasphemed God demonstrated publicly that the spirit of Elijah rested on Elisha.*

A v25 Samaria

Elisha's return (see v13a) brings the story to a close. The introductory formula in v1 and v25 serve as closure, demarcating the episode as a unified narrative unit. Elisha is back in Samaria. In this round trip, Samaria to Samaria, he traveled exactly the same route Elijah did, and therefore is a prophet just like Elijah was. The geography attested the fact that Elisha was a prophet in the spirit of Elijah.

Main point: *The spatial movements confirmed that Elisha was a prophet in the spirit of Elijah, marking him out as a prophet of God.*

SUMMARY

In this period of transition in Israel, God showed that even though Elijah was gone, God was not gone; he was still with Israel. God did this by giving them a new prophet: Elisha. Elisha was like Elijah, the power and presence of God was still at work in Israel, and this was demonstrated

Exegesis and Interpretation of the Narrative Structure 147

by various events that validated the prophetic ministry of Elisha. The validations are external evidence of an internal impartation of the Spirit to Elisha; he was the true heir (significance of v9 "double portion of the spirit") of the ministry of Elijah.

EXAMPLE 7

Genesis 25:19–34

The structure is based on the narrative constituent of narrative technique:

  A vv19–21 Narration
      B vv22–23 Discourse
          C ***vv24–28 Narration***
      B vv29–34a Discourse
  A vv34b Narration

Description of the Structure

This is a chiastic structure. The narrative units are matched on the basis of *narrative technique*; the narrator uses narration and discourse to structure the narrative. The central point of the narrative is the birth of the twins, their life's work and each of the sons are specially loved by one of the parents.

Focus Point

C vv24–28 Narration

The point of focus is vv24–28, which describes the birth and the naming of the boys. The love each parent has for a specific son is mentioned. Thus the scene is set for later events.

    Verse 24 affirms the explanation God gave in v23. God told Rebekah "two nations are in your womb; and two people shall separate from your body"; now in v24 we read "and when her days to bring forth were fulfilled, behold! Twins were in her womb." She gave birth to twins who were separated "from your body." The oracle of v23 had its initial fulfillment.

    The two matching units emphasize the naming of the two boys. In the first unit vv25–26, the two boys are named, and in the second unit (vv27–28), their names are elaborated on, with descriptions of their work and their relationship with their parents. They are named in terms of their "profession" (v27): "skillful hunter" and "dweller in tents," and then they are named in terms of their relationship with their parents (v28).

Esau's name was based on a physical quality, he "came out red, all over like a hairy robe" (v25). His body was covered in red hair from which his name derived. Jacob's name was based on a physical appearance: "his hand was holding on to the heel of Esau" (v26), which pointed to a character trait; one who grabbed the heel, or supplanter/deceiver (Gen 27:36). These are the names given to the boys, as the expression "and they called his name" indicates.

The reference to the age of Isaac (v26b) concludes the section dealing with the birth and naming of the boys.

The next section (vv27–28) *names the boys from a different perspective*. They were first named according to their professions. "Esau became a man acquainted with hunting, a man of the field"; he was a hunter of game. Jacob, on the other hand, "was a simple man living in tents"; this seemed to refer to Jacob as one who led a pastoral life, looking after sheep/cattle and moving from place to place; a tent-dweller.

They are then *named from the perspective of their relationship to the parents* in v28. The fact that each of the parents loved a different son is already an indication that the destinies of the boys are going to be very different. But the focus is on the characterization of the boys.

It is interesting that in the description of the relationships in vv27–28, the Rebekah-Jacob relationship is unqualified; Rebekah loved Jacob unconditionally. It was not the case between Esau and Isaac, as Isaac loved Esau because "venison was in his mouth," that is, Esau satisfied Isaac's love for venison, and he was loved for this reason.

Main point: At birth, Jacob and Esau were given names based on their physical features, their character traits, the work they did, and their relation to their parents.

A vv19–21 Narration

The unit begins with the words "and these are the generations of Isaac, Abraham's son" (v19). This indicates that a new narrative unit begins at this point. It does not have its normal function of listing the genealogical history of the patriarch, as no sons were born to Isaac yet.

Isaac's age when he married Rebekah is given next (v20); he was forty years old. When this is compared with v26b, it becomes clear that Rebekah had been barren for twenty years. This explains why there was no genealogy of Isaac. Isaac waited for a long time, praying *earnestly* to the Lord for his wife. After twenty years "the Lord was entreated for him" (v21); the Lord was prevailed upon as a result of Isaac's earnest praying and answered his prayer for Rebekah, "and his wife conceived" (v21b–c).

Main point: Isaac waited and prayed earnestly to the Lord for twenty years before sons were born to him.

B vv22–23 Discourse

Rebekah became worried when the children in her womb began "to struggle together" (v22). She was concerned that she might lose them. The expression "if thus" (literally), can be translated as "if it be so." Rebekah asked why her children were struggling if they are the work of God. She was puzzled by what was happening in her womb, as she knew that her conception was the work of God in answer to Isaac's earnest and persistent prayer. In v21, God answered Isaac's prayer and Rebekah conceived. And because it was God who enabled her to conceive, she went to him to find out what was going on (v22).

God told her (v23) that the struggle of the children in her womb was a struggle about their role and destiny. "The nation of whom the younger son will be the founding father will be stronger than the nation of whom the elder son will be founding father," and "the elder will serve the younger." The future destiny of the two sons had been determined by God.

Main point: Rebekah learnt that the twin's struggle represented a future struggle between two nations founded by the twins, the outcome of which had been decided by God.

B vv24–34a Discourse

This narrative unit is the first example of the struggle referred to in v23. The struggle will be repeated in chapter 27. The narrative unit has a *ring pattern*.

A

²⁹ And when Jacob had cooked stew, Esau came in from the field and he was famished;
³⁰ and Esau said to Jacob, "Please let me have a swallow of that red stuff there, for I am famished."
Therefore his name was called Edom.

B

³¹ But Jacob said, "First sell me your birthright."
³² "See I am going to die and what good is this, a birthright to me?"
³³ª And Jacob said, "First swear to me";

A

³³ᵇ so he swore to him, and sold his birthright to Jacob.
³⁴ª Then Jacob gave Esau bread and lentil stew.

The pivot B, vv30–33a, in which the struggle between the twins takes place, describes how *Esau and Jacob gave themselves a name,* in contrast to vv27–28 where they were given names. Esau named himself Edom, derived from the expression "that red stuff" (literally the red, this red) by selling his birthright (vv32–33) for "a swallow of that red stuff." In this way, Esau gave himself a name, as v30 affirms, "therefore his name was called Edom." Esau gave himself a new name derived from trading his birthright for the red stew. In this way, he brings the nation of Edom into existence. In Hebrew the link between red and Edom is much clearer; red = *hāʾāḏom* and Edom = *ʾeḏôm*.

Jacob, by holding his brother to ransom, "first swear to me" (see v34a), gave himself the name "supplanter"; he took over and became "first-born," the possessor of the birthright by holding his brother to ransom. He took advantage of his brother's hunger to get the birthright. From that point onwards his new name was supplanter.

It is interesting that the narrator *did not* give this meaning to the name of Jacob. He did, however, give a meaning to the name of Esau (v30b). The meaning supplanter is derived from *ʿāqēḇ,* "heel," and from there the English proper name "Jacob." Supplanter is the meaning given to Jacob's name first by Esau in Genesis 27:36 (*ʿqoḇ* overreach) and later by the prophet Hosea in 12:4 (see also Jer 17:9). The point is that neither the narrator nor God, whose viewpoint is represented by the point of view of the narrator, indicate that Jacob's action is a negative one; this only came later. Jacob's behavior and actions are described factually, without commentary or ethical judgment, unlike that of Esau, whose behavior is judged in v34.

It was through this struggle that the prediction of v23 was fulfilled. God determined the destiny of the two boys, "the older shall serve the younger" but God did not predict how the boys would realize that destiny or how the prediction would be fulfilled; the boys, however, through their *decisions* and *actions* determined the fulfillment of the destiny declared by God in v23. Put differently, God decreed their destinies; they determined the fulfillment of their destinies by their decisions, choices, and actions.

Main point: Esau and Jacob fulfilled God's prediction in v23 by their decisions, choices, and actions.

A v34b Narration

The verse is dominated by four verbal phrases describing the actions of Esau:

1. He ate.
2. He drank.
3. He rose.
4. He went on his way.

This staccato-like description depicts Esau as cold and emotionless regarding what he had just done. He had just traded his birthright for a plate of lentil stew and bread. It is clear that the birthright did not really matter to him, as he himself stated, "I am about to die, so of what use then is the birthright to me?" (v30b). His actions reflect this attitude. He placed very little value on the birthright. This is borne out by the narrator's comment "thus Esau despised his birthright" (v34c). His birthright of course refers to the rights he had as the firstborn ($b^e k or$). This root is quite similar to the root for the word blessing ($b^e r\hat{a}k\hat{a}h$), which is the subject of the second struggle in chapter 27. Esau despised ($yib\ ez$) his birthright; he treated it with contempt, and this is reflected in his actions described in v34: "he ate, he drank, he rose, and he went on his way."

The behavior of Esau and Jacob is compared, and from the negative ethical comment about Esau's actions (v34), we can infer what the narrator thought about Jacob. In this incident, the narrator does not see Jacob as a supplanter. We can infer that the narrator, and by implication God, sees Jacob in a much more positive light, as someone who knew what was of value; *he valued the birthright whereas Esau despised it*. Jacob had the correct sense of values. If a meaning was to be given to Jacob's name in this context, it should be: having a sense of what is valuable and what is not valuable and relentlessly pursuing that which is of worth and value (cf. Matt 13:45–46). Is this not why Jacob became the heir of the Abrahamic promise and not Esau?

This picture of Esau is very similar to the picture we have of Saul in 1 Samuel. God rejected Saul as king, and God was about to tear away the kingdom to give it to David. In chapter 28:25, the narrator comments about Saul and his men, "and they ate, and they arose, and they went away into that night," which spelt the end of Saul's kingship. And so it was with Esau and his birthright.

Main point: Esau's treatment of the birthright was judged as an act of contempt for that which is of worth and value, while Jacob is seen as a person who values what is of worth.

6

Sermon Construction Based on the Exegetical, Theological, and Preaching Ideas

INTRODUCTION

IN THE PREVIOUS CHAPTER, the process of narrative exegesis was described and illustrated. The aim of the process is to determine the meaning and significance of the narrative units, establish the focus point of the story, and formulate the main points of the narrative units. The results of this work are now used in formulating the exegetical, theological, and preaching ideas, which will be used when crafting the sermon.

The main points are synthesized to form the exegetical idea, which serves as the basis for the theological and preaching ideas.

The starting point for the formulation of the *main points* and the *exegetical, theological, and preaching ideas* for sermon crafting is the concept that a sermon has a *single idea* it wants to communicate to listeners. Robinson says "to ignore the principle that a central, unifying idea must be the heart of an effective sermon is to push aside what experts in both communication theory and preaching have to tell us."[1] Bruce Waltke makes the point that the recent developments in the "grammar of poetics" actually support this emphasis of the one main idea.[2] Fitzgerald, quoted by Achtemeier asks the question: "what single thought do I wish to leave with the congregation? Out of all the ideas in these two or three Scripture passages for next Sunday . . . what single emphasis will speak most strongly to the people in the pews?" This emphasis on the

---

1. Robinson, *Expository Preaching*, 37, 33–50; see also Anderson, *Preaching*, 39–59; Willhite, "Bullet versus Buckshot," in, *Big Idea*, edited by Willhite and Gibson, 13–23.

2. Waltke, "Interpretation Issues," 41–44.

single idea is also true of narratives.³ Brink says that according to Henry James, "begin die roman by 'n kernidee, of 'n kompleks van idees, wat uit gedruk word in storievorm" (translation: "the novel has its origin in a core idea or a complex of core ideas which are expressed in the form of a story").⁴ Amit agrees that a story is formed around a central idea, which the narrative exegesis attempts to determine.⁵ Kugel says, "one of the most striking things research has noted about the stories we have been reading in Genesis is their sparse, bare-bones quality. Indeed, one would not be wrong to highlight this quality in referring to them collectively as the Bible's schematic narratives. A schematic narrative *has a point to make, and the entire text is designed to make it*" (my emphasis).⁶ Thompson remarks, "one analyzes a story, asking not only, How does the story end? but What is the point? Generations of literary critics have assumed that the narrative, composed of a sequence of events, also has a message."⁷

In a sense, the process involves decomposing the narrative, getting back to the basic idea which is the basis of the story. This core idea is the message of the narrative.⁸ Erickson remarks, "it is essential in exegesis to summarize in a sentence or two the main thrust, the central burden and message of an entire book (assuming there is one) . . . [for] a good story always has a point to make."⁹

Together, the three ideas form the foundation upon which the sermon is crafted. Basing the sermon on the exegetical, theological, and preaching ideas is linked to the nature of the biblical text, as Erickson remarks, "a biblical text in this sense is *three*-dimensional, rounded: it represents the *God-dimension*, the '*original human-dimension*' and (third) the later, *secondary human-dimension*" (my emphasis).¹⁰ The use of the three ideas in sermon construction has been fully developed and advanced primarily by Robinson and others.¹¹

3. Achtemeier, *Preaching*, 11–12.
4. Brink, *Vertelkunde*, 13.
5. Amit, *Book of Judges*, 130.
6. Kugel, *How To*, 146–47.
7. Green and Pasquarello III, *Reading, Preaching*, 85.
8. Ross, *Creation & Blessing*, 42, 46; Mathewson, *Art*, 81.
9. Erickson, *Beginner's Guide*, 67, 134.
10. Ibid., 101.
11. Robinson, *Expository Preaching*; Willhite and Gibson, eds., *Big Idea*; Anderson, *Preaching*; Willhite, *Preaching*.

A more complete description follows of the key concepts that facilitate the transition from exegesis and interpretation to sermon crafting:

CONCEPTS NECESSARY FOR SERMON CRAFTING

Exegetical idea: A summary in about two sentences of the focus point and the main points of the different narrative units. It is written in past-tense verbs and reflects the language, time, and culture of the original audience, and excludes application language. It captures the essence of the whole narrative in the words of the narrative text and it is based on the exegesis of the text. It answers the question: what did this narrative mean *then*?

Theological idea: The theological idea rewrites the exegetical idea in language that is transcultural, timeless, and universal. This makes the exegetical idea relevant and applicable to any person, living anywhere, at any time. The theological idea is not limited and restricted to the people of the Bible; it speaks to everyone. It answers the question: what does the narrative mean *now*? It reveals the universal and enduring principle of the narrative. The theological idea works with the similarities between the situation of the original audience and the present audience.

Preaching idea: The exegetical idea is rewritten in language which is contemporary, personal, local, and situation-specific, and which captures the attention of the audience. The rewritten exegetical idea is called the preaching idea. It links and relates the exegetical idea to a local, real, specific situation here and now and calls for a response. How does the exegetical idea link, apply, and relate to this specific situation? The preaching idea must be written in such a way that it will be remembered by the listener. Diagrammatically:

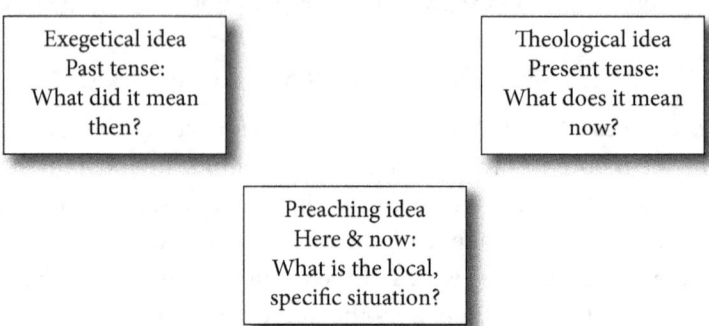

Wright, in reviewing Mathewson's *The Art of Preaching Old Testament Narrative,* remarks that one weakness of the "big idea" approach is that the "rich and many layered biblical passages may be rendered monotonous. Finding ideas or concepts in a text is certainly a part of biblical exegesis . . . but it is by no means the whole. What the text is *doing* is as important as what the text is *saying.* There is the danger that we will forget the time-conditioned character of the text in pursuit of a 'timeless' truth."[12] The discussion in the introduction about the issue of synchrony versus diachrony speaks to this weakness.[13] However, the remark that "the ideational language fundamentally conflicts with what makes a story a story" is untenable in view of what literary critics and biblical scholars say (see notes 4, 5, 6, 8, and 9). The concerns raised by Wright, however, need to be taken into account in any approach to Old Testament narrative.

The formulation of the exegetical, theological, and preaching ideas, based on the exegesis of the narrative text will be illustrated below using the narratives exegeted in chapter 5. The exegetical content of the narratives will not be repeated here. The purpose is to demonstrate the movement from the focus and main points to the formulation of the exegetical, theological, and preaching ideas.

The interrelationship between the focus point, the main points, and the three exegetical ideas are examined here. Careful attention is given to the manner in which the focus point and the main points provide the

---

12. Wright, *Quarterly*, 165–67.

13. See Jonker, *Exclusivity and Variety*; Fishbane, "Reviews," 103–4; De Moor, *Synchronic or Diachronic*.

basis for and develop the exegetical idea. The contribution that the focus point and the main points make to the development of the exegetical idea will be examined.

The exegetical idea provides the foundation to develop and formulate the theological idea and the preaching idea. The procedure for formulating the exegetical idea is as follows:

1. Write down all the main points in chronological order, starting with the main point of the focus point.

2. Summarize the essential ideas of the main points in a two-sentence statement. This is the exegetical idea.

The focus and main points of the passages exegeted in chapter 5 will be used here to illustrate the formulation of the exegetical, theological, and preaching ideas.

FORMULATING THE EXEGETICAL, THEOLOGICAL, AND PREACHING IDEAS

Example 1

~ GENESIS 25:20–26

The chiastic structure of this narrative unit is based on the narrative constituents of time and action (event):

    A   v20 Isaac married Rebekah at age forty
        B   v21a Isaac prayed for Rebekah's barrenness and God answered
            C   vv21b–22b Rebekah conceived but a struggle in her womb threatened the pregnancy
                D   vv22c–23 Rebekah asked God, who told her of the destiny and future of the twins in her womb
            C   v24 Rebekah carried the pregnancy to full term
        B   vv25–26a Two sons were born and named
    A   v26b Isaac was sixty years old when Rebekah gave birth to the twins

Focus Point

25:22b–23

Main point: Rebekah, concerned that her pregnancy would be prematurely terminated, enquired of God who told her of the destiny and future of the twins in her womb.

25:20

Main point: Isaac married Rebekah when he was forty years old, which affirmed the faithfulness of the servant, rewarded Abraham for his faith and emphasized that God kept his promise.

25:21a

Main point: Rebekah's barrenness threatened the Abrahamic promissory-covenant.

25:21b–22a

Main point: The answer to Isaac's prayers was under threat, as was Rebekah's future due to the possibility of an early termination of the pregnancy.

25:v24

Main point: Rebekah partially understood the significance of what she experienced as a threat to her pregnancy when she actually gave birth.

25:25–26a

Main point: The manner in which the twins were born signaled the continuation of the struggle outside the womb.

25:26b

Main point: Twins were born to Isaac when he was sixty years old, signaling that God is still at work to fulfill his promise to Abraham.

Summary

Isaac married, and twenty years later sons were born to him. But during the nine months of pregnancy, it was under threat from the struggle of the twins in her womb, which symbolized the future struggle and conflict between the sons. However, the oracle of God provided some answers, but Rebekah did not have a full understanding of the significance of v23b and its outworking in history. She had enough information to help her deal with her present situation. After a wait of twenty years, sons are born to Isaac, signaling that God's promise to Abraham is still on track.

Formulation of the Exegetical Idea

Main point: Rebekah, concerned that **her pregnancy would be prematurely terminated**, enquired of God who told her of **the destiny and future of the twins in her womb**.

Main point: Isaac married Rebekah when he was forty years old, which affirmed the faithfulness of the servant, rewarded Abraham for his faith, and emphasized that **God kept his promise**.

Main point: Rebekah's barrenness **threatened the Abrahamic promissory-covenant**.

Main point: The answer to **Isaac's prayers was under threat**, as was Rebekah's future due to the possibility of an early termination of the pregnancy.

Main point: Rebekah carried the pregnancy to full term, which symbolized **that God would also ensure that the Abrahamic promissory-covenant was fulfilled**.

Main point: The manner in which the twins were born signaled the continuation of the struggle outside the womb.

Main point: Twins were born to Isaac when he was sixty years old, signaling that **God was still at work to fulfill his promise to Abraham**.[14]

Exegetical Idea

The threat to the Abrahamic promissory-covenant was under the control of God, who would ensure that the promissory-covenant was fulfilled.

---

14. Note: The italicized phrases of the main points are used to formulate the exegetical idea below.

Theological Idea

The promises of God to his people may at times seem under threat, but he is in control and will fulfill his promises.

Preaching Idea

God is committed to your personal, and our corporate, spiritual and material wellbeing and integrity, despite the circumstances.

Example 2

～ GENESIS 24:1–67

The concentric structure is based on the narrative constituents of character and action (events):

> A   **vv1–9 Abraham made his servant swear an oath**
>> B   vv10–31 The servant was guided by God to the house of Nahor
>> B   vv32–61 The servant convinced the family his mission from God and departed with Rebekah for Canaan
> A   **vv62–67 The servant fulfilled the oath he swore**

Focus Point

24:1–9 and 24:62–67

Main point: The servant, having sworn an oath, arrived back with the right wife for Isaac, affirming Abraham's trust in God and proving that God had passed the "test."

24:10–31 and 24:32–61

Main point: The servant persuaded Rebekah and her family to let her go to Canaan with him by demonstrating that his mission was ordained of God.

Formulation of the Exegetical Idea

Main point: **The servant**, having sworn an oath, ***arrived back with*** the right wife for Isaac, ***affirming Abraham's trust in God and proving that God had passed the "test."***

Main point: The servant persuaded **Rebekah** and her family to let her go to **Canaan** with him by demonstrating that his mission was ordained by God.[15]

Exegetical Idea

The servant arrived back in Canaan with Rebekah, which was an affirmation that his mission was a success and of Abraham's trust in God, who had passed the test.

Theological Idea

The success and progress of the people of God are affirmations of their trust in him, and the truth that he rewards those who trust him.

Preaching Idea

Your spiritual and material progress is an affirmation that God is faithful and that he rewards faith in his trustworthiness.

Example 3

JUDGES 1:1—2:5

The structure is based on the narrative constituent of event (action):

- A vv1–2 God said Judah must lead the war to take the land and assured them of victory
    - ***B vv3–36 The successes and failures of the tribes in taking the land***
- A vv1–5 Failure to take the land was blamed on the people's covenant unfaithfulness

---

15. Note: The italicized phrases of the main points are used to formulate the exegetical idea below.

Focus Point—1:3–36

1:3–7

Main point: Judah had both success and failure in its campaign against the Canaanites and Perizzites.

1:8

Main point: The town of Jerusalem was utterly destroyed and Adoni-Bezek was killed in the process.

1:9–10

Main point: The regions of the Negev were utterly destroyed.

1:11–15

Main point: Caleb's wholehearted commitment to God was held up as an example of what was required for complete success in taking the land.

1:16–18

Main point: Simeon occupied his allotted territory successfully with the help of Judah and the Kenites.

1:9–20

Main point: The Judah-alliance had partial success in possessing their allotted territory because they lacked the character trait of wholehearted commitment to God, symbolized by Caleb.

1:21

Main point: The tribe of Benjamin failed to take its allotted territory.

1:22–29

Main point: The house of Joseph failed because it covenanted inappropriately, lacked self-belief and settled for short-term socio-economic gains.

1:30

Main point: Zebulun failed because they chose to use the inhabitants as a source of income rather than achieving God's purpose.

1:32

Main point: Asher was assimilated by the Canaanites and stood to lose their identity.

1:33

Main point: Naphtali failed to take possession of the land allotted to him because he chose to fail.

1:34–36

Main point: Dan failed because of a lack of determination, and because they did not receive help from the greedy house of Joseph.

2:1–2

Main point: God told the tribes he was their leader, that the land was already conquered, they just had to go in and take it.

2:3–5

Main point: God declared that the inhabitants will continue to be a snare, because the tribes failed to meet their covenant obligation to possess the land.

The formulation of the Exegetical Idea

Main point: Judah had both **success and failure in its campaign** against the Canaanites and Perizzites.

Main point: The town of **Jerusalem was utterly destroyed** and Adoni-Bezek was killed.

Main point: The regions of the **Negev was utterly destroyed**.

Main point: Caleb's **wholehearted commitment to God was held up as an example of what was required** for complete success in taking the land.

Main point: **Simeon occupied his allotted territory successfully** with the help of Judah and the Kenites.

Main point: The Judah-alliance had **partial success in possessing their allotted territory** because they lacked wholehearted commitment to God, symbolized by Caleb.

Main point: The tribe of **Benjamin failed** to take its allotted territory.

Main point: **The house of Joseph failed** because it covenanted inappropriately, lacked self-belief and settled for short-term socio-economic gains.

Main point: **Zebulun failed** because they used the inhabitants as a source of income rather than achieving God's purpose.

Main point: **Asher was assimilated** by the Canaanites and stood to lose their identity.

Main point: **Naphtali failed** to take possession of the land allotted to him because he chose to fail.

Main point: **Dan failed** because of a lack of determination, as well as not receiving help from the greedy house of Joseph.

Main point: God told the tribes he was their leader, that the **land was already conquered**, they just had to go in and take it.

Main point: God declared that the inhabitants will continue to be a snare, because they **failed to meet their covenant obligation to possess the allotted territory**.[16]

Exegetical Idea

The tribes failed to possess their allotted territories because they lacked the requirement for complete success: wholehearted commitment to God.

---

16. Note: The italicized phrases of the main points are used to formulate the exegetical idea below.

Theological Idea

The people of God will fail in their possession and appropriation of all that God had already accomplished for them if they lack wholehearted commitment to God.

Preaching Idea

To appropriate and enjoy all that God has for you requires wholehearted commitment to him.

Example 4

∽ Job 1:13–22

Labeling based on the narrative constituents of character and action (event):

A vv13–15		Messenger one: the Sabeans took the oxen and the donkeys and killed the servants
B v16		Messenger two: the fire of God burnt up the sheep and the servants
C v17		Messenger three: the Chaldeans took the camels and killed the servants
D vv18–19		Messenger four: a great wind destroyed the house and killed the children
E v20		Response of Job: he mourned and he worshipped
F v22		**Narrator's comment: Job did not blame God**

Focus Point

1:22

Main point: **Job remained unshakable** in his understanding of himself and his understanding of God.

1:13–19

Main point: **Job** was struck by tragedy and he **lost almost everything he possessed**.

1:20–21

Main point: **Job** responded to his tragedy by **mourning and worshipping God** because he understood that life and wealth are gifts of God and not rewards for how good we are.[17]

Exegetical Idea

Job remained unshakable in his faith in God, even though he lost almost everything. He worshipped him while mourning, because he understood that life and wealth were gifts from God.

Theological Idea

Christians remain unshakable in their faith in God in the face of loss and tragedy because they understand that life and wealth are gifts from God and not rewards for their good behavior.

Preaching Idea

A right understanding of life and wealth is key, if your faith in God is to survive loss and tragedy.[18]

Example 5

~ JUDGES 9:7–21

The structure is based on the narrative constituent of action (event):

A vv7–9	Attempt one unsuccessful: the olive tree refused to reign over the trees
B vv10–11	Attempt two unsuccessful: the fig tree refused to reign over the trees
C vv12–13	Attempt three unsuccessful: the vine refused to reign over the trees
D vv14–15	Attempt four successful: the bramble-bush agreed to reign over the trees

---

17. Note: The italicized phrases of the main points are used to formulate the exegetical idea below.

18. Note: Beginning with example 5 the main points are not repeated twice as was the case previously.

E vv16–21   ***Jotham's speech: he challenged the integrity of the Shechemites' actions***

Focus Point

9:16–21

Main point: **Jotham** used a parable to **warn the Shechemites** that **destruction will befall them** because **they acted dishonorably and insincerely** towards the memory of Gideon (Jerubbaal).

9:7–9

Main point: The **olive tree rejected the invitation of the trees** as of far less value and worth than its normal role, symbolizing God's disapproval of what the Shechemites had done.

9:10–11

Main point: **The fig tree rejected the invitation of the trees** because she felt the new position had far less honor

9:12–13

Main point: The **vine refused the invitation of the trees** because of its superior role of serving gods and men, once again symbolizing God's disapproval of what the Shechemites had done.

9:14–15

Main point: The **bramble-bush accepted the invitation**, but warned that should the trees act dishonestly and without integrity, they would be destroyed.[19]

Exegetical Idea

Jotham, using a parable, told the Shechemites that destruction awaits them because they acted dishonorably and insincerely when they appointed Abimelech as their king.

Theological Idea

---

19. Note: The italicized phrases of the main points are used to formulate the exegetical idea below.

The people of God bring his judgment upon themselves when they act dishonorably, insincerely, and without integrity.

Preaching Idea

You bring God's judgment upon yourself when you act dishonorably, insincerely, and without integrity.

Example 6

2 KINGS 2:1–25

The structure is based on the narrative constituent of space (geography):

> A   v1 Gilgal
> > B   vv2–3 Bethel
> > > C   vv4–5 Jericho
> > > > D   vv6–7 Jordan
> > > > > E   v8 Parting the waters of the Jordan
> > > > > > F   ***vv9–13 Elijah departed and his mantle and ministry passed over to Elisha***
> > > > > E   v14 Parting the waters of the Jordan
> > > > D   vv15–18 Jericho
> > > C   vv19–22 Purifying the waters of Jericho
> > B   vv23–24 Bethel
> A   v25 Samaria

Focus point

2:9–13

Main point: **The prophetic ministry transitioned from Elijah to Elisha** as they crossed the Jordan implying that prophets are not trained, anointed, and appointed.

2:1

Main point: **A new phase in the prophetic ministry** within Israel was about to begin.

2:2–3

Main point: **Elisha demonstrated the true character of a "son of the prophet"** in his commitment to Elijah, but had a concern about his future ministry as a prophet.

2:4–5

Main point: The future of Elisha as a prophet was under threat, so he thought, with the imminent departure of Elijah his master.

2:6–7

Main point: Elijah and Elisha stood on the banks of the Jordan River opposite the sons of the prophets, faced with **the challenge of crossing the river in full flow**.

2:8

Main point: Elijah and Elisha crossed the Jordan River together, which **confirmed that Elisha** would have a future in prophetic ministry.

2:14

Main point: **Elisha parted the waters** of the Jordon, just like Elijah did, which **confirms that the God who was with Elijah was now also with Elisha**.

2:15–18

Main point: **The sons of the prophets acknowledged that Elisha** was indeed a prophet like Elijah, after they returned home empty handed from their search for Elijah's body.

2:19–22

Main point: **The removal of the barrenness** caused by the water at Jericho **proved that Elisha was a prophet in the spirit of Elijah**.

2:23–24

Main point: **God's divine judgment** on the young men who mocked Elisha and thus blasphemed God **demonstrated publicly that the spirit of Elijah rested on Elisha**.

2:25

Main point: **The spatial movements confirmed that Elisha** was a prophet in the spirit of Elijah, marking him as a prophet of God.[20]

Exegetical Idea

The incidences which pointed to the transition of the prophetic ministry from Elijah to Elisha showed that prophetic ministry was a divine calling and not just a matter of training.

Theological Idea

Ministry and transitions in ministry must be a matter of divine calling and not just training and the choice of people.

Preaching Idea

The requirements change in service and ministry in the Church should fulfill.

Example 7

～ Genesis 25:19–34

The structure is based on the narrative constituent of narrative technique:

    A   vv19–21 Narration
       B   vv22–23 Discourse
          C   ***vv24–28 Narration***
       B   vv29–34a Discourse
    A   v34b Narration

Focus point

25:24–28

Main point: At birth, **Jacob and Esau were given names** based on their physical features, a character trait, the work they did, and their relation to their parents.

---

20. Note: The italicized phrases of the main points are used to formulate the exegetical idea below.

25:19–21

Main point: Isaac waited and prayed earnestly to the Lord for twenty years before **sons were born to him**.

25:22–23

Main point: Rebekah learnt that **the struggle between the twins represented a future struggle** between two nations founded by the twins.

25:29–34a

Main point: **Esau and Jacob fulfilled the prediction of v23** as predicted by God by **their decisions, choices, and actions**.

25:34b

Main point: **Esau treated** his valuable birthright **with contempt**, while **Jacob** is seen as a person who **values what is of worth**.[21]

Exegetical Idea

The real character of Esau and Jacob became evident from their decisions, actions, and choices.

Theological Idea

The real character of God's people will become evident from their decisions, actions, and choices.

Preaching Idea

The real you will become evident from your decisions, actions, and choices.

CONCLUSION

With the exegetical, theological, and preaching ideas in place, the transition can be made to the writing of the sermon manuscript. The next chapter illustrates different sermon formats available to the preacher for the task of sermon crafting.

---

21. Note: The italicized phrases of the main points are used to formulate the exegetical idea below.

7

Sermon Formats and the Structured-Repetition Approach

INTRODUCTION

THE PREVIOUS CHAPTERS DISCUSSED the various phases involved in a structured-repetition approach. In this chapter, the approach is illustrated with a number of narrative passages. There are also four fully developed sermon manuscripts in which the work done up to chapter 6 is applied using four sermon formats: didactic, third-person narrative, story-frame, and story-reflection-story. This chapter demonstrates the effective integration of exegesis and sermon crafting using a structured-repetition approach to Old Testament narratives. It also shows the flexibility of the approach by applying it to a variety of sermon formats.

The focus here is on the transition from the exegetical task to the homiletic task. The transition moves from exegesis to interpretation to application, which aims to make the message relevant to the listeners through personal and contemporary language.

The sermon manuscripts presented here to illustrate the various formats reflect my own personal teaching-preaching style and presentation.

EXAMPLE 1: DIDACTIC FORMAT

Introduction

The didactic sermon format, also known as the traditional format, is the best-known sermon format and is used by many, if not most, preachers in preaching. It is also known as the argumentative format, because it is based on the Aristotelian model of persuasive argument. Information and argument are used to persuade; the format focuses on the mind and intellect of the person. It aims to change the listener's mind or way of thinking.

The process of preparing a didactic sermon manuscript using a structured-repetition approach is as follows:

1. The *preaching idea* is the theme of the sermon.
2. The introduction of the sermon develops the *exegetical idea*.
3. The *main points* form the headings or points of the sermon outline; they form the skeleton of the sermon outline.
4. The *exegetical content* of each narrative unit is the basis for the body of the sermon, and provides the content for each of the main headings or points of the sermon. It is important to note that each person will develop the exegetical content and write the manuscript in his own style. The development of the exegetical content into the sermon manuscript is not just a matter of repeating the exegetical content. It involves a *rewriting* of the exegetical content in the way the person is going to present or preach it. It conforms to personal preaching style. At this point there is room for creativity and personal innovation.
5. A *conclusion* is then developed.

Text: 2 Samuel 13:1–22

CLOSURE

The first step in the exegetical process is to establish where the narrative begins and ends. In this case it is fairly straight forward; there are a number of indications in the narrative text that this is a self-contained narrative unit.

Verse 1a reads: "now it was after this." This is the usual formula in Old Testament narrative indicating the beginning of a new narrative episode. Verse 23a reads: "now it came about after two full years," again the formula indicates that a new narrative unit begins at v23, which means that the previous narrative episode ends at v22. Thus the narrative text begins at v1 and ends at v22.

In addition, both v1 and v22 have a ring structure based on the repetition of the narrative constituent of character, which confirms the limits of the narrative text:

Verse 1

    A "Absalom the son David
        B had a beautiful sister whose name was Tamar
    A Amnon the son of David . . . "

Verse 22

    A "Absalom did not speak to Amnon
        B because of Tamar his sister
    A Absalom hated Amnon"

It is clear that 2 Samuel 13:1–22 is a self-contained narrative text.

Exegesis of the Structure

The structure is uncovered according to the process described in chapter 2.

The structure is based on the narrative constituent of event (action) and space:

A vv1–8a   Amnon used Jonadab's plan and succeeded to get Tamar into his house by herself
B vv8a–14 Amnon raped Tamar ignoring her protests and her alternative suggestions
C vv15–19 Amnon ordered Tamar out of his house ignoring her protests
D vv20–22 Absalom consoled Tamar, while David was very angry but did nothing

Description of the Structure

The structure is linear, consisting of four narrative units and unit C vv20–22 is the *focus point*. It is characterized by movement in space; Tamar moved from Amnon's house to Absalom's house. The movement from the house of the one brother to the house of the other brother suggests a feud between them (see also v4 where Amnon referred to Tamar as "my brother Absalom's sister"). This suggests that Amnon, in raping

Tamar, was trying to hurt Absalom. Tamar was a pawn in the fight between the two brothers.

The rape scene is the longest of the units, which focuses the attention of the reader on the rape event and on Tamar, the rape victim.

The introductory formula "now it was after this" indicates the beginning of a new episode. While 2 Samuel 13:1 suggests that this episode is a continuation of chapters 11–12. The broader context for the interpretation of the narrative structure is therefore 2 Samuel chapters 11–12.

Another indication of the continuity between chapters 11–12 and this episode is 13:21. The introductory formula at v23 "now it came about after two full years" marks the start of a new episode, so this episode begins at 13:1 and ends at v22.

Focus Point

C vv20–22
In v20, Absalom spoke to Tamar. His house must have been near Amnon's for him to be able to intervene as quickly as he did after the rape happened. There is no indication that Tamar went directly to his house, the text just says "and she went away, crying aloud as she went." She was walking, in no particular direction. Absalom must have heard the crying, came out to investigate, and found that it was Tamar.

Absalom's question is very significant. He asked, "Has Amnon been with you?" Why would Absalom suspect that Amnon was responsible for what had happened to Tamar? And particularly that what had happened was of a sexual nature, as the expression "with you" suggests? This implies that he was aware that Amnon wanted to sleep with Tamar (v2). Absalom's question also suggests possible tension and conflict between the two brothers. He did not wait for her reply, a further indication that he was sure Amnon was guilty of raping Tamar, a conclusion he arrived at from the state of Tamar described in v18a and v19, as well as knowing that Tamar would not consent to sexual relations with Amnon (vv12–13).

Absalom's advice was strange: "keep silent, my sister, he is your brother; do not take this matter to heart" (v20b). It would appear that Absalom did not want people to know what had happened to Tamar (a tough task given that she was walking around crying). He got her to stop crying, and he stopped her from going to David to report the matter (v21), saying, "Do not take this to heart." He did not mean that what happened to her was not serious and did not matter, for he himself treated it as a serious matter (v22). Absalom's intention was to deal with the matter himself, as a private and personal matter, an issue between him and Amnon (v22). Honor and shame played an important role in ancient societies, and the way to dishonor a man was through the women connected to him. So by raping Tamar, Absalom's sister, Amnon sent a message to Absalom about what he thought of him. It is for this reason that Absalom wanted to keep the news from becoming public and reaching the king (v20b). He was going to settle the matter himself. It also reflected his lack of confidence and trust in David, feeling that David was going to do nothing about it, as (v21) proved. He felt he had to take action if his honor and the honor of his sister were going to be restored.

Verse 21 describes David's response to the news about Tamar; he was "very angry." There is no indication that he expressed that deep anger; it appears that he internalized it and then left it at that. But David's response is bracketed by Absalom's response, v20 and v22; it is in the middle of Absalom's response in v20 and v22, and it contrasts with his reaction. The framing highlights the inappropriateness of David's response; it was a very sad and disappointing reaction. By placing David's response in this contrasting context, the narrator makes a connection between chapters 11–12 and chapter 13, and suggests that David already shared the blame for what happened to Tamar and for the events in 13:24–33. The narrator uses this structural arrangement to evaluate David's conduct.

Verse 22 describes Absalom's response to the event. Verse 22a is the effect and v22b supplies the reason for the attitude and behavior of Absalom. But v22 is the clearest example of the trouble in the family when compared with v1:

Verse 1	Verse 22
"Absalom the son David had a beautiful sister whose name was Tamar and Amnon the son of David loved her."	"Absalom did not speak to Amnon . . . Absalom hated Amnon because he had violated his sister Tamar."

Two things jump out from the comparison: first, in v22 any reference to familial relationship is missing compared to the twice repeated "son" in v1; there is also no reference to "David" in v22, as is the case in v1, which places the spotlight on him and his inaction and further suggests trouble in the family; trouble between the two "brothers" and the father. Second, Tamar is pivotal in both verses; she was at the center of events in this episode. It is significant that Absalom speaks of Amnon as Tamar's "brother" (v20), but in v22 there is no familial reference, showing the intensity of his hatred for Amnon.

The episode ends by emphasizing Absalom's hatred for Amnon and his caring for Tamar, while David, the father of the family, was "very angry" but did nothing. The family is torn apart because David did nothing (v21). David was right to feel deep anger, but in this context it was not enough. The contrast of v20 and 22 with v21 puts the spotlight on David's inaction. Given what had happened, doing nothing was the wrong response. The situation called for action and David failed. This pattern in vv20–22 is diagrammatically presented as follows:

V20 Absalom found and consoled and cared for Tamar
V21 David heard what happened and was "very angry"
V22 Absalom hated Amnon because he violated Tamar

And yet the events that play out in this episode were because David did act; he did something, as chapters 11–12 make clear. However, when he should not have acted he did, and when he should have acted he did not, with disastrous consequences for his family. This link with what happened previously is indicated by the connection of 13:1 to chapters 11–12 through the introductory formula "now it was after this." The demonstrative pronoun "this" refers to chapters 11–12, showing that the behavior of David in 2 Samuel 11–12 had unintended consequences for his family, in this case, the rape of Tamar. Lust and its disastrous consequences seemed to have followed this family.

Main point: *The family was ruined. Tamar was violated, Absalom hated Amnon, and David, though very angry, did nothing.*

A vv1–5
At one level, this can be read as a story in which Amnon, in his obsessive lust, raped his half sister Tamar as a way of dishonoring and humiliating Absalom and so demonstrate his power over Absalom, assisted and abet-

ted by their father David who did nothing when he heard what Amnon had done. This resulted in Absalom's hatred for Amnon.

There is, however, a second level at which the story must be read, which is indicated in the text in v1a by the words "now it was after this."

Two important points flow from v1a. The first is syntactical and is related to the phrase "now it was after this." The phrase means that the events of chapter 13 happened after the events of chapters 11–12, and the events of chapter 11–12 will have some bearing on our understanding of this episode. Secondly, v1 sets up a triad, with Tamar as the pivot:

X   "*Absalom the son of David*
Y   had a beautiful *sister whose name was Tamar*
X   *Amnon the son of David* loved her."

This arrangement functions as an announcement statement for the episode, telling the reader what the episode is going to be about. It shows that the episode is about Absalom, Amnon, Tamar, and David. The presence of David in this arrangement provides the link to chapters 11–12.

In v2a, Amnon "made himself ill" and in v5 he is told "pretend that you are ill." What is the difference? In v2a, the source of his illness is his obsessive lust for Tamar caused by her beauty and his belief that it was impossible for him to have sexual intercourse with her because she was a virgin (contra v13b). So he made himself sick by stressing about his lust for Tamar. So he was distressed to the point of illness:

a) Because of his half-sister Tamar
b) Because she was a virgin
c) Because she was beautiful (v1)

And because she was all this, but especially point (b), Amnon could not act upon his lust. The first sickness expressed this inability to get Tamar alone with him, as Alter comments, "the last phrase [to do anything to her] here has a definite negative connotation . . . and makes clear the narrow carnal nature of Amnon's 'love' for Tamar. Sexual tampering with a virgin had particularly stringent consequences in biblical law."[1] The first sickness was mental and emotional rather than physical, brought about by Amnon himself.

---

1. Alter, *David Story*, 256.

The second sickness, v5a, was pretence, feigning, and deception. Here, the illness is used to overcome his perceived inability to be alone with Tamar so he could use her to satisfy his sexual desire.

Verse 2b reads "and it seemed hard [impossible] in the eyes of Amnon to do anything to her." What does this mean? Amnon felt that he could never be alone with Tamar because according to cultural norms, a virgin could not ordinarily visit his house without an escort. I say ordinarily because as the succeeding events indicate, a situation had to be created which would legitimize her visit to his house unaccompanied (v9b).

Amnon had a friend named Jonadab; and it is likely that he was an advisor, rather than just simply a friend. Alter remarks on the title given to Jonadab: "*rēʿa* . . . in a royal context is also the title of someone who played an official role as the king's, or the prince's companion and counselor."[2] This is also suggested when he is described as "a very shrewd man." The question—"Why are you so depressed morning after morning" (v4)—asked by Jonadab, shows that he was a regular at the palace complex. The word used to describe the look on Amnon's face is the Hebrew word *dal*, which means "poor" in Leviticus, but here it means "dejected." The look was similar to the disappointed, dejected, defeated look a poor person would have after attempting to get something to eat all day and returning home empty handed. This was the physical expression of Amnon's mental and emotional state.

After hearing the reason for Amnon's state, Jonadab presented Amnon with a plan to get Tamar into his house, alone. Jonadab's plan would provide a valid reason for Tamar to be alone in the house with Amnon, which was perhaps all Jonadab intended (see v4). For Amnon, however, the plan would make what he wanted to do very easy. He would be alone in the house with Tamar and could do what he always wanted to do. So Jonadab advised: pretend that you are sick and ask the king to send Tamar to your house to make food for you. In this way, so Jonadab thought, Amnon would be alone with Tamar, and would have the opportunity to declare his love (v4) to her. I think Jonadab interpreted Amnon's depression (v4) as love sickness.

But the plan that Jonadab came up with (v5), and its aftermath (vv17–18), made it clear that Amnon did not really love Tamar and was not interested in marrying her (13b). He only wanted to have sexual

2. Ibid.

intercourse with her to humiliate Absalom. The plan was based on deception. For Amnon, this meant he would have the opportunity to "do anything to her" sexually (v2). This point is clear from the words used for "food," which indicated Amnon's intentions. Jonadab used the terms *leḥem . . . habbiryâh* for food (v5); Amnon used the terms *ûtlabbēb . . . lᵉbibôt* (v6); David used the term *habbiryāh* (v7); the narrator used the terms *ûtlabbēb . . . lᵉbibôt*; Amnon used *habbiryāh* (v10); the narrator used *hallᵉbibôt* (v10). Only Amnon and the narrator used the term "cakes" and its cognate "make." As Fokkelman[3] explains, the use of the term "cakes" has a sexual connotation. Amnon was very clear about what he wanted. Everyone else was deceived by him, except Absalom (v20).

B v6
Amnon put Jonadab's plan into action, and pretended to be sick and deceived the king. The king visited him and he asked that Tamar be sent to his house. If he really loved her and wanted to marry her, as it seems Jonadab thought (v4), and as Tamar showed was a real option (v13c), he had the opportunity to ask the king to give Tamar to him in marriage. He did not do this because he did not want to marry her; he wanted to have sexual intercourse with her, motivated by his lust and desire to humiliate Absalom.

C v7–8a
David sent a message to the palace instructing Tamar to go to Amnon's house and prepare food for him. Tamar went to the house of Amnon as instructed by the king. Finally, Tamar was in his house by herself. The plan worked and Amnon had Tamar where he always wanted her, in his house, unescorted.

Main point: Amnon, in his desperation to satisfy his lust, deceived and used Jonadab and David to get Tamar into his house unescorted.

A vv8b–14
This unit details the rape. What seemed impossible (v2c) was now possible for Amnon, with Tamar alone in the house. He refused to eat the cakes Tamar made and ordered all the servants out of the house. He then ordered her to bring the cakes to him in "the chamber" (the inner room), which she did, and fed him there. Then he grabbed hold of her

---

3. Fokkelman, *King David*, 105.

and said, "Come lie with me, my sister" (v11). She protested, vv12–13, citing four reasons: he would be breaking the law of the land, v12b; the consequences for her, given that she was his sister—the personal shame and suffering she would have to endure, v13a; the consequences for him—he would be regarded as a fool or scoundrel, a low-life and common criminal, v13b; and there actually was an alternative, v13c. She attempted to reason with him, "but he would not listen to her" (v14a, cf. v16).

Amnon's view of what he was doing was different from Tamar's view. He said, "Come, *lie* with me," (*šikbî*, v11; see also v20); but she said, "Do not violate me" (*tᵉʿannēnî*), v12; see also v22a. For Amnon this was merely a sex act, calculated to hurt Absalom. For Tamar it was much more than just an act of sexual intercourse because the rape had more severe consequences for her, for her person (violate me), v13a. It was not just a sex act; it was the destruction of a life. His lust for her was so strong that he refused to listen to her. He was prepared to destroy Tamar's life if it meant he could satisfy his lust and humiliate Absalom. The rape, and therefore Tamar, was a means to an end: satisfaction of his sexual urges and dishonoring Absalom and so demonstrating his power over him. The narrator devotes six and a half verses to the rape, making it the main event in the narrative.

Main point: Amnon, overcome by his lust, ignored Tamar's attempts to reason with him and raped her.

B vv15–19

The events that flow from the rape are described in this unit. The focus is on the sudden and violent turn around in the feelings of Amnon and his treatment of Tamar as a result. This sudden change demonstrates that he did not love her (v4). He may have been attracted to her (v1) and lusted after her, but he certainly did not love her. He also saw her as a means to humiliate Absalom.

The term love is used four times: v1, 4, 15 (2x). The term hate is also used four times in v15, but with a difference: adverbs are used to qualify hate: "a very great hatred . . . the hatred . . . was greater than the love." In contrast, the word love has no adverbs qualifying it. This brings the intense hatred he had for her and Absalom into focus; hatred overshadowed and vanquished love. In the text, Amnon said he loved Tamar (v4), but the sudden and radical change showed that he never really loved her. In fact, Amnon despised Tamar (v15): "for the hatred with which he hated her was greater than the love with which he had loved her." This is also clear in verses 1, 4, and 15:

A   Amnon David's son *loved her* . . . Amnon said to him "I *love* Tamar" (vv1, 4)
Then Amnon hated her
B   with a very great hatred; for the hatred with which he hated her(v15a–b)
A   was greater than the *love* with which he had *loved her* (v15c)

This pattern confirms that Amnon never loved Tamar; he found her repulsive, contemptuous, and recoiled from her: "get up, go away." The point is further confirmed when comparing vv1b–2 with vv15–19.

In v16, Tamar again protests "no, because this wrong in sending me away is greater than the other that you have done to me." This is a strange reaction until one understands the implication of her being sent away.

Tamar is concerned about the future to which Amnon had condemned her; a future without the opportunity for her to get married at all, indicated in v20b "so Tamar remained and was desolate in her brother Absalom's house," which was probably for at least two years (cf. v23; Gen 38:11b).

For the second time it is said of Amnon "yet he would not listen to her" (v16). His desire to have her sexually made him deaf to the voice of reason. Furthermore, he showed his hatred by calling Tamar "this woman" (v17). She was no longer "my sister." The description of her being thrown out by the servant is interrupted by the narrator's comment that Tamar was a virgin (v18a), which explains her protest in v16 and Amnon's feeling (v2) that it was impossible for him "to do anything to her."

In v19, Tamar mourns the shame, the loss, and the destruction of her bright future. She mourned the loss of her virginity and all that it meant. The rape had utterly destroyed her; in fact, Amnon had utterly destroyed her in his passionate lust for her, his hatred for Absalom, and his intense desire to get even with him.

Consumed by lust, Amnon destroyed Tamar; "and she went away, crying as she went." She walks without any direction, symbolizing the directionless path ahead of her. There was no future for her, and she left his house mourning this loss.

*Main point: **After Amnon raped Tamar, he sent her away with contempt to face a doomed future.***

FORMULATION OF THE EXEGETICAL IDEA

Main point: **Amnon's lust ruined the family**; Tamar was desolated, Absalom hated Amnon, and David, though very angry, did nothing.

Main point: **Amnon, desperate to satisfy his lust**, deceived and used Jonadab and David to get Tamar into his house unescorted.

Main point: **Amnon**, overcome by his lust, ignored Tamar's attempts to reason with him and **raped her**.

Main point: After Amnon raped **Tamar**, he sent her away with contempt to ***face a doomed future***.

Exegetical Idea

Amnon, driven by his obsessive lust for Tamar, raped her with disastrous consequences.

Theological Idea

Christians, driven by an obsession of any kind, will behave in ways that are destructive and disastrous.

Preaching Idea

Flee obsessions of any kind, because it has disastrous and destructive consequences.

Sermon

READING: 2 SAMUEL 13:1–22

Theme: **Flee obsessions of any kind, because it has disastrous and destructive consequences.**

INTRODUCTION

Prostitution is said to be the oldest trade in the world; it is as old as human civilization itself, we are told.

Well, there is a human trait expressed in human behavior that is even older than prostitution; it has its origin in primordial time, right at the beginning before the birth of human civilization. It is well-known yet much denied reality called lust; that intense desire to possess a person, a thing, or even an experience on one's own terms. The Bible refers to this when it tells us:

"When the woman saw that the tree was good for food, and that it was a delight to the eyes, and that the tree was *desirable* to make *one* wise, she took from its fruit and ate; and she gave also to her husband with her, and he ate" (Gen 3:6) (my emphasis).

Here is that wanting to have something on one's own terms. We read about it again a couple of chapters later, in a more intense description:

"The wickedness of man was great on the earth, and that every intent of *the thoughts of his heart was only evil continually*" (Gen 6:5) (my emphasis).

We know this today as lust. And it is common to both Christians and non-Christians alike, causing havoc. And the story before us speaks to this matter of lust and obsession telling us to flee obsessions of any kind, because of its disastrous and destructive consequences:

For lust drives you to deceive and use people, including those close to you and who care about you—vv1–8a

We are introduced to the characters in v1 at the beginning of the story. They are the sons of David, Absalom, and Amnon, and the daughter of David: Tamar. She was the biological sister of Absalom but the half-sister of Amnon. We are told that Amnon was in love with Tamar, v1. A careful reading of v1, however, shows that we have a triangle in which Absalom, Amnon, and Tamar are the main role players with David an agent. His only role was to instruct Tamar to go to Amnon's house to make food for him, v6.

Amnon appeared to be so deeply in love with Tamar that it distressed him to the point that he was sick with love; a love-sick puppy. And on a first reading it would seem that Amnon's distress was caused by his love for Tamar. The Hebrew verb in v1 is a *hithpael* verb, which is a reflexive verb. This means that Amnon was making *himself* sick. In other words he kept on stressing to the point where he made himself emotionally sick, and his emotional sickness could be seen in his physical demeanor. For this reason, when Jonadab saw his face, he asked: "Why do you, the king's son, look so haggard morning after morning?" (v4a). Now Amnon himself gives the reason for the stress he was experiencing: "I'm in love with Tamar, my brother Absalom's sister." So, Amnon's love was the reason for his mental, emotional, and physical state.

But according to v2b, there was another reason for his state, the real reason: "on account of his sister Tamar, for she was a virgin, and it seemed impossible for him to do anything to her" (NIV). The real reason Amnon was stressed to the point of emotional sickness was because he desired to be sexually intimate with Tamar; he wanted to have sexual intercourse with her, this is the meaning of the somewhat obscure expression "to do anything to her." So the source of his sickness was his desire for sexual relations with Tamar, which could not be fulfilled, and not his love for her. To put it simply: Amnon *lusted* after Tamar, and this *lust* and obsession of wanting to have sex with her drove him to the point where he was emotionally stressed. Lust was the reason for Amnon's mental, emotional, and physical condition.

The depiction of Amnon in vv1–2 as a person controlled by lust gives us important insights into the concept of lust. So what is lust in the first place? It can be defined as follows: "it is striving for an object which may be a person, a thing, an experience."[4] In the case of Amnon, it is expressed in the following way, "to do anything to her." He had this intense desire to do "something" to her (v2) and strove to achieve this objective, to the point where it made him sick. The other element of lust is that it is based on "a false evaluation of the possessions and the evils of life."[5] For Amnon, the issue is about sexual intimacy with Tamar which as v2 says, "it seemed impossible for him." This evaluation is proved false in v13: "please speak to the king, he will not keep me from marrying you." So Amnon's situation is a classic case of lust. And as far as the basic nature of lust is concerned, it comes down to getting what you want on your terms. Amnon wanted sex, but on his terms, and that is the essence of all types of lust.

The stumbling block to him satisfying his lust was a cultural prescription. Culture dictated that virgins were not allowed to visit a man's house unaccompanied. In this way, virgins were protected from violations of their virginity, jeopardizing their chances of marriage and the honor of the family.

4. Schönweiss, "Desire," 456.
5. Ibid.

In walks the inimitable Jonadab. He was a friend of Amnon; but he was also a relative: an uncle (the brother of David), and an advisor, as the expression "morning after morning" (v4) suggests. He was a frequent visitor to the palace and had an official position at the palace, in all probability an advisor or counselor of Amnon. He asked Amnon, "Why do you, the king's son, look so haggard morning after morning?" (v4); to which Amnon replied, "I'm in love with Tamar" (v4). But this was a lie of course, as v2 makes clear; it was lust, not love that made him so sick. And Jonadab, who appears to be a jovial, too-eager-to-please character, was deceived by Amnon and provided him with a plan to overcome his obstacle, v5. The plan was simple but effective, as it would become clear later: pretend you are sick; your father will visit you, and when he visits you ask him to send Tamar to your house to make food for you.

I do not think that Jonadab was aware that Amnon, driven by lust, was going to have sex with Tamar, and was going to do so forcibly; for if he knew that he would never have suggested the plan. I think he thought Amnon was only looking for an opportunity to declare his love for Tamar to her.

The plan worked, and on hearing that Amnon was "sick" David visited him (v6) and he made his request. David instructed Tamar, "go to the house of your brother Amnon and prepare some food for him" (v7). And so David was also deceived by Amnon, and by his brother Jonadab.

Now the deception of David was understandable, although he is not totally blameless. Even though he was the king, he violated the cultural prescription and protocol and placed Tamar in a position where Amnon could violate her. Could it be, I ask, that having just lost a child (11:23), David wanted to be a good father, showing care, and so unwittingly broke cultural protocol and prescription in instructing Tamar to go to Amnon's house on her own?

The deception of Jonadab, however, is easier to understand. We are told he was "a very shrewd man" (v3); and from the tone of the question in v4 it appears that he was kind of a "happy chappy," eager to please the prince to advance his career at the palace. So, that he was duped is understandable, and almost expected. One could say that he might have been shrewd, but he was not very wise, and there is a difference. And so, although both David and Jonadab were deceived, they themselves were not completely blameless and contributed to their own deception. The plan worked, and finally Amnon had Tamar in his house and on her own (v8). But to achieve this, he had to deceive a friend, a close confidant and counselor, and his father. This is the extent to which lust drove him. He allowed himself to be so controlled by lust that he was prepared to use those closest to him, who cared about him, to satisfy his lust.

For lust makes one behave in a totally irrational manner—vv8b–14

Once Amnon had Tamar in his house, he sent the servants out of the house, went into the inner room and told Tamar to bring the food to him there. When she was in the inner room and about to feed him, he grabbed hold of her and said to her: "Come, lie with me," v11. She resisted and attempted to reason with Amnon:

First, she pointed out the gravity of what he wanted to do. He said to her "come, lie with me"; she replied, "no my brother, do not violate me." Amnon saw it as just sexual intercourse, but Tamar pointed out that this was not just sexual intercourse, it was worse: it was a violation of her, a virgin in Israel. And the violation of a virgin had very serious and destructive consequences.

Second, she pointed out that this was not just sex, it was a violation of the identity of the nation, what Israel stood for as a people of God, "such a thing is not done in Israel"; it was a "disgraceful thing" (see Judg 19:23; 20:6); it was an abomination in Israel. As a people of God, Israel was expected to act differently to the surrounding nations, and Amnon was not doing that. In fact, he was guilty of breaking the covenant; what he wanted to do was evil and ungodly.

Third, she gave him an alternative: "please speak to the king, for he will not withhold me from you." But he was not going to speak to the king because he had no intention to marry her; he had an opportunity to speak to the king, v6a, after he professed to Jonadab that he was in love with her, v4b. So he refused the alternative she gave him.

Refusing to listen to her, and being stronger than she was, he "violated her and lay with her." In v14, the narrator combines Amnon's view of what he was doing and Tamar's view of what he was doing, by placing "violated [*wayeʾannehâ*] her" first and "lay [*wayyiškab*] with her" second, he puts the emphasis on the true nature of the act. This was a rape and not just an act of sexual intercourse. It was also a symbol of power over Tamar, because the text says, "since he was stronger than she." To describe the act of rape, the narrator uses the Hebrew root *ʿânnî*, poor, powerless, to make this point. Thus Tamar becomes the victim of uncontrolled and obsessive lust. Moreover, by violating Tamar, Amnon was doing what his father David did (chapter 11); he took what was not given to him (see 11:27; see also 11:1, 12:9).

Sexual lust led to Amnon's irrational behavior, the use of force, and the violation of Tamar: actions which had their origin in the refusal to see reason.

For lust causes the destruction of people and their futures—vv15–19

In these verses, we encounter a sudden and radical change in Amnon, but not a surprising change given what he set out to do. We read: "then Amnon hated her with a very great hatred; for the hatred which he hated her was greater than the love with which he loved her." This contrasts with "the hatred which he hated her *was greater than* (my emphasis) the love with which he loved her" and raises the question whether he really loved her (see v4b). The answer to that question is no.

The destructive impact of what had been done to her is reflected in her words: "This wrong in sending me away is greater than the other you have done to me." If he had raped her and then asked the king to marry her (v13b), she would have had a future, but now her future was basically destroyed. Her words in v13a—"as for me, where could I get rid of my shame?"—are echoed here. Where was she to go? Home? (see v21). Amnon had destroyed her life, her future. And the destruction of her future is descriptively expressed in v18 when the narrator says, "Now she had on a long sleeved garment; for in this manner the virgin daughters of the king dressed themselves in robes." She was dressed like a virgin, but she was no longer a virgin; that had been taken away from her and with it her future. Thus the destruction of her future was symbolized in her torn clothing.

Moreover, the destruction of her future is also demonstrated by her actions, "and Tamar put ashes on her head, and tore her long-sleeved garment which *was* on her; and she put her hand on her head and went away, crying aloud as she went" (v19). She is in mourning; mourning the loss of her virginity and her future. And the words "went away . . . as she went" give the impression of someone walking aimlessly, in no particular direction, for she had no direction in which to go; she had no future, it had just been taken from her.

Verse 20 describes her situation thus: "so Tamar . . . was *desolate* [emphasis mine] in her brother Absalom's house." Tamar's future was destroyed, for lust destroys people and their futures.

For lust ruins relationships—vv20–22

The rape of Tamar, rooted in the lust of Amnon, had wider consequences. Apart from the desolation it caused Tamar (v20), it also ruined relations within the family, as vv21–22 indicates, ". . . King David . . . was very angry . . . Absalom did not speak to Amnon either good or bad; for Absalom hated Amnon because he had violated his sister Tamar." The family was torn apart. Amnon did not only destroy the life of one person, and it would still have been a very serious matter if he had done that alone; but even worse, he was responsible for the ruin of the relationships within the whole family. This ruin of the family relations overshadowed relationships in the family for years to come; it had both immediate and long-term consequences which brought incredible pain and suffering to the family. The life of the family was never the same again. That's what lust does.

Conclusion

The lust we encounter in the rape of Tamar is sexual lust. But as we all know, sexual lust is just one type of lust. There is the intense, obsessive desire to "own" and control a person, and then there is the well-known lust for material things. All the types of lust

1. Drive us to deceive and use people, even those close to you and who care about you.
2. Make us behave in a totally irrational manner.
3. Cause the destruction of people and their futures.
4. Ruin relationships.

So how do we deal with lust? It's profoundly simple, yet tough: Flee! Not just sexual lust, but all types of lust in terms of the exhortation of Paul (1 Tim 6, 2 Tim 2): sexual, material, experiential, and the lust of persons. Flee! Notice that fleeing is a deliberate choice and decision when you become aware of some danger. And to stay aware of the danger of lust is to continually evaluate one's attitude and thinking about sex, people, material possessions, and the desire for experience in the light of the

Word of God. Part of that evaluation process is to deliberately be part of a community where everyone is held accountable. This is what it means to flee lust of all types.

EXAMPLE 2: THIRD-PERSON NARRATIVE

In this format, the sermon describes the narrative from a past perspective, and the narrative text features regularly in the sermon manuscript.

Text: Ruth 4:1–10

CLOSURE

The story moves from the threshing floor (3:6), to the city (3:15c), and finally to the gate (4:1), which indicates that we have a new episode starting with 4:1.

In 3:13, Boaz commits to redeeming the land. The commitment is fulfilled when Boaz redeemed the land (4:9), publically affirmed his intention to marry Ruth (4:10), and the transaction attested by the community. The community also spoke a blessing upon him and Ruth (4:12–13). The end of the episode is marked at 4:12. The episode begins in 4:1 and ends in 4:12.

EXEGESIS OF THE STRUCTURE

Labeling based on the narrative constituents of geography (space) and character:

> A v1ab Boaz waited at the gate for the kinsman-redeemer
> > B v1c The kinsman-redeemer joined Boaz at the gate
> > > C vv2–4a Boaz presented the situation to the kinsman-redeemer and elders
> > > > **D v4b The kinsman-redeemer said he intended to redeem the land**
> > >
> > > C v5 Boaz pointed out the implication of redemption
> >
> > B v6–8 The kinsman-redeemer decided not to exercise his right to redeem
>
> A v9–10–12 Boaz bought the land and affirmed his intention to marry Ruth, as witnessed by the community

Description of the Structure

The structure is a concentric pattern with v4b as the pivotal point. The division into narrative units is based on the interaction between Boaz and the kinsman-redeemer at the gate of the town. Boaz aims to ensure that the kinsman-redeemer gives up his right of redemption, so that he is able to buy the land from Naomi and automatically gain the right to marry Ruth.

Focus Point

D v4b
The kinsman-redeemer was informed that (a) Naomi planned to sell the land that belonged to Elimelech, her deceased husband; (b) he was the nearest relative and had first opportunity to redeem the land. In this half-verse, he *decided* to redeem the land. Thus the pivotal matter in the narrative unit 4:1–10 is the kinsman-redeemer's decision to buy Elimelech's land from Naomi. The kinsman-redeemer posed a threat to Boaz's intention to marry Ruth (3:9–13). This half-verse, which is the focus point is important; it will determine the progress of the story and how it ends.

Main point: The kinsman-redeemer informed the "community court" that he intended to exercise his right of redemption and buy the land from Naomi.

A v1ab Boaz
After the night's events at the threshing-floor, Boaz hurried to the city gate at daybreak (3:13). The gate was the city's only entry and exit point. If Boaz was going to find the kinsman-redeemer this was the right place to be. In addition, "and when morning comes" (v13, repeated twice) was the best time if Boaz was to resolve the matter of marriage to Ruth that very day (v18b). Once a person left the city it would be difficult to contact him/her again.

A variety of activities took place at the gate of the town. For example, the market place was near the gate, and people met in the gateway for social events. The community assemblies and gatherings to transact legal matters also took place at the gate. So it was a strategic place and Boaz positioned himself there.

Boaz's actions and thinking described in this unit demonstrates that he is a wise person who thinks strategically. It also underlines his commitment and serious intention to marry Ruth.

Main point: Boaz took action to fulfill his promise to settle the matter of Ruth's future that day.

B v1c kinsman-redeemer
Boaz asked the kinsman-redeemer to join him at the city gate. The text reads "and he turned aside"; he changed course, he changed direction. He was on his way out of the city, but he interrupts his plans to join Boaz at the gate as requested. This willingness to change his program for the day to accommodate Boaz was part of the kinsman-redeemer's character; he was a reasonable, thinking person. Without knowing why Boaz wanted to see him, he agreed to join him at the gate. This action was also part of the hospitality that characterized ancient societies.

Main point: The kinsman-redeemer accepted Boaz's invitation to join him at the gate, without knowing the reason for the invitation.

C vv2–4a Boaz
Boaz asked ten elders of the city to join him at the gate for a legal council meeting; an assembly of city elders was constituted. Some of the city people also gathered to see what was going on (v9). The gate was often used for legal meetings (Deut 16:18; 21:19; 25:7,); and a seat "among the elders in the gates" (Prov 31:23) was a high honor, while "oppression in the gates" was a synonym for judicial corruption (Job 31:21; Prov 22; Isa 29:21; Amos 5:10).[6]

Main point: Boaz set up a "community court" at the gate.

C v5 Boaz
The kinsman-redeemer heard the reason for Boaz's' invitation, and decided to exercise his right to buy the land Naomi was selling. In v5, Boaz informed him of the implications of buying the land: "You must also acquire Ruth the Moabitess, the widow of the deceased, in order to raise up the name of the deceased on his inheritance." So the matter was not a simple one of buying a piece of land. It involved taking up the kinsman-

---

6. Harris et al., *Wordbook*, 945–46.

redeemer responsibility to ensure that Mahlon's name continued by marrying Ruth and conceiving children with her.

Main point: Boaz explained the implications of buying the land to the kinsman-redeemer.

B v6 kinsman-redeemer
His reason for not buying the property is particularly significant. He reasoned that if he bought the land and raised children with Ruth, he would put his own estate at risk because neither the children nor the land would be his. The land would be the inheritance of the children he would have by Ruth and therefore he stood to lose his investment (see v5, v10). Given this, he felt it was "impossible" for him to exercise his right as the nearest kinsman-redeemer. The "impossibility" and "I cannot redeem it" (v6) are stated three times and mean "it would not be wise for me to redeem it"; it would be unwise to take such a risk. The kinsman-redeemer's approach was rational, logical, and sensible. It made sense not to take the risk presented to him by Boaz. He did not want to take such a risk "lest I ruin my own inheritance." The word "ruin" derives from the Hebrew verb *šaḥat*, meaning a pit, and from this, other meanings are inferred: destruction, grave, corruption. Another possibility is that it comes from *šâḥat*, "to go to ruin"; the word is not used in its root form. It is possible that these words have the same form but with different meanings: *šaḥat*, "sink down" (not really "dig"), Prov 2:18, and the other from *šâḥat*, "go to ruin." It is difficult to prove that these are two different words, but the general concept of loss, destruction, or ruin is clear from the context.[7]

The kinsman-redeemer may have overstated the case of his potential loss. He really did not want the responsibility that came with buying the land, unless he was implying that to buy the land he would have to mortgage his existing property and if he could not repay the loan he would lose everything. If this was the case, then what he said makes sense: this would indeed be a huge risk to take. It appears that his refusal was very sensible. The main point of the thrice-repeated "I cannot redeem it" shows the kinsman-redeemer is wise, thinking, logical, and sensible, by highlighting his aversion for risk.

---

7. Holladay, *Lexicon*, 364, 366.

This trait of being wise, thinking, logical, and sensible is also evident in the story as a whole when the actions and decisions of the characters are scrutinized:

- a. Elimelech was wise in chapter 1 when there was a famine in Bethlehem (the house of bread).
- b. Orpah was wise when she was persuaded by Naomi to go back to her father's house.

Three of the six characters (Elimelech, Orpah, and kinsman-redeemer) in the narrative took sensible and wise decisions. But this wise and reasonable approach robbed them of a greater future prospect, as 4:16–22 and Matthew 1:1–6a demonstrate. In avoiding risk and taking the safest option, they denied themselves the opportunity to be part of something great, something of universal history-making significance: an event that changed the course of history. They played it safe and lost this opportunity.

Main point: The kinsman-redeemer took what seemed to be a sensible decision and refused to buy the land when he heard the implications of doing so.

A v7–10 Boaz

The narrator enters the story at this point and explains an old custom that was about to take place. The explanation was for the benefit of the readers who, at the time the book of Ruth was written, would have been unfamiliar with the practice of legalizing the purchasing of land. Verse 7 is very difficult to translate and the following translation is suggested to clarify the custom:

"Now this was *the custom* in former times in Israel concerning the redemption and the exchange *of land* to confirm any matter: a man removed his sandal and gave it to another; and this was the *manner of attestation* in Israel."

The italicized expressions are not in the text, they are supplied for clarification. To enhance the sense of the verse, a semi-colon should be place after the supplied expression "of land," and the next expression, "any matter," should be clarified with a bracketed explanation as follows (in this case the purchase of land, cf. Deut 25:8–10). Putting all this together, the verse would read as follows:

Sermon Formats and the Structured-Repetition Approach

"Now this was *the custom* in former times in Israel concerning the redemption and the exchange *of land;* to confirm any matter (such as purchase of land, cf. Deut 25:8–10), a man removed his sandal and gave it to another; and this was the *manner of* attestation in Israel."

The term "attestation" (*hatt^e'ûdâh*) means "to solemnly affirm." This can be done by a person or an inanimate object like a stone / heap of stones (the Ark, the Commandments, etc.). So by removing a sandal and giving it to another, the object and the action attest to the validity and legality of the transaction. In this narrative unit, the basic idea is repeated three times: *'ēdîm* (v9 witnesses); *'ēdîm* (v10 witnesses); *'ēdîm* (v11 witnesses). So the nearest relative took off his sandal and handed it to Boaz, attesting that Boaz has the legal right to redeem the land Naomi was selling. The transaction is completed in the presence of witnesses: the elders and the community. He addressed them (v9) and affirmed that they are witnesses of the transfer of the right of redemption to him; his purchase of the land of Elimelech; and his decision to marry Ruth and raise children for Mahlon. Verses 9–10 are framed by the repetition of the expression:

"You are witness today . . . " (v9)

" . . . you are witnesses today" (v10)

In v10, Boaz states that the elders and the community witnessed that "I have bought . . . all that belonged to Elimelech and all that belong to Mahlon and Chilion." The Hebrew verb *qânîtî* is translated by the New American Standard Bible as "bought" and "acquired." "Bought" refers to the land, and "acquired" refers to Ruth, drawing a distinction between the acquisition of a person and a thing. Is there a difference between the two ideas? From v10b it is clear that *qânîtî* has the sense of "marry," as Boaz expressed the purpose of the acquiring as follows: "in order to raise up the name of the deceased on his inheritance." Boaz married Ruth so the children of the marriage would inherit the land he just bought, of which Ruth's deceased husband was the heir. Therefore "acquire" is an appropriate translation. This was not just a commercial transaction, as the nearest relative thought at first (v4). When he realized that the transaction was to ensure that the name of dead would not disappear (v5), he was not prepared to take on this responsibility and so refused. In v10, Boaz was saying, "I'm not just buying a piece of land, I am taking on the responsibility of raising seed for Mahlon." It was about ensuring the future of a relative, the family, clan, and tribe.

The expression "on his inheritance" is peculiar. It suggests that even though Ruth's husband is dead, the land was still his; although Boaz bought the land, it still belonged to Ruth's deceased husband. This is in keeping with the law that the land remained within a family, clan, and tribe. So even though Boaz paid for the land, he did not own it, he held it for the heirs of Mahlon.

The transaction was attested by the community witnesses, v11a, which completed the legal process. That they witnessed more than a transaction in which land exchanged hands was confirmed in vv11b–12; the community expressed a covenantal blessing upon the couple, and in this way Ruth is incorporated into the covenant people.

*Main point: **Boaz exercised the right of kinsman-redeemer and purchased the land in the presence of the elders and the community who blessed him.***

Formulation of the Exegetical Idea

Main point: ***The kinsman-redeemer*** informed the "community court" that he ***intended to exercise his right of redemption*** and buy the land from Naomi.

Main point: ***Boaz took action to fulfill his promise*** to settle the matter about Ruth's future that day.

Main point: ***The kinsman-redeemer accepted Boaz's invitation to join him at the gate***, not knowing the reason for the invitation.

Main point: Boaz set up a "community court" at the gate.

Main point: Boaz explained to the kinsman-redeemer the implications of buying the land.

Main point: ***The kinsman-redeemer took a seemingly sensible decision*** and refused to buy the land when he heard the implications of doing so.

Main point: ***Boaz exercised the right of kinsman-redeemer*** and purchased the land in the presence of the elders and the community who blessed him.

Exegetical Idea

The kinsman-redeemer made a seemingly sensible decision when he offered the right of redemption to Boaz, which robbed him of an historic opportunity.

Theological Idea

God's people may make "sensible" decisions and in the process lose the opportunity to make history with God.

Preaching Idea

Play it safe and lose the chance to make history.

Sermon

Reading: Ruth 1:1–16 and 4:1–12

Theme: **Play it safe and lose the chance to make history.**

His head throbbed, his heart ached, and an irrepressible inner voice kept on nagging "give up and go, pack up and go" as Elimelech dragged his weary feet along the dusty track that led from his fields to his home, the place he had known so well and had come to love. It had taken him a long time to reach this point. But there was no other way out. It was time to pack and go.

Now it was the time when the judges were judging. A time in which "every man did what was right in his own eyes" (Judg 17:6). It was a time of social and political upheaval, instability, and chaos. There were land invasions, for "the Medianites would come with the Amalekites and the desert tribes . . . and they would camp on the land and destroy the crops . . . They would come with their livestock and tents, as thick as locusts . . . They came and devastated the land" (Judg 6:1–6).

There was also a brutal rape; some men of the town Gibeah of Benjamin surrounded the house in which a visitor to the town had lodged for the night, and demanded that he be brought out so that the men of the city could have sex with him. When the visitor's host saw that they were about to break down the door, he sent out his concubine and "they raped her and abused her all night long and did not stop until morning" (Judg 19:22–25).

Intimidation and exploitation were rife, as Micah experienced. The tribe of Dan took his priest and gods from his house. And when he confronted them, they said "you had better not say anything else unless you want these men to get angry and attack you. Then you and your whole family would die . . . Micah saw that they were too strong for him, so he turned and went back home" (Judg 18:19–26).

And if that was not enough, the tribe of Dan felt a lack of security and extreme vulnerability. They were looking for a place to call home and came upon Laish "that town of peaceful and quiet people." They killed all the inhabitants and burnt the town. The men from Dan then rebuilt the town and settled down there themselves. They changed the name from Laish to Dan" (Judg 18:27–32).

Then the land received a devastating blow. There was *no bread in the house of bread* [for that was what Bethlehem meant] because "there was a famine in the land" (Judg 1:1).

So, day after day Elimelech stood on the hills outside Bethlehem, 800 meters above sea level. Casting his eyes heavenwards he prayed, hoped, agonized, and willed the precious rain to fall from the red-hot brassy skies, but nothing happened. He wished for bread to silence the unbearable moans and groans of his two little boys—the product of their pangs of hunger. But the wish never became a reality.

At the same time, just 80 kilometers northwest of Bethlehem, by the shortest available route, is the Plains of Moab.

On a clear day, the Plains of Moab could be seen from the hills outside Bethlehem. It was near the northern tip of the Dead Sea. This was also the beginning point of the Jordan River. So the Plains of Moab was a very fertile area, rich in agriculture. The lush green fields of Moab were a stark contrast to the brown and dusty fields of Bethlehem.

Day after day, the fertile land beckoned to Elimelech. "Come," it said. "Come over here."

It made perfectly good sense for Elimelech to spell out the solution to the problem of famine: M-O-A-B.[8] "There is no other sensible way to avoid the pain, suffering, loss, and hopelessness that came when famine struck," Elimelech said to himself. "And to remain in Bethlehem of Judah meant death; no future. The agony of the past months has been too much. If I want to avoid losing my family now that my crops are gone, I better leave; No! I must leave."

---

8. Luter and Davis, *Ruth & Esther*, 25.

Sermon Formats and the Structured-Repetition Approach   199

And so Elimelech did the sensible thing. He took whatever belongings he had, his wife Naomi, and the two little boys Mahlon and Chilion, and they left for the Plains of Moab. And after a tricky and potentially dangerous trek "they entered the land of Moab and remained there."

But it wasn't long before their actions started to look less sensible, as the events which followed their arrival in Moab showed: things went horribly wrong. Shortly after their arrival in Moab, Naomi was dealt a heavy blow: Elimelech died and she was left a widow. But she was comforted by the knowledge that she had two young men who could take care of her.

But after some years, the two boys decided to marry. Mahlon married the Moabitess Ruth and Chilion married Orpah. There was joy and contentment in Naomi's home again. She could smile, although the pain caused by the death of Elimelech lingered on. And so it was that they stayed in the land for ten years.

But then tragedy struck again. Not just one, but both the boys died. Naomi was now in dire straits. A widow in a foreign country, destitute, with no family, no income, no security, and no future. And so she became a very bitter person. "Is this what doing the sensible thing comes to?" she questioned. "What am I to do now?"

But with God, good news is never far away. For "some time later Naomi heard that the Lord had blessed the people by giving them a good harvest" (1:6). The house of bread had bread again. It was clear to Naomi what she had to do. She had to return home of course; home to the once windswept, dusty roads of Bethlehem of Judah.

Naomi immediately called her daughters-in-law and told them the good news. She told them of her plan to return home. She gathered together what little possessions she had and got ready to leave Moab with her daughters-in-law.

They had covered only a short distance to Bethlehem when Naomi's bitterness overpowered her. She turned around to her daughters and said, "Go back home and stay with your mother." She prayed a prayer for them saying,

> May the Lord be as good to you as you have been to me and those who have died. And may the Lord make it possible for each of you to marry again and have a home. (1:6–7)

They protested. But Naomi was persistent, persuasive, and determined. And she told them, "you must go back my daughters, why do you want to come with me?"

And with a string of questions she gave them the physical (biological) (1:12b), the social (1:12b), the personal (1:13a), and the theological (1:13b) reasons why going with her to Bethlehem was not the sensible thing to do. "Mission impossible," Naomi announced to her daughters.

Now who would not be persuaded by such common sense? Orpah was persuaded: she said to herself, "what Naomi says makes a lot of sense. After all I have more of a chance of a future here in Moab than in Bethlehem of Judah. The advantages of Moab are better than what I will get in Judah. In Moab I would be among my own people; I will have no language problems, no cultural barriers to cross, no uncertainty of what to do and what not to do; what is acceptable and what is not acceptable. What is more, Moab has always been a good country economically; we have always had enough to eat; there have been no shortages here in Moab."

To crown it all, the road to Bethlehem for three single-woman travelers is very risky. I agree with Naomi, it does not make much sense to leave this place of fullness. I think the smart and sensible thing is to stay!

She "kissed her mother-in-law good bye and went back home" (1:14).

And so it was that the two widows continued the rest of the journey to Bethlehem of Judah, alone and in silence.

They arrived in Bethlehem of Judah and saw what they had heard about earlier. For "the barley harvest was just beginning when they arrived in Bethlehem" (1:22).

Harvest time was that time of the year when all people could talk about was money, finance, trade, and deals. It was like budget time in South Africa when the preoccupation of the people, newspapers, radio, and television are finances, stock markets, rebates, tax cuts, increases, and saving money, money, money.

Even Boaz is introduced to us in terms of his financial position. For we read, "Naomi had a relative, a rich and influential man." Literally the text reads, "a heavy, weighty man." This had nothing to do with his waistline of course, but meant that he was a heavyweight, financially and socially.

Sermon Formats and the Structured-Repetition Approach

The wealthy Boaz went to Bethlehem to check on the progress of the harvesting of his crops. When he arrived, he saw a strange young woman in his fields and asked his foreman about her. He was told that she was Ruth the Moabitess, Naomi's daughter-in-law, who had returned with Naomi from the Plains of Moab. Since he had already heard of all the noble things Ruth had done, he showed her kindness. She stayed in his fields that day at his encouragement. When Ruth arrived home she told Naomi about her day, and how kind Boaz was to her.

Naomi immediately planned, plotted, and engineered a meeting between Ruth and Boaz that night at the threshing-floor. The meeting resulted in a virtual marriage between Ruth and Boaz. But there was a small problem. In the words of Boaz, "I am a close relative but there is a man who is a closer relative than I am."

So, early the next morning Boaz hurried to the gate of the city. The gate of the city was an interesting and strategic place. It was the place to be if you were looking for a person; it was the place where people met to socialize, but more importantly, it was the place where justice was dispensed and where legal agreements were made.

Boaz waited at the gate. Soon he saw the nearest relative. His name? Mr. "so-and-so" (this is what his name literally means in Hebrew). Boaz invited him and ten elders of the city to sit down, and then he said to Mr. so-and-so:

"Naomi, who has come back from the land of Moab, wants to sell the piece of land, which belonged to our brother Elimelech. So I thought to inform you saying, 'Buy it before those who are sitting here and before the elders of my people. If you want to redeem it, then redeem it, but if not tell me that I may know, for there is no one to redeem it but you and I am after you.'"

It was the custom in those days for a relative to take over the land of a family member who was in financial trouble. In this way, the land stayed within the family. The relative also had to take care of the person in trouble. This was known as the custom of the kinsman-redeemer (Lev 25:23–27). So when Mr. so-and-so heard that Naomi was selling the land, which belonged to his brother, he had both the right and the duty to buy it. He said to Boaz, "I will [buy] it."

But then the genetic trait of his wily old forefather Jacob reared its head, and Boaz pulled the rug from under the feet of Mr. so-and-so. He said, "On the day that you buy the field from the hand of Naomi, you must also acquire Ruth the Moabitess, the widow of the deceased, in order to raise up the name of the deceased" (4:5).

Immediately there was a problem. Mr. so-and-so suffered from material tunnel-vision: everything was looked at from the viewpoint of material gain. He was also a shrewd businessman. When he heard what Boaz said he was worried. He made a few quick sums in his head. You could hear his computer humming as he made his calculations. He said to himself, "Buying the land and taking Naomi is one thing. For in that case I would add the land to my present properties and so enlarge my estate. There would also be only one extra mouth to feed, one extra person to take care of. But, marrying Ruth as well? Now that's a different kettle of fish. For then there would be two people that I will have to take care of. And since I would have to raise children for Mahlon, Ruth's dead husband, I would lose my investment. The sons I raise for Mahlon will inherit the land for which I paid. No! I cannot take that risk."

Let's be fair. No person with common sense would accept a deal that could result in losing all his wealth. In addition, there would be the extra wife and children to take care of. On top of this one would have, thrown in for good measure, a determined, persuasive, and manipulative mother-in-law like Naomi. Anyone faced with this situation would be expected to do the sensible thing and walk away. This is exactly what Mr. so-and-so did. He walked away. And he said to Boaz, "I will give up my right to buy the field because it would mean that my own children would not inherit it. [In fact I would utterly destroy my own inheritance, he said.] You buy it; I would rather not [buy it]" (4:6).

Sensible? Yes. But very regrettable.

And so the land was sold; Ruth was married, and Boaz found a wife. The village, once caught in the pangs of hunger, and the pain and destruction of famine, rejoiced. Yes, Bethlehem was alive and vibrant again.

Naomi had a grandchild. She was no longer the bitter old lady from Moab, but the great grand-mother of David, who was the father of Perez, who was the father of Joseph, who was the husband of Mary, the mother of Jesus Christ, the son of the living God.

And Elimelech? He was safe, safe from the pain and suffering of the famine, but also "safe" from experiencing the miracle of God (1:6). He lived a life of safety based on avoiding tragedy, and yet it struck anyway; he lived a risk-free life based on sensible choices, but it was a regrettable life. He missed out on what God did for his people. He robbed his children of seeing the mighty works of the God of Israel performed in the giving of a good harvest to the nation.

And Orpah? Well, we don't know whether she eventually married and enjoyed all the advantages Moab had to offer. She disappeared from biblical history. It could have been otherwise. But her sensible risk-free, short-term benefit choices possibly, no, certainly, robbed her of the opportunity of becoming a mother in Israel. She missed a golden opportunity to be named among those who are called blessed. She robbed herself of a place on the grand stage of the history of God with his people by merely doing the sensible thing.

Mr. so-and-so the materialist went on working, making money, working; forever the man with no name. The very thing feared by people in those times happened to him. He died an anonymous person. Who would remember him? He tried to secure his future; but by making the sensible, risk-free, short-term choice, he lost the future instead.

All three people, Elimelech, Orpah, Mr. so-and-so, made sensible choices that avoided difficulties; risk-free choices, choices with short-term benefits and gains. But the choices turned out to be regrettable. No, much more than regrettable. They were costly. It cost them the opportunity of being part of the grand purposes of God for Israel and the world. But why? Because they opted for the expected, safe, and logical option.

And what about us? How often do we do the same: settle for the sensible, safe, risk-free choices when it comes to the things of God? Our personal lives? You do remember times when you took the safe, sensible way out.

Maybe it was in your relationships with your son, daughter, husband, wife, a colleague at work, a close friend, in the Church's ministry.

Now when you look back, it is with regret. Why? Because that sensible, risk-free decision robbed you of the opportunity of experiencing the miracle of God; the opportunity to deepen a friendship; the opportunity of service and ministry; the opportunity of personal growth.

Think again when you are tempted to make a choice purely based on common sense, for the safe decision can be costly.

EXAMPLE 3: STORY-REFLECTION-STORY FORMAT

This format is one of many illustrated by Wijngaards.[9] The biblical text is read and followed by a reflection with explanation and application.

Text: Genesis 38:1–30

CLOSURE

The traditional narrative introductory formula "and it came to pass" (v1) begins in chapter 38; a new character, Judah, is also introduced. Chapter 39 takes up the story of Joseph, which began in chapter 37 with the opening words "now Joseph had been taken down to Egypt." This is therefore a stand-alone, self-contained episode.

EXEGESIS OF THE NARRATIVE STRUCTURE

The structure is based on the narrative constituent of character:

> A   **vv1–11 After the deaths of Er and Onan, Judah sent Tamar home to wait for Shelah**
>> B   vv12–23 Tamar deceived Judah and is impregnated by him
>> B   vv24–26 Tamar presents to Judah his pledge and he declared her righteous
>
> A   **vv27–30 Twins are born with the younger supplanting the elder**

DESCRIPTION OF THE STRUCTURE

This is a chiastic structure with the outer matching units A and A as the point of focus. The units B and B in the center develop A and A. In A and A, Tamar's "death" was reversed with the birth of the twins. Widowhood in her father's house (v11) held the potential of her "death" as a woman: never being married and never bearing children. The birth of the twins meant she had a future again.

A reversal also happens in B and B. Judah was told that Tamar was pregnant. He decided to do the right thing according to the law: let her be burned, the punishment for adultery. Tamar presented Judah's pledge as proof that she was innocent. She averted a travesty of justice and also ensured that Judah did not destroy his future by destroying his posterity. In keeping the law, as he thought he did, he would have unwittingly deprived himself of a future.

---

9. Wijngaards, *Communicating*, 108–11.

Shelah disappeared from the story; he played no further part in the narrative after Tamar was sent to her father's house. And with his "disappearance" from the narrative, hopes for descendants for Judah also disappeared. But Judah had descendants he was not aware of through Tamar. And so Judah's attempt to secure his future by not giving Shelah in marriage to Tamar failed; yet he had a future he did not foresee: God secured Judah's future.

God is not mentioned again after v10, so his involvement is not immediately clear. It is depicted in the reversal that happened during the birth of the twins described in vv27–30. Zerah put out his hand while Tamar was in labor, and the midwife tied a scarlet ribbon around his hand, marking him as the first born. But then the other twin, "broke through" while Zerah was pulling his hand back (v29) and was born first. He was given the name Perez; he was the elder of the two twins because he came out first, even though Zerah had the ribbon on his arm. It is in this reversal that we see the hand of God at work. Tamar and God working together secured the future of Judah by ensuring he had posterity, in a way he did not plan.

Focus Point

A vv1–11 and A vv27–30

The first narrative unit, vv1–7, begins with the phrase "and it came about at that time." This refers to chapter 37 and places the story after the reported "death" (disappearance) of Joseph. At that time "Judah went down, away from his brothers"; this suggests that they were together, probably looking after Jacob's flock, when Judah decided to leave them to visit his friend the Adullamite (v12).

Judah *saw* the daughter of Shua and married her (v2). He is described as *seeing and acting* again in v15 and v24b. He acts rather impulsively: he saw and he took, just as he heard and pronounced the death sentence on Tamar.

Judah's wife bore him three sons Er, Onan, and Shelah (see 1 Chr 2:3). Er died because what he did "was evil in the eyes of the Lord" (vv3–7). Notice the text does not give details of what the evil is, it simply says that he was evil (*wayᵉhî ra'*). *Wayᵉhî* is a verb from the root *hayah* (to be), and when used of action is translated "and it happened," or "and it came to pass" (see v9), but when used of things and persons it refers to the essence, nature of a thing or a person. Thus the text says Er was by nature an evil person. Compare this to the description of Anon in v10a. This implied that he also did evil things, and so God killed him for his evil deeds; God judged him and took his life. Er's death sets in motion the main events of the story.

At the time, Judah lived "in Chezib" (*bikzîb*) (v5). The proper name *kzb* derives from the noun *kâzâb*, with the root meaning "lie, falsehood."[10] The main events of the story played out in Chezib, and the name of the place announced the theme of the story: lies and falsehood. We see this in Judah (see 37:25–35), Onan (vv8–9), Judah (v11), Tamar (vv13–17), and the birth of the children (vv27–30). A trail of deception, started by Jacob, continued in the family tree, and the events in this chapter are an example of this.

In vv8–10, Judah, in keeping with ancient Near Eastern custom, instructed Anon (the second-eldest son) to fulfill his responsibility as brother-in-law by marrying Tamar and raising "seed"; an inheritance for Er, the eldest brother. Anon spilled his seed because he knew the children would not be his. And what he did was "evil in the eyes of the Lord" and God killed him (vv8–10). This is the only time in the story that God acts directly; all the other times he acted indirectly.

In v11, Judah sent Tamar to her father's house after the death of Onan to wait until Shelah, his third and youngest son, was older. He would then let Shelah marry her (v11a). Judah did this because he thought his sons had died because they married Tamar (v11b). The narrator, however, tells us the real reason for their deaths; they "did evil in the eyes of the Lord."

The second half of the verse, v11b, suggests Judah did not intend to carry through his promise, for he said to himself "lest he also die like his brothers" (see v14b). If marrying Tamar meant death, then whether Shelah married her now or when he had grown up would not make a difference. Therefore Judah was never going to allow Shelah to marry Tamar and his sending her to her father's house to wait for Shelah was a falsehood. In other words, Judah was protecting his own seed, his posterity, and his future. Judah was trying to secure his future by not giving Shelah to Tamar in marriage, for he feared (v11) Shelah would also die like his brothers. Judah deceived Tamar when he made a promise he did not intend to keep (v26). So Judah tried to hold on to his son and his

---

10. Holladay, *Lexicon*, 154.

future. Yet is it interesting to notice that after v11, Shelah "disappears" from the story and from Israel's history; he is not heard of again. In this sense, Judah's fears became reality; he lost his future; his son disappeared, or so it would seem (see Matt 16:25; 10:39; Luke 14:27, 17:33; John 12:25; 1 Pet 2:21, Rev 12:11).

Main point: Judah had three sons two of whom died because they did evil. He refused to let Tamar marry Shelah, fearing his death.

vv27–30

In vv27–30, Tamar gave birth, and it became known that she was carrying twins. During the birth, one of the twins put out a hand and the midwife tied a scarlet ribbon around his hand identifying him as the first born (v28); as he drew back his hand, however, the second twin came out and the midwife exclaimed "what a breach you made for yourself" (v29) and he was named Perez, which means "breach or to burst forth." The twin who was born after Perez came out with the ribbon around his wrist and was named Zerah, which means, "a dawning of brightness." So Perez, though younger, was regarded as the older of the twins. Judah had a future, but in a way he did not plan. On the other hand, justice was maintained because Tamar was vindicated (see v26).

The supplanting of Zerah by Perez symbolized the deception that was taking place at the time. It is similar to the supplanting of Esau by Jacob in Gen 25.

It signaled that a change was about to happen. The birth process is a chiasmus:

A	B
Perez the twin born first	Zerah the twin with the ribbon
B	A
Zerah the twin born second	Perez the twin without the ribbon

But there is another significance to the supplanting taking place in this story. By referring to the switching in Genesis 48:8–22, chapter 38 becomes connected to the Joseph story in chapters 39–50. So chapter 38 is not an interruption, but rather a continuation of the larger story of the fulfillment of God's promise to Abraham.

The chiasmus referred to above represents the activity of God to secure Judah's future. Judah tried to secure his own future by denying Tamar her legal right, marriage to Shelah. But Shelah disappeared from the story and plays no part in the story from v11, suggesting that the future of Judah was at risk. First Tamar vv12–18, and now God vv27–30, secured Judah's future for him through her right doing and the unseen working of God. God appears only twice in this story: directly in v7a, and indirectly in vv27–30. He was active at the beginning and at the end, and in between he let people, events, and history take its course, using it to advance his purpose and plan as the chapters following this story show.

The birth and naming of Zerah indicates that *change* is about to take place in the history of Jacob; his name means the "dawning of brightness"; his birth signaled that brightness was about to dawn, especially given the darkness of chapter 37, as well as the earlier chapters of Genesis. Beginning with Genesis 25:19–26 Jacob's life has been one of struggle and conflict, but that was about to change, as signaled by the birth of Zerah. A chiasmus stands at the turning point of a new phase in Jacob's life. As already mentioned, a chiasmus also stands at the end of Jacob's life story, and this is clear from what immediately follows.

Joseph's sons were born to him in Egypt. Joseph visited Jacob just before he died and took his sons Ephraim and Manasseh to Jacob so he could meet them. When Joseph presented his sons to Jacob, he positioned Ephraim on the left of Jacob because he was the youngest and Manasseh on Jacob's right because he was the eldest. Before blessing them, Jacob made a switch: he placed his right hand on Ephraim's head and his left hand on Manasseh's head, thus giving Ephraim the blessing of the eldest son (Gen 47:29—48:22). Joseph tried to rectify this but Jacob stopped him. This is another chiasmus:

         A   B

Manasseh . . . . Ephraim

         B   A

Ephraim . . . . Manasseh

Sermon Formats and the Structured-Repetition Approach 209

This chiasmus symbolizes the *beginning* of the fulfillment of the promise made in Gen 15:12–16; the promise that Abraham's descendants will return to the land God promised him. It is completed with the Exodus from Egypt, which in turn brings Jacob's story to an end. The promise finds its final fulfillment with the conquest and occupation of the land. The birth and the blessing stories clearly demonstrate the link between chapter 38 and the rest of the Genesis story.

While Shelah disappeared from the story and Israel's history after v11, Perez and Zerah (v29) are mentioned again in Ruth 4:16–22 and Matthew 1:3–6a. So Judah had posterity after all; he had a future through Tamar (vv12–23), although he did not plan it that way.

Main point: Tamar gave birth to twins, thus securing Judah's future. During the birth Perez supplanted Zerah, symbolizing God's involvement.

B vv12–23

In vv12–19, Tamar's actions were deliberate; she wanted: a future and protection for herself, as well as an inheritance for Er. She was about to force the hand of Judah into doing what he was legally obligated to do. Her concern was not only posterity for Er, she also wanted Judah do what was right: end her widowhood and secure her future and status in the community (v11a, v14, and v15).

Verses 12–15 began a new phase in the story, introduced by the death of Judah's wife: the completion of the period of mourning and the start of the season of sheep-shearing. Tamar had been denied marriage to Shelah (v14). When she heard that Judah was on his way to Timnah to shear sheep, she took action. She dressed like a prostitute and positioned herself along the road at the entrance to the town of Enaim. Judah approached what he thought was a prostitute (*zônâh*) (v15b). The incident starts with the phrase "when Judah saw her" (v15a). Previously, Judah acted on what he saw and set in motion a series of events that ultimately sent Tamar into widowhood (v2, v11). Now Judah also acted on what he saw, which set in motion a series of events that would have a different outcome for both him and Tamar.

In verses 16–18, Tamar and Judah spoke to each other for the first time since she was sent into widowhood. He said, "Let me come in to you." This phrase is mentioned twice in v16. It is the opposite of what happens in v11; there he sent her *away from him*, now *he wanted to come into the woman he sent away.* When he sent her away, he was in control. Now she was in control; the tables are turned.

In v17, he made a promise: "I will give you a kid." What Tamar also wanted was a "kid" but not from the flock, from him personally; she wanted seed of another kind, not the kind he is offering. But remembering the past and knowing that Judah could not be trusted (v11 v14b), she asked for a pledge (vv16b–18a). This time he would have to do what he promised, she was now in control. This control is indicated by the fact that nine of the sixteen personal pronouns used in the dialogue refer to Tamar and seven to Judah. It is all about her; it was about her taking what he was not willing to give. She put him in a situation where he had no alternative but to give to her what he failed to give in vv10–11.

Verse 18a describes the next event in a very cold, matter of fact, staccato tone: "he gave them to her . . . went in to her . . . she conceived by him." The emotionless, staccato description (see Gen 19:34) of the sex act affirms that Judah believed she was a prostitute. But it also symbolizes the way Tamar had been treated by him all along; without feeling, concern, or care.

"And he gave them to her" (v18b), refers to his "seal, cord, and staff" as a pledge. The signet ring, girdle, and staff represented Judah's legal identity. It says "and he went in to her, and she conceived." By impregnating her, he gave her dignity back to her and removed her widowhood, now that she was pregnant with his children. Ironically, the very person Judah feared would destroy his future was in fact the person who secured his future, as vv27–30 will later show.

Verse v19 forms a frame with v14b. Verse 19b reads: "taking off her veil she put on her garments of widowhood." In v14 she *takes it off* and in v19 *she puts it on*; the situation is reversed to apparent normality: Tamar is home and a widow once again, but this time a pregnant widow. This foreshadows the change in her status that is about to take place. Her position changed from widow to prostitute to widow, and finally to that of mother and "wife" with a future. She had turned the tables. She was deceived by Judah (v11, v14), now she had deceived him (v14a, vv15–18).

It is impossible not to be reminded of the Jacob-Esau, Jacob-Laban, and Jacob-Joseph deceptions; the latter being the most recent one. Judah was involved in that deception, and what he did to his father is done here to him. The role of clothing is also significant. In the Jacob-Joseph incident it was a robe of many colors, here it is the widow and prostitute clothing. And even though the text does not explicitly express a negative judgment on the deception committed by both Judah and Tamar, the consequences of the deception expressed the negative view of the narrator. Judah had to live with the fact that he fathered children with his daughter-in-law, and Tamar lived with v26b "and he did not lie with her again."

So Judah, on his way to Timnah, stopped and impregnated a prostitute, and in return he gave her his staff, girdle, and signet ring as a pledge.

Judah tried to redeem his pledge, vv20–23, but he failed, which is underscored by the repetition of the inability of his friend the Adullamite to find the *zōnā* (prostitute) with whom Judah had sexual intercourse:

"and Judah sent the kid . . . but he did not find her" (v20)

"I sent this kid, and you did not find her" (v23)

The failure frames the unit. The confusion about the identity of the person Judah had slept with contributed to the failure. Judah thought he had slept with a professional prostitute (v15), and the Adullamite went looking for "*qâdês*"; a "cultic prostitute." The anonymity of the person Judah slept with is confirmed in v20 when he referred to her as "the woman." It also reminds us about the anonymity in which Tamar had lived in her father's house.

The failure to find the prostitute is rather ironic. When Judah had to keep the promise he made to Tamar, (v11) he did not. Now that he actually took steps to do what he promised, he failed. His failure to realize his intention to keep his promise is reinforced by v14b; it suggested that Judah was not the type of person who kept his promises. At a different level, the failure was important because if he had recovered his pledge, Tamar would have failed completely to secure posterity for Er and restore her position and status in the community; she would have failed to ensure that Judah carried out his legal responsibility.

Main point: Judah has sexual intercourse with a prostitute and gave her a pledge; his friend did not redeem it because the prostitute was not found.

B vv24–26

It is now three months after the events of vv13–19. The phrase *"it was told Judah"* refers to a report that was given to Judah. It was based on what the community *saw*; once again Judah acted on what *was seen*, just as he did on two previous occasions (v2, v15). The report was presumably given by people in the community, and by reporting Tamar's pregnancy to Judah, the community recognized his responsibility for his widowed daughter-in-law.

In v24, she was accused of "illicit sexual intercourse" (*zânâh*). This word regularly refers to "illicit heterosexual intercourse" committed by women,[11] normally with married men (adultery). Tamar is accused of adultery. Though it was not known who was responsible for Tamar's pregnancy, there was no doubt that she was pregnant. It was also clear that it was Judah's responsibility to deal with her adulterous pregnancy. He commanded, "Bring her out and let her be burnt." The community will execute punishment; it will be done publicly because what Tamar did affected the community, and the community must put it right.

Judah pronounced judgment on Tamar's illicit sexual intercourse. The punishment for commercial and cultic prostituting was set out in the law in Lev 21:9, 19:29, and Deut 22:21, 23:17–18. But the punishment Judah pronounced went further than what the law required; "let her be burnt" was only applicable to the daughter of a priest (Lev 21:9), not Tamar. So why did Judah act so harshly? It may have been guilt that was driving Judah; he knew he had wronged Tamar and now he sought to get rid of his "problem" by acting harshly. He prescribed a more serve punishment than what the law required and therefore more than what God required because he was aware of his own failure to do right by Tamar.

In v25, Tamar responded by sending Judah the pledge items with the message "look and *see* if you *recognize*" (my emphasis) these things. Notice once again the reference to "see," for Judah acts based on what he sees. Presenting the pledge at this point confirmed that Tamar's actions described in vv13–19 were part of a carefully designed plan. She was determined to make sure that right triumphed and that Judah fulfilled his obligation.

"[A]nd Judah looked" (v26); he recognized that the items belonged to him. In that moment he was also forced to recognize her. The ano-

---

11. Harris et al., *Wordbook*, 246–47.

nymity of vv20–23 (see also v11) was gone. Moreover, he also recognized that he failed to fulfill his duty, for he said "I did not give her to my son Shelah." In doing this, Judah acknowledged his error. There is a change in Judah here. As quick as he was to pronounce judgment, he was also quick to acknowledge that he was wrong. He acknowledged that he failed in his duty to Tamar: "I did not give her to my son Shelah." He admitted that his actions caused Tamar to do what she did, and therefore he could not judge her. There is a change in Judah; in v24 he was self-righteous, here he was humble, and this change foreshadows the change that is to happen from chapter 39 onwards.

The way in which he justified Tamar was by declaring, "She is more righteous than I" (v26a). How can Tamar be "more righteous" when she deceived Judah, vv13–19? The word "righteous" is used here in a legal, rather than moral, sense. It means doing what the law required. He did not do what the law required, but she did. It was not her responsibility to do what the law required: ensure that seed was raised up for Er. That was his responsibility.

Verse 26b: "and he did not lie with her again"; he did not take her to be his wife, which would have been illegal. She was now available to another man, enabling Tamar to have a future. She got back the most important thing: recognition and respect in the community and a future; she took back the right to be married again. The children born to her would of course be Judah's, securing his future.

Main point: Judah declared that Tamar should be burnt to death, but when presented with the pledge he acknowledged he was in the wrong, not Tamar.

Formulation of the Exegetical Idea

Main point: Judah had three sons, two of whom died because they did evil. He refused to let Tamar marry Shelah, fearing his death.

Main point: Judah had sexual intercourse with a prostitute and gave her a pledge. His friend did not redeem it because the prostitute was not found.

Main point: Judah declared that Tamar should be burnt to death, but when presented with the pledge he acknowledged he was in the wrong, not Tamar.

Exegetical Idea

Judah tried to preserve his seed to secure his future, but discovered it cannot be done without God or by unjust means

Theological Idea

Christians who try to secure the future in their own way will discover that it cannot be done without God nor by unjust means.

Preaching Idea

It is impossible to secure your future without God and just behavior.

Sermon

READING: GENESIS 38:1–30

Theme: **It is impossible to secure your future without God and behaving justly.**

INTRODUCTION

Of all God's creatures, human beings are the only ones who ask the question, "What is going to happen?" We are the only creatures concerned with the future, making preparations for the future, and not just the immediate future but the long-term future. To this end, we emphasize education; we try to make sure that we have a good pension to retire on; we take out life insurance policies; invest in our health, and so on. Our goal is to secure the future.

If you were living in the ancient Near East or in Israel, you would secure your future in one way primarily: offspring. You would make sure you have children and enough of them. No wonder the Psalmist can say:

> Sons are a heritage from the Lord,
> Children a reward from him;
> Like arrows in the hand of a warrior
> Are the sons born in one's youth.
> Blessed is the man, whose quiver is full of them
> They will not be put to shame
> When they contend with their enemies in the gate.

Apart from the idea of God's sovereign involvement in procreation reflected here, the Psalm also points to the security benefits of many sons: "They will not be put to shame, when they contend with their enemies in the gate." In other words, they will be a bulwark for the city.

When it comes to the military, political, social, and economic security of the city and the family, it helps to have many sons. In fact, there is a biblical story that illustrates this point in the encounter between Jacob and his sons and the Hivite Hamor and his son Shechem in Genesis 34.

But life proves that despite the preparations, provisions, and plans we make to secure our futures, things do not always work out the way we plan. There is always some surprise waiting for us in the future. And it is this reality that raises the question: can we really make sure of the future? Can we really secure our future? The answer to that question is yes. But this affirmation depends on what we believe.

As we accompany Judah the son of Jacob in his attempt to secure his future, we will come to understand just what is necessary to secure the future.

Story, vv 1–7

¹ And it came about at that time that Judah departed from his brothers, and visited a certain Adullamite, whose name was Hirah.
² And Judah saw there a daughter of a certain Canaanite whose name was Shua; and he took her and went in to her.
³ So she conceived and bore a son and he named him Er.
⁴ Then she conceived again and bore a son and named him Onan.
⁵ And she bore still another son and named him Shelah; and it was at Chezib that she bore him.
⁶ Now Judah took a wife for Er his first born, and her name *was* Tamar.
⁷ But Er, Judah's first-born, was evil in the sight of the Lord, so the Lord took his life.

Reflection, vv 1–7

The events in our story take place after the death of Joseph, reported by his brothers to their father in chapter 37. The brothers are in the field tending the flocks of Jacob.

Judah leaves his brothers to visit his friend Hirah, an Adullamite who lived in the village Chezib. The name of the village means "lie or falsehood." In a way, it tells us what is coming in the rest of the story, what the story is going to be about.

At Chezib, Judah saw and married Shua. He is described as "seeing and acting" again in v15 and v24b. He is characterized as a person who acts rather impulsively; he saw and he took, just as he would later hear and pronounce the death sentence on Tamar.

Shua gave birth to three sons, Er, Onan, and Shelah. The eldest son, Er, died because he did an evil deed in God's sight, and we are not told what the specific evil deed was. But the Hebrew phrase "because he did evil" can be translated, "because he was an evil person," from which it follows that he did evil things.

So Judah suffered his first setback. Is this God punishing him for his part in the events of chapter 37? We will have to wait and see.

Story, vv8–11

⁸ Then Judah said to Onan, "go in to your brother's wife, and perform your duty as a brother-in-law to her, and raise up offspring for your brother."
⁹ And Onan knew that the offspring would not be his; so it came about that when he went in to his brother's wife, he wasted his seed on the ground, in order not to give offspring to his brother.
¹⁰ But what he did was displeasing in the sight of the Lord; so he took his life also.
¹¹ Then Judah said to his daughter-in-law Tamar, "remain a widow in your father's house until my son Shelah grows up"; for he thought, "*I am afraid* that he too may die like his brothers." So Tamar went and lived in her father's house.

Reflection, vv8–11

Judah, in keeping with ancient Near Eastern custom and the Mosaic Law (Deut 25:5–10), instructed Onan, the second eldest son, to fulfill his responsibility as brother-in-law and marry Tamar. In this way he would raise "seed"; an inheritance for Er, his eldest brother. It was not just a matter of bringing children into the world as heirs of Er, it also meant taking responsibility for the children and everything that it involved (see Ruth chapter 4). So Onan deliberately spilled his semen (seed) because he knew the children would not be his.

What Onan did was "evil in the eyes of the Lord." Onan violated the law of God. It was not the spilling of the seed that was the violation, but the refusal to raise heirs for Er, because without heirs, Er's inheritance (mostly land) was at risk. The land belonged to God and was given to Israel as an inheritance and in fulfillment of God's promise to Abraham (Gen 12:1–3). Moses legislated that the land was to remain in the family (see 1 Kgs 21). Therefore, when Onan spilled his seed, he disrespected God, his law, and the sacred history of which he was a part. Moreover, by refusing to raise sons for Er, Onan ensured that the name of Er perished. For this reason, God judged and killed him (vv8–10). This act and v7 are the only times in the story that we see God acting directly; all the other times he acts indirectly. So Judah suffers a second blow for Onan dies.

He now faced a dilemma, a crisis. He had one son left, Shelah. The right thing to do was to let him marry Tamar and raise children for his eldest brother Er. But doing this meant that Shelah might also die. And if Shelah also died, then Judah had no hope of posterity, heirs, descendants. Judah's name would die when he died; he would not be remembered and would have no future. So he sent Tamar home to her father to wait there to be married to Shelah. But of course, Judah had no intention of letting that happen.

If marrying Tamar meant death, then whether Shelah married her now or when he had grown up would make no difference, either way he would have died. Thus Judah deceived Tamar, acting unjustly towards her in an attempt to preserve his own seed and future. He was willing to sacrifice her future to secure his own. Will he succeed?

We have an indication that he will not succeed when we observe that no mention is made of Shelah after v11. He "disappears" from the rest of the story; symbolically he dies as well, and so Judah fails in preserving his seed and securing his future his way. In fact, Shelah not only disappears from this story, but also from much of Old Testament and Israelite history.

So Tamar went to her father's house where she waited to be given in marriage to Shelah.

Story, vv 12–19

[12] Now after a considerable time Shua's daughter, the wife of Judah, died; and when the time of mourning was ended, Judah went up to his sheepshearers at Timnah, he and his friend Hirah the Adullamite.

¹³ And it was told to Tamar, "Behold, your father-in-law is going up to Timnah to shear his sheep."

¹⁴ So she removed her widow's garments and covered *herself* with a veil, and wrapped herself, and sat in the gateway of Enaim, which is on the road to Timnah; for she saw that Shelah had grown up, and she had not been given to him as a wife.

¹⁵ When Judah saw her, he thought she *was* a harlot, for she had covered her face.

¹⁶ So he turned aside to her by the road, and said, "here now, let me come in to you"; for he did not know that she was his daughter-in-law. And she said, "what will you give me, that you may come in to me?"

¹⁷ He said, therefore, "I will send you a kid from the flock." She said, moreover, "will you give a pledge until you send *it*?"

¹⁸ And he said, "what pledge shall I give you?" And she said, "your seal and your cord, and your staff that is in your hand." So he gave *them* to her, and went in to her, and she conceived by him.

¹⁹ Then she arose and departed, and removed her veil and put on her widow's garments.

Reflection, vv12–19

Judah's wife Shua died, and Tamar was still waiting to be given in marriage to Shelah, who had grown up by now.

The end of the period of mourning for Shua coincided with the start of the sheep-shearing season and Judah made plans to visit his sheep shearers. When Tamar was told that Judah was on his way to visit his sheep shearers at Timnah, she jumped into action to get what she wanted, what Judah had denied her, and what she had a right to receive: posterity for Er and a future for herself.

She took off her widow's clothes and put on the clothes of a prostitute and stationed herself at the entrance of the village Enaim, which was en route to Timnah.

When Judah reached the entrance and saw (remember this?) the prostitute, he said to her "let me come in to you"; let me have sexual intercourse with you. He did not know that it was his daughter-in-law Tamar he was speaking to.

Ironically, this was the first time he had spoken to her since sending her home to her father's house. The phrase "let me come in to you" is mentioned twice in v16. It is the opposite of what happens in v11;

then he sent her *away from him*, now *he comes into her*. There he was in charge and in control, now she was—the tables were turned on him.

Now Judah thought the person he was speaking to was a "*zônâh*," a professional prostitute. He did not know that it was his daughter-in-law Tamar. The "prostitute" asked him about her payment and he promised to send her a kid when he arrived at Timnah. She then asked for his staff, girdle, and signet as a pledge in lieu of payment. Tamar did this because she knew that Judah could not be trusted (v11 v14b). She asked for a pledge (vv16b–18a) to make sure that this time he would have to do what he promised. She was now in control. This is indicated by the fact that nine of the sixteen personal pronouns used in the dialogue refer to Tamar and seven to Judah. It was all about her; it was about her not receiving what she should have received. What he was not willing to give, she was now taking. She put him in a situation where he had no alternative but to give to her what he failed to give her in vv10–11.

Judah complied and gave her the pledge she asked for. He had sexual intercourse with her and went merrily on his way, but the "prostitute" was impregnated as a result of the encounter.

Tamar went home, took off the prostitute clothes and put on her widow's clothes. It is interesting to note how v19 and v14 reflect each other. Verse v19 forms a frame with v14b. Verse 19b reads, "taking off her veil she put on her garments of widowhood." In v14, she takes off her widow's clothing and in v19 she puts it on; the situation returns to apparent normality. Tamar is home, a widow once again; however, this time she is a pregnant widow. And what happens here foreshadows the change in her status that is about to take place. Her position changed from widow to prostitute to widow, and finally to that of mother and "wife" with a future. She had turned the tables. She was deceived by Judah (v11, v14), now she had deceived him (v14a, vv15–18). Tamar had taken back what had been taken from her. And the deception of Judah by Tamar also signals that Judah would fail in his attempt to secure his future his way, especially now that Tamar was pregnant.

STORY, VV20–23

[20] When Judah sent the kid by his friend the Adullamite, to receive the pledge from the woman's hand, he did not find her.

²¹ And he asked the men of her place, saying, "where is the temple prostitute who was by the road at Enaim?" But they said, "there has been no temple prostitute here."

²² So he returned to Judah, and said, "I did not find her; and furthermore, the men of the place said, 'there has been no temple prostitute here.'"

²³ Then Judah said, "let her keep them, lest we become a laughingstock. After all, I sent this kid, but you did not find her."

Reflection, vv20–23

Judah arrived at Timnah. His first order of business was to redeem his pledge. He sent his friend the Adullamite with the kid, as promised, to redeem his pledge.

But he failed, and his failure is underscored by the repetition of his friend's inability to find the *zōnā* (prostitute):

> "and Judah sent the kid . . . but he did not find her" (v20)
>
> "I sent this kid, and you did not find her" (v23)

The failure encloses the unit. It is reinforced by the confusion about the identity of the person with whom Judah slept. Judah thought he slept with a professional prostitute (v15), but the Adullamite went looking for "*qâdêš*," a "cultic prostitute." The anonymity of the person Judah slept with is affirmed in v20 when he referred to her as "the woman." The anonymity signals the fact that Judah was going to fail in his attempt to redeem his pledge.

It is an ironic situation. When Judah had to keep his promise, he did not. Now that he wanted to do so, he could not. His failure to keep his promise reinforced v14b: Judah was the type of person who did not keep his promises. At a different level, the failure was important because he had retrieved the pledge, and Tamar would have failed completely to restore her position, secure her future, and protect her legal rights. She would have failed in ensuring that Judah carried out his legal responsibility.

Tamar did everything in her power to ensure that justice was done. She may not have been an Israelite, or may have had very little knowledge of the God of Israel, but she did what his law prescribed: ensure that justice is done. So Judah failed once again, and his failure underscores that he would not secure his future in his way.

STORY, VV 24–26

²⁴ Now it was about three months later that Judah was informed, "your daughter-in-law Tamar has played the harlot, and behold, she is also with child by harlotry." Then Judah said, "bring her out and let her be burned!"
²⁵ It was while she was being brought out that she sent the pledge to her father-in-law, saying, "I am with child by the man to whom these things belong." And she said, "please examine and see, whose signet ring and cords and staff are these?"
²⁶ And Judah recognized *them*, and said, "she is more righteous than I, inasmuch as I did not give her to my son Shelah." And he did not have relations with her again.

REFLECTION, VV 24–26

It is now three months later and Judah is back from his visit to Timnah. Judah heard from the community that his daughter-in-law was pregnant. The community informed him because they knew that Tamar, being a widow, was still under the authority of Judah. The community understood that she was pregnant as a result of *zānâ*, a term used to describe the act of "illicit heterosexual intercourse" committed by women.

Judah instructed that she be brought out of her father's house and be burned to death. But the punishment for commercial and cultic prostituting is recorded in Lev 21:9, 19:29, and Deut 22:21, 23:17–18, and Judah's punishment goes further than what the law required. Death by burning was only applicable in the case of the daughter of a priest (Lev 21:9), and therefore not applicable to Tamar. So why did Judah act so harshly against Tamar? Was he driven by guilt? He knew that he was wrong in not giving her in marriage to Shelah; moreover, he feared giving Shelah in marriage to Tamar because Shelah might die like his other two sons. This was an opportunity to get rid of his "problem." Could this be the reason why he prescribed a more severe punishment than what the law prescribed, and therefore more than what God required?

As Tamar was brought out of the house, she took the pledge with her and sent it to Judah saying "I am with child by the man to whom these things belong . . . examine and see, whose signet ring and cords and staff are these." Notice here once again the reference to "see," for Judah is the kind of person who acts based on what he sees. Presenting the pledge now underlines the purposefulness of Tamar's actions described in vv13–19; she had a plan and implemented it carefully. It also displayed her determination to ensure that the right thing was done to her, and that Judah fulfilled his obligation.

When Judah recognized that the items were his, he did the right thing; he declared that Tamar was justified because "I did not give her to my son Shelah." He was quick to pronounce judgment, but also quick to acknowledge that he was wrong. He justified Tamar by acknowledging that he failed in his obligation.

Judah exonerated Tamar, saying, "She is more righteous than I" (v26a). What does this mean? How can Tamar be "more righteous" when she deceived Judah (vv13–19)? The word "righteous" is used here in a legal sense, not a moral sense. It means "doing what the law required." Tamar did what the law required and Judah did not.

The narrator concludes this unit with the comment, "and he did not lie with her again" (v26b); he did not take her to be his wife, which would have been illegal. She was now available to another man. The children born to her would of course be Judah's. She got back the most important thing: recognition and respect in the community and a future. She took back the right to be married again. Judah was not going to secure his future in the way he planned.

Story, vv27–30

²⁷ And it came about at the time she was giving birth, that behold, there were twins in her womb.
²⁸ Moreover, it took place while she was giving birth, one put out a hand, and the midwife took and tied a scarlet *thread* on his hand, saying, "this one came out first."
²⁹ But it came about as he drew back his hand, that behold, his brother came out. Then she said, "what a breach you have made for yourself!" So he was named Perez.
³⁰ And afterward his brother came out who had the scarlet *thread* on his hand; and he was named Zerah.

Reflection, vv27–30

Tamar gave birth and discovered there were twins in her womb. As she was giving birth, one of the twins put out a hand and the midwife put a scarlet ribbon around his hand marking him as the first born (v28). As he drew back his hand, the second twin forced his way out of the womb

Sermon Formats and the Structured-Repetition Approach

and the midwife exclaimed "what a breach you made for yourself." He was named Perez, which means "breach or burst forth." The twin with the scarlet ribbon came out next, and he was named Zerah, which means "a dawning of brightness." So Perez, though younger, was the oldest of the twins by virtue of the fact that he came out first, while Zerah, who was marked as the eldest, came out second and was therefore the youngest. The birth of the twins meant that Judah had a future, in a way he did not plan. Tamar was vindicated and Er had posterity, his name would live on.

But the supplanting of the one twin by the other has its own significance. It points to the function of the story as a whole. The story indicates that *change* was about to take place in the history of Jacob; it signaled the dawning of brightness, especially given the darkness of chapter 37. The birth process is a chiasmus:

> A   B
>
> Twin with the ribbon . . . . second twin
>
> B   A
>
> Second twin . . . . twin with the ribbon

The supplanting here is a repeat of Gen 25:19–26. Beginning with this incident, Jacob's life was one of struggle and conflict, but that was about to change, signaled by the birth of Zerah, "a dawning of brightness."

But the chiasmus also announced a new beginning in the life of Jacob, which starts with Joseph in Egypt (chapter 39). So chapter 38 is not an interruption, but rather a continuation of the larger story; it is a hinge that links the past with the present and the future.

The chiasmus is at the turning point of a new phase in Jacob's life, and a chiasmus also stands at the end of Jacob's life.

Joseph's sons were born in Egypt, and they were the last of Jacob's grandsons to be born. Joseph visited Jacob just before he died, and took his sons Ephraim and Manasseh so Jacob could meet them. Joseph placed Manasseh on Jacob's right because Manasseh was the eldest and he placed Ephraim on Jacob's left because he was the youngest. But in blessing them, Jacob makes a switch: he puts his right hand on Ephraim's head and his left hand on Manasseh's head, thus giving Ephraim the blessing of the eldest son, Genesis 47:29—48:22. So we have another chiasmus:

A	B
Manasseh . . . . Ephraim	
B	A
Ephraim . . . . Manasseh	

This chiasmus also symbolized a change; the *beginning* of the fulfillment of the promise made in Gen 15:12-16; the promise that Abraham's descendents would return to the land God promised him. It began with the Exodus from Egypt, which brought the life story of Jacob to an end. The promise finds its final fulfillment with the conquest and occupation of the land.

So, the chiasmus we have in vv27-30 symbolizes God's presence and activity and shows how God secured Judah's future. Judah tried to secure his future by denying Tamar her legal right, marriage to Shelah. But Shelah disappeared from the story, and Judah's future was at risk. First Tamar, vv12-18, and then God vv27-30, secured Judah's future for him. Nothing that he did himself secured his future. It was Tamar's actions and the unseen hand of God that ensured Judah's future. Judah was given a future, but not in the way he planned.

Conclusion

The future cannot be secured without God, for "man proposes but God disposes," as the saying goes. We may plan, but God is the final arbiter of those plans, as we have seen in Judah's story.

This understanding of the future is true not only of the Old Testament; it holds true for the New Testament as well, illustrated by the following story:

There was once a rich man who had a fertile farm that produced fine crops. In fact, his barns were overflowing every year. He was doing so well that he began planning for the future. He said to himself, "I think it's time that I tear down my barns and build bigger ones. Then I'll have room enough to store everything. I can then sit back and say to myself, My friend, you have enough stored away for years to come. Now take it easy! Eat, drink, and be merry!" But God said to him, "You fool! You will die this very night. Then who will get what is stored in your barns?" Yes, a person is a fool to store up earthly wealth and to make preparations for the future but not have a rich relationship with God. (Luke 12:15–21).

It is impossible to secure the future without God.

EXAMPLE 4: FRAME-STORY FORMAT

The format is used by Holbert.[12] A story is used to introduce the subject and the sermon is concluded with a story.

Text: 2 Chronicles 25:1–28

CLOSURE

Chapter 25 is the beginning of the reign of a new king in Judah. Amaziah was the son of Joash, who was murdered. The chronological description in v1a indicates the start of the reign of a new king, and the start of a new episode in the story of the kings of Israel and Judah. Chapter 24:27b: "then Amaziah became king in his place," indicates that a new episode begins in chapter 25. The death of Amaziah, 25:27b–28, signals the end of this episode. This is a self-contained narrative unit that forms part of the larger narrative of the kings of Israel and Judah.

EXEGESIS OF THE NARRATIVE STRUCTURE

The structure is based on the narrative constituents of character, time, and technique:

> A v1–4 Amaziah revenged his father's death, respecting the law
> > B v5–13 Amaziah, listened to the prophet and was victorious over Seir
> > > C ***vv14–16 Amaziah turned to idolatry and his destruction was prophesied***
> > B v17–24 Amaziah, over-confident, fought Joash and was defeated
> A vv25–28 Amaziah's servants plotted against him and he was murdered in Lacish

---

12. Holbert, *Preaching*, 93–115.

Description of the Structure

This is a concentric structure. Amaziah had mixed fortunes during his reign, illustrated by the reversal of his victory over Seir/Edom (25:5–13) and his defeat by Israel in 25:17–24; thus a reign that began in victory ended in defeat.

The pivot of the concentric structure is his idolatry, the reason for his mixed fortunes. The other reason was his youthful, foolish, and arrogant over-confidence and pride, v1, v16, and v19. He suffered the same fate as his father, murdered by his own servants.

Focus Point

C vv14–16

In these verses, Amaziah turned from the worship of God, who gave him victory over Seir/Edom, to the worship of the gods of Seir/Edom. He turned to idols after a successful war against Seir v14a. This was his folly; he turned to gods that were not able to fight. It was illogical, irrational behavior that had its root in arrogance (v16a). For this reason, God decided to destroy him. God sent a prophet to tell him what God was about to do. God was offering him the opportunity to turn away from his idolatry. The question of the prophet—"why?"—gave Amaziah a chance to turn the anger of the Lord away (v15a). He rejected the opportunity and so rejected the Lord, and God now would reject him: "I know that the Lord has planned to destroy you." Note that the prophet's knowledge of the plan of God was based on v16b "because you have done this [that is, v14] and have not listened to my counsel." The prophet must have given counsel to Amaziah when he confronted him, v15b. In all probability, the prophet told Amaziah to repent and return to God and obey him with his whole heart.

Verse 16 describes Amaziah's attitude. He told the prophet:

1. "Have we appointed you a royal counselor," which meant the prophet was not part of the inner circle, one of his personal advisors who told him what he wanted to hear, cf. v7, v17.

2. "Why should you be struck down?" He threatened to kill the prophet of God.

The prophet predicted his end, v16c. There is a causal link between *the prophet's knowledge* about what God was about to do and *the reason for his knowledge* about what God was about to do. His knowledge was not due to a special revelation; it was a conclusion drawn from Amaziah's behavior: "because you have done this" (that is, turned to idols) and because you "have not listened to my counsel." This was the prophet's source of the knowledge of what God intended to do to Amaziah.

Main point: Amaziah, in his half-hearted commitment to God, turned to idolatry. This would ultimately result in his destruction.

A vv1–4

This unit describes Amaziah. Verses 1–2 give some background:

> He was young—twenty-five years old, v1a.
> He had a mother to guide and counsel him, 1b.
> He did what was right, v2a.
> He did not do right with his whole heart, v2b.

Each of the half-verses has a counter-point: *young* but had *a mother*; *do right* but *not wholeheartedly*. The statement in v2 "not . . . with his whole heart" is an *announcement* phrase, stating up front what the theme of the narrative unit is and what Amaziah's main character trait was: half-heartedness and indifference.

In vv3–4, Amaziah does the right thing. He obeyed what was written in the Law of Moses regarding each person being responsible for their own sin (see Deut 24:16). He did not kill the children of his father's murderers, but he could also have spared the lives of his father's conspirators and murderers. He could have served God with his whole heart; showing mercy and compassion. He could have decided not to kill his father's murderers. As king, it was in his power to do it. An act like that would have been a sign of wholehearted commitment to God.

This description of Amaziah doing the right thing in v2b is preceded by an odd reference to the presence of his mother in Jerusalem. He was persuaded by his mother's influence (v1) to do the right thing. If she had not been there, he probably would have killed the children as well. The reference to his half-heartedness (v2b) pointed to his immaturity as a young king with a great deal of power. *His mother proved to be his saving grace.*

The servants in v3a are the counselors of the king. The text refers to them as *his* servants; they are officials advising and serving the king in the palace. Therefore "servants" in v3 and the "royal counselors" in v16 (see v17) are the same. The noun in v3 is *'ebed* and in v16 *yôēṣ* but in the story both words refer to court/palace officials. The first time the word *yôēṣ* is used is in Exod 18:19. Jethro saw that Moses carried the huge administrative burden and said to him, "I shall give you counsel, and God be with you." He then gave him an organizational plan and advised him how to carry out the administrative responsibilities for ruling and judging his people. The terms "servants" and "counselor" mean palace officials who carry out administrative duties.

Main point: Amaziah did what was right, but in a half-hearted manner.

B vv5–13

The passage describes how Amaziah prepared to go to war against the Edomites. He took a census of the males twenty years and older and there were 300,000 fighting men. He divided them into companies of thousands and hundreds, each with their own commander. He also hired 100,000 men from Israel (Ephraim).

Now "a man of God" (v7) warned him against taking the Israelite soldiers with him (vv8–9) because God had turned against Israel/Ephraim. If he took the men from Israel with him he would suffer defeat. *Amaziah listened to the "man of God"* and sent the soldiers home. So the man of God brought him to his senses and saved him from defeat. This incident illustrates Amaziah *doing the right thing*.

The soldiers were extremely angry with Amaziah, and on their way back to Israel they raided some of the Judean towns, plundering them and killing 3,000 of the inhabitants (v10, v13).

Amaziah *"strengthened himself"* (v11); the Revised Standard Version translates *"took courage."* The courage is based on what the man of God told him, that God would give him the victory if he sent the Israelites back home. He led the army into battle and killed 20,000 soldiers of Seir. He had success, as predicted by the man of God (v8b, v9b).

But there are also examples of Amaziah's half-hearted commitment:

1. He took a census, v5. Whenever the king in the Old Testament took a census without specific instructions from God, it was seen as an act of disobedience.

2. He hired the 100,000 soldiers from Israel, v11. So although he listened to the man of God, he behaved like a self-sufficient king, not needing the help of God (see vv8–9). He was his own man.

All the acts of Amaziah described in this chapter were carried out *without consulting God* (vv3–4, 5–13, and 17–24). God did not spare him from the consequences of his foolish decisions.

Amaziah's half-hearted obedience resulted in suffering for his own people; his folly and arrogance caused pain. And this was not just expected suffering because of war; it was suffering caused by the half-hearted commitment of Amaziah to God.

Main point: Amaziah defeated the Edomites, but caused his people pain, suffering, and death because of his half-hearted commitment to God.

B vv17–24

Amaziah's behavior in this unit was a reaction to what had happened in v13. But there are two indications that Amaziah's actions were not just politically motivated: v17 "Amaziah took counsel and sent to Jehoash . . . the king of Israel." He consulted his young political advisors (cf. v16a, v3b), who counseled him to take revenge on Jehoash and Israel, but he did not include the man of God, and therefore God, in this decision. In v19, "you said, 'you have defeated Edom. And your heart has become proud in boasting.'" He was motivated by arrogance, pride, and a false sense of confidence in his own ability, forgetting the real reason for his success (see v9b, v11–12). It was this pride that motivated his challenge to Jehoash, king of Israel (v17).

Jehoash tried to dissuade Amaziah, using a fable (v18–19), but he stubbornly refused to listen (v20). His refusal was part of God's plan to judge him for his idolatry, given the previous narrator comments (v13, v16b).

Jehoash defeated Amaziah, ransacked Jerusalem and the temple, and took the treasurers and some of the people of Judah as captives to Samaria (vv21–24), while Amaziah himself remained in Jerusalem. This fulfilled the prophet's words in v16.

Amaziah, smarting from the actions of the Israelite soldiers in v13 and emboldened by his defeat of the Edomites and the advice and support of his counselors, sent out the challenge to Jehoash to face him in war. This resulted in his defeat and ultimately his death.

*Main point: Amaziah was defeated by Jehoash, and **his officials and some Judeans were taken to Samaria** because of his half-hearted commitment to God.*

A vv25–28

Amaziah became aware of a conspiracy in the palace to kill him and fled to Lachish. But the court officials who conspired against him sent men to Lachish, and he was murdered there. The murder is reported in a matter-of-fact manner, without any emotion. The narrator gives the reason for his death as follows: "from the time that Amaziah turned away from the Lord" (v27a; see also v2, v16b). His death was the result of his half-hearted commitment to God. He died in exactly the same way his father did, described in chapter 24. He was brought back from Lachish and buried in Jerusalem (in the city of Judah), with his fathers. The man of God's prophecy in v16 was fulfilled.

Main point: Amaziah suffered the same fate as his father, murdered by his court officers because of his half-hearted commitment to God.

Formulation of the Exegetical Idea

Main point: **Amaziah**, in his half-hearted commitment to God, **turned to idolatry**. This ultimately resulted in his destruction.

Main point: Amaziah did what was right, but in a half-hearted manner.

Main point: **Amaziah** defeated the Edomites, but **caused his people pain, suffering, and death** because of his half-hearted commitment to God.

Main point: Amaziah was defeated by Jehoash, and **his officials and some Judeans were taken to Samaria** because of his half-hearted commitment to God.

Main point: **Amaziah** suffered the same fate as his father, **murdered by his court officers**, because of his half-hearted commitment to God.

Exegetical Idea

Amaziah's half-hearted commitment to God resulted in unwise decisions, which brought suffering upon his people and led to his murder.

Theological Idea

Christians' half-hearted commitment to God will result in unwise decisions, actions, and pain, and could even lead to death.

Preaching Idea

Serving God half-heartedly has disastrous consequences; it is costly.

Sermon

Reading: 2 Chronicles 25:1–28; Revelation 3:14–16

Theme: **Serving God half-heartedly is costly.**

Introduction

It was Thursday evening—the time when Bramway Baptist Church Council has its regular quarterly meeting. As the council members settled down, the minister said, "Folks, we are at the end of the first quarter of the new church year. Tell me how you feel. Tell me how things are in your life, before we get to the agenda."

One by one, the people around the table told their story. The common thread running through their stories was "I am tired, physically weary." People were not complaining or dejected, they just felt tired, as the service and ministry of the past three months had affected them physically.

Now someone looking in from the outside and listening to them would have said, "these folks really have their lives out of balance. They are too committed to the church, too committed to ministry, too committed to God."

Last week Saturday was the funeral service of Uncle Jeff. He was eighty years old when he died—well known in his town and within the Christian community. Several people paid tribute to Uncle Jeff, speaking particularly about his passion for lost people; how he left no stone unturned to make sure people heard the Good News. Why, just before he was admitted to hospital he was sitting at the entrance of the local shopping mall handing out tracts to passersby—Uncle Jeff was "on fire for God"—totally committed to God.

Now how would our world judge his life? "Unbalanced! Too busy in the church; too sold out to God. He should have had more balance in his life," some might say.

And yet, every tribute spoke of what a great father and husband he was. Being "sold out to God" and being a great father and husband were not mutually exclusive for Uncle Jeff. Society would, and we might, judge these people who are "on fire for God" as unbalanced. But God promises to reward them.

There is a flip side of course. There are many Christians who are unbalanced, but that is not the issue. The issue is really that today the balance has shifted heavily in the direction of our own personal concerns; personal priorities; personal desires, dreams, and plans. People like Uncle Jeff and the council members have the balance tipped more in the opposite direction. They believe God is serious about us being seriously committed to him; it makes a difference to God how we serve him. They believe this because there are many stories in the Word of God that shows that half-hearted commitment to God is costly.

I want to share one such story with you; a story which makes this point emphatically. It is about Amaziah, who served God half-heartedly at great cost to himself and his people.

It's the year 796 BC. For the previous forty years, Judah was ruled by the very young king Joash. He was only seven years old when he was installed as king of Judah by Jehoiada the priest, with the help of the Levites, captains, and the clans of Judah. Athaliah, who had usurped the throne, was killed. So the real power behind the throne was the priest Jehoiada. Under this priestly guidance, the king introduced major changes in the cultic and religious life of the nation.

During the last years of Joash's reign, however, the king began to listen more and more to the voice of his counselors. Jehoiada fell out of favor and was murdered. Joash himself suffered the same fate at the hands of some of the very same court officials to whom he listened.

Amaziah stepped into this situation when he became king. He was twenty-five years old; older than his father, but apparently not any wiser.

After he stabilized the political situation, he executed his father's murderers (v3). Although his father was dead, he still had his mother. She is mentioned only once in the story, v1a. She is mentioned against the background of two statements about Amaziah: "he did right in the eyes of the Lord but not wholeheartedly"; and he did not murder the children of the officials who murdered his father (v4), in accordance with the law (see Deut 24:16). It is strange that it is said that he did not serve God wholeheartedly in the same breath that it is said that he did not kill the children of his father's murderers. One would think that by not killing the children of his father's murderers, he was serving God with his whole heart! The mention of his half-hearted commitment to God in the midst of his gracious act suggests that if he was serving God with his whole heart, he would have spared the lives of the fathers also. Yes, the palace officials deserved to die, but as king he could have spared their lives; he had the power to do so but not the heart, because his heart was not wholly owned by God. His half-hearted serving of the Lord was reflected in his immaturity. He did not have a heart for God and so did not wholly serve God; to act like God; to show grace, even though he had every reason and right to kill the palace officials.

His indifference in his service of God pointed to his immaturity, not only politically but spiritually too.

Immaturity in spiritual matters is the fruit of a half-hearted commitment to God.

But there was more to come, as we see from vv5–13. Amaziah was preparing for war against Edom (Seir). He had 300,000 fighting young men to send to the front, but decided that this was not enough and hired an extra 100,000 soldiers from Israel to reinforce his troops (vv5–6). The man of God warns against this (v7) because God was against Israel (Ephraim). He was told that God would make sure that he was defeated (vv8–9) if he ignored the warning. Amaziah listens to the counsel of the man of God, but under protest, because he was concerned about the monetary loss he would suffer, "but what shall we do for the hundred talents which I had given to the troops of Israel?" (v9). This was his main concern: what was going to happen to my money? Nevertheless, he sent the 100,000 troops back to Israel.

Now for the twist. We read that Amaziah, *"strengthens himself"* (v11) then led the army into battle. He went in the strength of his own might, the might of his 300,000 strong fighting forces. This is confirmed by v19a, which literally reads "you said, 'behold, I have defeated Edom.' And lifted you up your heart to boast." So although he listened to the man of God, (see v10), he behaved like a self-sufficient king, not needing the help of God. Still, he was successful, killing 20,000 soldiers of Edom

(Seir). He had the victory and success predicted by the man of God in vv8–9.

Meanwhile, the returning Israelite soldiers were extremely angry with Amaziah, and on their way home they raided some of the Judean towns, plundering them and killing 3,000 people (v10, v13). People suffered and died because of Amaziah's initial unwise action. God kept his word, as spoken by the man of God, but God did not let Amaziah off the hook for the unwise decision of hiring the men from Israel, which showed his insensitivity to God's decision about Israel. He prepared for war without consulting God, and his indifferent attitude and half-heartedness towards God brought this pain, suffering, and death upon his people. So it was that Amaziah's half-hearted commitment to God led to unwise choices and self-sufficient arrogance which caused his people to suffer pain, material loss, and even death. Amaziah's half-hearted service to God is evident from his insensitivity to God's judgment of Israel; his self-centered arrogance, and his preoccupation with money.

Indifference in one's commitment to God causes others to suffer.

The peak of Amaziah's half-hearted commitment is revealed in his postwar behavior. I suppose, in an effort to remind him of his convincing victory over Edom, and as a means of feeding his ego, he turned to the worship of the gods of Edom, gods who were not able to save their people from defeat at the hand of Amaziah. He brought them with him to Judah, set them up "as his own gods" and worshipped them (v14). *How irrational can a person be?*

The expression "as his own gods" affirms what was just said. His irrational worshipping of the gods he conquered was, paradoxically, the worship of himself, his strength (v11), which he believed gave him the victory over Edom (see v19). The worship of self often results in irrational actions. As a result, God decided to destroy Amaziah (v15a, 16a).

This arrogant self-importance can be seen clearly in his response to the man of God's question, "why do you consult this people's gods . . . ?" First, the question "why" was an opportunity presented to Amaziah to avert the anger of the Lord (v15a), but he did not take this opportunity and set himself on the road to self-destruction.

Second, his response to the question was, "Have we appointed you a royal counselor?" (v16); implying that the prophet was not part of the inner circle, who told him what he wanted to hear (cf. v7, v17). He

Sermon Formats and the Structured-Repetition Approach 235

had no need to consult God; no need to hear from God because he had self-appointed men of wisdom to counsel him. Moreover, he said "why should you be struck down?"; he threatened to kill the prophet of God and this was not just an empty threat (v3). So God decided to destroy him.

The key to understanding his illogical behavior in this narrative unit is in v16a: *his arrogance*. Thus it was that Amaziah's half-hearted commitment to God resulted in his self-destruction.

Indifference in one's commitment to God leads to irrational behavior that is rooted in arrogance and ends in self-destruction.

Amaziah was angered by the actions of the Israelite troops (v13) and sought revenge. He sent a challenge to Jehoash the king of Israel, "come let us face each other" (v17): come and face me on the battlefield and I will show you who is stronger and greater. The implication is that what Jehoash's troops did to the towns and inhabitants of Judah would be child's play in comparison to what Amaziah would do to Jehoash and his troops. This confidence and arrogance is a result of the victory over the Edomites and his ownership of the gods of the Edomites, which made him feel invincible (v19a), and the support of his counselors (v17).

Using a parable (vv18–19), the king of Israel sent the following message, and I paraphrase: "Young man stay home, don't be stupid; you are going to get killed and your people will be destroyed." I am sure his counselors advised him that Jehoash was all big talk. To stay home would send the wrong message. So he stubbornly refused to listen to Jehoash (v20). The narrator comments that his refusal was part of God's plan to judge him for his idolatry and apostasy (v14, v16b). The words "Amaziah would not listen, for it was from God," means his stubborn indifference handed him over to the judgment of God; no prophet was sent to warn him this time, whereas on two previous occasions he received a warning, v7, v15b. He sealed his own fate through his half-hearted commitment to God.

Jehoash (vv21–24) defeated Amaziah, ransacked Jerusalem and the temple, and took the treasurers and some Judeans as captives to Samaria. The prophet's words of v16 were fulfilled; God's plan to destroy Amaziah commenced. The defeat of his troops and taking Judaeans captive was the first stage of God's judgment on Amaziah. So Amaziah's half-hearted commitment to God resulted in defeat and humiliation not only for him, but also for his people.

Indifference in one's commitment to God leads to abandonment by God, resulting in defeat and humiliation.

But there was one more aspect to the judgment of God on Amaziah. He was left behind in Jerusalem by Jehoash. Was the destruction of Amaziah predicted in v16 going to be left unfulfilled? Or did the prophet mean the defeat of the army and the taking of captives when he used the word destruction? A reading of v25 seems to give this impression, for it says "Amaziah outlived his Israelite counterpart, Jehoash, by fifteen years." So for fifteen years it looked as if God's judgment was complete, until we read vv27–28. These verses record the fact that a conspiracy to kill Amaziah was hatched in the royal palace. The conspirators, though only identified as "they," must have been palace officials. Amaziah was aware of the conspiracy and escaped to Lachish. The palace officials sent men to Lachish, where he was killed.

Amaziah outlived the king of Israel, who defeated him, but he could not "outlive" or escape the consequences of his half-hearted and indifferent commitment to God. He died as predicted by the prophet in v16b.

Moreover, he died in exactly the same way his father died, killed by conspirators; killed by his advisors. He was brought back from Lachish and buried in Jerusalem ("in the City of Judah," v28) with his fathers. And so the curtain closes on the life of Amaziah. He did serve God, yes, but he served God half-heartedly and paid a personal price for it.

Half-hearted commitment to God has individual and personal consequences that are inescapable.

Conclusion

There is a story about a young minister who went to his first church with eager enthusiasm. To his disappointment, he found the worship services poorly attended and the spiritual life of the congregation at a low ebb.

He went from house to house seeking to renew an interest, but several people said the church was so dead that they did not care to attend. He discussed the situation with his church board and they agreed that the criticism was probably justified.

The pastor announced that since the church was considered dead, he would conduct its funeral the following Sunday.

The church was crowded that day. In front of the pulpit was a coffin. The minister eulogized the deceased. He told how much the church had accomplished in the past and expressed his sorrow over its untimely demise.

Then he invited the congregation to go forward and view the corpse. One by one the people looked into the casket; each was amazed to see his/her own face reflected in a mirror in the bottom of the coffin. Many were shocked and indignant, but then each member began to realize that his or her own spiritual indifference was the reason the church was dead.

The church was dead because they were spiritually dead. Half-hearted commitment to God is costly, individually and corporately. We can choose to serve God with indifference, with half-hearted commitment, but remember we will pay a price for it. Let those who hear, hear what the Spirit says to the Church.

Where do we begin as we confront our own half-hearted commitment? This verse from the hymn "You ask me why?" provides a place to start.

It says:

> You ask me why I find no rest nor gladness
> In paths where selfish ease would while my hours?
> And why I toil where hearts in bitter sadness
> Lie crushed beneath sin's fierce o'erwhelming powers?
> *It is because I know life's thread is slender.*
> But one short hour, one little stretch of road,
> Then yearns my heart with love divinely tender,
> To seek the lost and bring them home to God.

Then there is this encouragement from another great hymn of the faith:

> Go, labor on; spend and be spent,
> Thy joy to do the Father's will:
> It is the way the Master went;
> Should not the servant tread it still?

Half-hearted commitment to God is costly.

Conclusion

OF THE MANY TASKS the minister has, none is as demanding as preaching and teaching the word of God. The frequency with which it has to be done makes it particularly challenging; ministers preach a minimum of once a Sunday, as well as mid-week bible studies, marriage ceremonies, funerals, to mention just a few occasions.

The expectation of the congregation makes the task even more demanding: people go to a place of worship and expect "to hear from God." They expect that what they will hear will address their situation, their questions, struggles, and concerns, and they expect the message to be different, new, fresh, relevant, and to give guidance as they struggle with religious, political, social, and economic questions that are often complex. They want to hear how to relate and respond to these issues as believers who trust that the Bible is his word.

Scripture is a rich and varied source for theology and truth and it equips Christians to deal with the issues and concerns raised above. But how do we access this rich source of information? Preaching is one method among many, but it is an important one. For ministers to access the richness and diversity of Scripture, they must be given tools. I believe the structured-repetition approach in this book is such a tool.

We have come to the end of our journey, during which you were introduced to a structured-repetition approach to Old Testament narrative. It is an approach that practically integrates hermeneutics and homiletics; it presents to ministers another way of accessing the Old Testament biblical narratives meaningfully, and allows faith communities and the world to hear God's word in fresh and new ways, adapting to different times and new circumstances. It aims to help us hear the voice of the God who speaks and who says, "My thoughts are not your thoughts nor are your ways my ways" (Isa 55:8). And if the approach to Old Testament narrative presented here helps someone hear the thoughts of God and have a better understanding of his ways, then it would have accomplished its purpose.

However, the approach presented here does raise some concerns, some of which are addressed below:

1. Subjectivity is a concern. Interpreters perceive structures in narratives, episodes, and narrative units that are not supported by the text; they see structures in the text that are not there. This concern is informed by the desire and the importance of objectivity in biblical interpretation, which is correct. But it must be conceded that an "either or" approach to the relationship between subject-object is not true to life and to what actually happens in the academic, scientific, and even legal spheres, to name a few. The demand for controlled subjectivity is correct, but the expectation of absolute objectivity is unrealistic. In this regard, Trible remarks, "the question assumes a total divide between objectivity and subjectivity . . . To the extent that the words 'objective' and 'subjective' are useful, one must allow for both in scholarly endeavors. Each corrects and is corrected by the other; neither gains ascendancy . . . The answer continues by observing that subjectivity characterizes all biblical methods. Subjects (i.e., scholars) devise methods, subjects use methods, and subjects draw different conclusions from the use of methods."[1]

   I believe the concept of narrative text developed here goes some way in mitigating the subjectivity by identifying the narrative structure based on the constituent elements that constitute a narrative text. In this way, control is exercised, as Simon Bar-Efrat indicates, "it is definitely undesirable to base the structural analysis partly on verbal elements, partly on elements of technique and partly on characters, on events, on themes or on other varieties of narrative or conceptual content [He further advises that it] . . . should be borne in mind, however, that the interpretation of structure is much more prone to subjectivity than its mere description. In order to endow the proposed interpretation with a high degree of probability and convincing power it is recommendable to look for data in the text, apart from the structure, that confirm or support it."[2] For this reason,

---

1. Trible, *Rhetorical Criticism*, 230–31.
2. Bar-Efrat, "Observations," 172.

I have limited the narrative constituents that form the basis for identifying narrative structure to no more than three, mainly because the other two are required by the first narrative constituent, for example, character requires either place, action or speech.

Subjectivity also involves "filling the gaps" in narratives. It seeks answers and provides information to questions the reader has, even though the specific, literal text does not provide the answers. Such gap filling has to be informed by the context of the particular narrative, episode, or narrative unit, in addition to applying general hermetical principles for it to be valid. This is, once again, controlled subjectivity.

2. The text can be dehistoricized by focusing on the text itself. Again, to do so would be against the text itself. The text is both form and content. History is an element of the content, and this might not be true to the same degree in fictional writing, but in biblical narrative it stands. Therefore if the text, made up of form and content, is taken seriously, the historical element of its content must also be taken seriously, staying true to the nature of the text itself. This also holds true for the religious and theological dimension of the biblical text.

3. It is possible to feel that this approach cramps a person's style or predisposes a minister to a didactic sermon format and style. But this tendency is not inherent to the approach, nor is it unique to this specific approach. It is the bane of all hermeneutic and homiletical methods. It is a matter of choice, rather than predetermined by the method.

4. Can this approach be applied to texts other than Old Testament narrative? It can, based on the premise that any meaningful text is structured because meaningful communication requires structure. A structured-repetition approach can be used for any structured text. Therefore, the approach not only applies to the Old Testament, but also to the New Testament.

A Structured-Repetition Approach to the proclamation of Old Testament narratives is presented here in the belief that it is an option which can enhance the preaching task of ministers and be a blessing to the Church.

Bibliography

Achtemeier, E. *Preaching from the Old Testament*. Louisville: John Knox, 1989.
Adam, P. *Speaking God's Word: A Practical Theology of Preaching*. Leicester: InterVarsity, 1996.
Alter, R. *The Art of Biblical Literature*. New York: Basic, 1981.
———. *The Story of David: A Translation with Commentary of 1 and 2 Samuel*. New York: Norton, 1999.
Amit, Y. *Reading Biblical Narratives: Literary Criticism and the Hebrew Bible*. Translated by Yael Lotan. Minneapolis: Fortress, 2001.
———. *The Book of Judges: The Art of Editing*. Translated by Jonathan Chipman. Leiden: Brill Academic, 1999.
Anderson, K. C. *Preaching with Integrity*. Grand Rapids: Kregel, 2003.
Arp, T. R. *Perrine's Story and Structure*. 9th ed. Fort Worth: Harcourt Brace College, 1998.
Baker, D. W., and B. T. Arnold, eds. *The Face of Old Testament Studies: A Survey of Contemporary Approaches*. Grand Rapids: Apollos, 1999.
Bar-Efrat, S. "Some Observations on the Analysis of Structure in Biblical Narrative." *Vetus Testamentum* 30:2 (1980) 154–73.
Barkhuizen, J. H. "Jona: Die Rekonstruksie van 'n Karakter." *HTS* 44:1 (1988) 55–70.
Bebbington, David. *Patterns of History: A Christian View*. Downers Grove: InterVarsity, 1979.
Berlin, A. *Poetics and Interpretation of Biblical Narrative*. Sheffield: Almond, 1983.
Boling, R. G. *Judges: A New Translation with Introduction and Commentary*. Vol. 6A of *The Anchor Bible*, edited by David Noel Freedman. Garden City: Doubleday, 1975.
Borden, P. "Is There Really One Big Idea in That Story?" *The Big Idea of Biblical Preaching: Connecting the Bible to People*, edited by K. Willhite and M. G. Scott, 67–80. Grand Rapids: Baker, 1998.
———. "The High Cost of Lamb (2 Samuel 11–12)." In *The Art of Preaching Old Testament Narrative*, edited by S. D. Mathewson. Grand Rapids: Baker, 2002.
Borgman, P. *Genesis: The Story We Haven't Heard*. Downers Grove: InterVarsity, 2001.
Bosman, H. L., et al. *Old Testament Storytellers*. Vol. 2 of *The Literature of the Old Testament*. Cape Town: Tafelberg, 1988.
Botha, J. *Semeion: Inleiding tot aspekte van die interpretasie van die Griekse Nuwe Testament*. Pretoria: NG Kerkboekhandel, 1990.
Bray, G. *Biblical Interpretation Past and Present*. Leicester: Appolos, 1996.
Brink, A. *Vertelkunde: 'n Inleiding tot die lees van Vehalende Tekste*. Cape Town: Academia, 1987.
Brown, C., ed. *The New International Dictionary of New Testament Theology*. 3 vols. Exeter: Paternoster, 1976–1978.

Bibliography

Chisholm, R. B., Jr. *Interpreting Historical Books: An Exegetical Handbook.* Grand Rapids: Kregel, 2006.

Claassens, J. L. M. "'n Kulturele verwysingsraamwerk vir die Japhthah verhaal (Rigters 10:6—12:7)." MA thesis, University of Stellenbosch, 1996.

———. " 'n Herwaardering van die Ou Testamentverhaal in die prediking: met spesifike verwysing na die Jefta-verhaal (Rig 11:1—12:7)." *NGTT* 37:4 (1997) 397–401.

———. "Theme and Function in the Jephthah Narrative." *JNSL* 23:2 (1997) 203–19.

Cloete, T. T. *Literêre terme en teorieë.* Pretoria: HAUM-Literêr, 1992.

Dancy, J. *The Divine Drama: The Old Testament as Literature.* Cambridge: Lutherworth, 2001.

Deist, F. E., and J. J. Burden. *An ABC of Biblical Exegesis.* Pretoria: van Schaik, 1980.

De Moor, J. *Synchronic or Diachronic? A Debate on Method in Old Testament Exegesis.* Leiden: Brill Academic, 1995.

De Siva, D. A. *Honor, Patronage, Kinship & Purity: Unlocking New Testament Culture.* Downers Grove: InterVarsity, 2000.

Dorsey, D. A. *The Literary Structure of the Old Testament: A Commentary on Genesis–Malachi.* Grand Rapids: Baker Academic, 1999.

Elliot, W. *Flow of Flesh, Reach of Spirit: Think Sheets of a Contrarian Christian.* Grand Rapids: Eerdmans, 1995.

Erickson, R. J. *A Beginner's Guide to New Testament Exegesis: Taking the Fear out of Critical Method.* Downers Grove: InterVarsity, 2005.

Fausset, A. R. *Fausset's Bible Dictionary.* Grand Rapids: Zondervan, 1949.

Fishbane, M. "Reviews of Recent Work on Biblical Narrative." *Prooftexts* 1 (1981). 99–104.

Fitzgerald, G. R. *A Practical Guide to Preaching: Helps and Hints for Sermon Preparation and Delivery.* New York: Paulist Press, 1989.

Fokkelman, J. P. *King David: 2 Samuel 9–20 & 1 Kings 1–2.* Assen: Van Gorcum, 1981.

———. *Reading Biblical Narrative: An Introductory Guide.* Leidendorp: Deo, 1999.

Gehart, M. "The Restoration of Biblical Narrative." In *Narrative Research on the Hebrew Bible*, edited by M. G. W. Amhai et al. Atlanta: Scholars Press, 1989.

Goldingay, J. *Approaches to Old Testament Interpretation.* Rev. ed. Leicester: Appolos, 1990.

———. *Israel's Gospel.* Vol. 1 of *Old Testament Theology.* Downers Grove: InterVarsity, 2003.

Gräbe, I. "Die Gelykenis van die Barmhartige Samaritaan: Narratiewe Tegnieke en Vergelykingskonstruksies." *HTS* 42:2 (1986) 265–81.

———. "Narratologiese Ondersoek en Eksegese van die Boodskap van die Evangelies." *HTS* 42:1 (1986) 151–68.

Green, J. B., and M. Pasquarello III. *Narrative Reading, Narrative Preaching: Reuniting New Testament Interpretation and Proclamation.* Grand Rapids: Baker Academic, 2003.

Green, J. P., Sr., trans. *The Interlinear Bible: Hebrew and English.* Vol. 2, *1 Samuel–Psalm 55.* Grand Rapids: Baker, 1976.

Greidanus, S. *The Modern Preacher and the Ancient Text: Interpreting and Preaching Biblical Literature.* Grand Rapids: Eerdmans, 1988.

Gros Louis, Kenneth R. R., et al., eds. *Literary Interpretations of Biblical Narratives.* Nashville: Abingdon, 1974.

Harris, Laird, et al. *Theological Wordbook of the Old Testament*. 2 vols. Chicago: Moody, 1980.

Holbert, J. C. *Old Testament Preaching: Proclamation and Narrative in the Hebrew Bible*. Nashville: Abingdon, 1991.

Holladay, W. *A Concise Hebrew and Aramaic Lexicon of the Old Testament*. Leiden: Brill, 1971.

Johnson, A. M., Jr. *Structuralism and Biblical Hermeneutics: A Collection of Essays*. Pittsburgh: Pickwick, 1979.

Jonker, L. *Exclusivity and Variety: Perspectives on Multi-dimensional Exegesis*. Kampen: Kok Pharos, 1996.

Jonker, J., and D. Lawrie. *Fishing for Jonah (anew): Various Approaches to Biblical Interpretation*. Stellenbosch: Sun, 2005.

Kawin, B. F. *Telling It Again and Again: Repetition in Literature and Film*. Boulder: University Press of Colorado, 1989.

Kubler, G. *The Shape of Time: Remarks on the History of Things*. New Haven: Yale University Press, 1962.

Kugel, J. L. *How To Read the Bible: A Guide to Scripture, Then and Now*. New York: Free Press, 2007.

Lambe, A. J. "Judah's Development: the pattern of Departure-Transition-Return." *JSOT* 83 (1999) 53–68.

Lion-Cachet, F. N. *In Die Werkswinkel Van Die Ou-Testamentiese Eksegese: Die verklaring van die Ou Testament in die Praktyk*. Potchefstroom: Potchefstroomse Universiteit vir Christelike Hoër Onderwys, 1987.

Long, V. P. *The Art of Biblical History*. Leicester: Apollos, 1994.

Long, T. *Narrative Structure as Applied to Biblical Preaching: A Method for Using the Narrative Grammar of A J Greimas in the Development of Sermons on Biblical Narrative*. Ann Arbor: University Microfilms International, 1982.

Luter, B., and B. Davis. *Ruth & Esther: God Behind the Seen*. Rossshire, Scotland: Christian Focus, 2003.

Klaus, N. *Pivot Patterns in the Former Prophets*. Journal for the Study of the Old Testament Supplement Series, 247. Sheffield: Sheffield Academic, 1999.

Malina, B. J. *The New Testament World: Insights from Cultural Anthropology*. Rev. ed. Louisville: John Knox, 1993.

Malina, B., et al. *A Time Travel to the World of Jesus: A Modern Reflection of Ancient Judea*. Cape Town: Orion, 1996.

Marais, J. "Narratiwiteit en die Ou Testament." *HTS* 49:3 (1993) 637–49.

Marquerat, D., and Y. Bourquin. *How To Read Bible Stories*. Translated by J. Bowen. London: SCM, 1999.

Mathewson, S. D. *The Art of Preaching Old Testament Narrative*. Grand Rapids: Baker, 2002.

Matthews, V. H. "The Anthropology of Clothing in the Joseph Narrative." *JSOT* 65 (1995) 25–36.

Millard, A. R., and D. J. Wiseman, eds. *Essays on the Patriarchal Narratives*. Leicester: InterVarsity, 1980.

Miller, J. H. "Narrative." In *Critical Terms for Literary Study*, edited by F. Lentricchia and T. McLaughlin. 2d ed. Chicago: University of Chicago Press, 1995.

Milne, P. J. *Vladimir Propp and the Study of Structure in Hebrew Biblical Narrative*. Sheffield: Sheffield Academic, 1988.

Muilenberg, J. "A Study in Hebrew Rhetoric." *Vetus Testamentum Supplement* 1 (1953) 97–111.

Niehof, M. "Do Biblical Characters Talk To Themselves? Narrative Modes of Representing Inner Speech in Early Biblical Fiction." *JBL* 11:4 (1992) 577–95.

Osborne, G. R. *The Hermeneutical Spiral: A Comprehensive Introduction to Biblical Interpretation*. Downers Grove: Intervarsity, 1991.

Parunak, H. Van Dyke. "Some Axioms for literary architecture." *Semitics* 8 (1982) 1–16.

———. "Transitional Techniques in the Bible." *JBL* 102 (1983) 525–48.

Pilch, J. J., and B. J. Malina, eds. *Handbook of Biblical Social Values*. Peabody: Hendrickson, 1998.

Polak, F. *Biblical Narrative: Aspects of Art and Design*. Jerusalem: Bialik Institute, 1994.

Pratt, R. L., Jr. *He gave us stories: The Bible Student's Guide to Interpreting Old Testament Narratives*. Brentwood: Wolgemuth & Hyatt, 1990.

Roberts, J. H., et al. *Old Testament and New Testament (OTE/NTE)*. Study Guide 101, University of South Africa, 1988.

Robinson, H. *Expository Preaching: Principles and Practice*. Leicester: InterVarsity, 2001.

Ross, A. P. *Creation and Blessing: A Guide to the Study and Exposition of Genesis*. Grand Rapids: Baker, 1998.

Rowe, J. C. "Structure." In *Critical Terms for Literary Study*, edited by F. Lentricchia and T. McLaughlin. 2d ed. Chicago: University of Chicago Press, 1995.

Ryken, L. *Words of Delight: A Literary Introduction to the Bible*. Grand Rapids: Baker, 1992.

Sailhamer, John H. *The Pentateuch as Narrative: A Biblical-theological Commentary*. Grand Rapids: Zondervan, 1992.

Schönweiss, J. "Desire." In *The New International Dictionary of New Testament Theology*, edited by C. Brown. Exeter: Paternoster, 1975.

Schutte, P. J. W. *'n Literer-Teoretiese Benadering tot die Uitleg van die Ester Verhaal*. MA thesis, Universiteit van Pretoria, 1989.

Ska, J. L. "Our Fathers Have Told Us: Introduction to the Analysis of Hebrew Narrative." In *Subsidia Biblica 13*. Rome: Pontifical Biblical Institute, 2000.

Sternberg, M. *The Poetics of Biblical Narrative: Ideological Literature and the Drama of Reading*. Indiana: Indiana University Press, 1985.

Talbert, C. H. *Literary Patterns, Theological Themes and the Genre of Luke-Acts*. Missoula: Scholars Press, 1974.

Teugels, M. "The Anonymous Matchmaker: An Enquiry into the Characterization of the Servant of Abraham in Genesis 24." *JSOT* 65 (1995) 13–23.

Thiselton, A. C. *New Horizons in Hermeneutics*. Grand Rapids: Zondervan, 1992.

Thompson, J. W. "Reading the Letters as Narratives." In *Narrative Reading, Narrative Preaching: Reuniting New Testament Interpretation and Proclamation*, edited by J. B. Green and M. Pasquarello III. Grand Rapids: Baker Academic, 2003.

Trible, P. *Rhetorical Criticism: Context, Method, and the Book of Jonah*. Minneapolis: Fortress Press, 1994.

Turner, L. A. *Announcements of Plot in Genesis*. Sheffield: Sheffield Academic, 1990.

Van der Toorn, Karel. *Scribal Culture and the Making of the Hebrew Bible*. Cambridge: Harvard University Press, 2007.

Vanhoozer, K. J. *Is there Meaning in this Text? The Bible, the Reader and the Morality of Literary Knowledge*. Leicester: Apollos, 1998.

Bibliography

Vosloo, W. "Die Tuinverhaal. 'n Naaratologiese ondersoek van Genesis 2–3." In *Mensetal oor God se Woord: Huldigingsbundel opgedra aan Prof. A.H. van Zyl*. Kaapstad: Lux Verbi, 1988.

———. *Great Tales . . . Greater Truths*. Pretoria: Orion, 1992.

Walkte, B. "Old Testament Interpretation Issues for Big Idea Preaching: Problematic Sources, Poetics, and Preaching the Old Testament, an Exposition of Proverbs 26:1–12." In *The Big Idea of Biblical Preaching: Connecting the Bible to People*, edited by K. Willhite and S. M. Gibson. Grand Rapids: Baker, 1998.

Walsh, J. T. *Style and Structure in Biblical Hebrew Narrative*. Minnesota: Liturgical Press, 2001.

Webb, W. J. *Slaves, Women and Homosexuals: Exploring the Hermeneutics of Cultural Analysis*. Downers Grove: InterVarsity, 2001.

Wilder, A. N. "Story and Story-World." *Interpretation* 36: 4 (1983) 353–64.

Willhite, K., and S. M. Gibson, eds. *The Big Idea of Biblical Preaching: Connecting the Bible to People*. Grand Rapids: Baker, 1998.

Willhite, K. *Preaching with Relevance, Without Dumbing Down*. Grand Rapids: Kregel, 2001

Wijngaards, J. N. M. *Communicating the Word of God*. Essex: McGrimmond, 1978.

Wood, D. *The Jacob Portfolio: Ambition, Love and God*. Leicester: InterVarsity, 1990.

Wong, G. T. K. *Compositional Strategy of the Book of Judges*. Vol. 111 of *Vetus Testamentum Supplements*. Leiden: Brill Academic, 2006.

Wright, S. Review of *The Art of Preaching Old Testament Narrative*, by Steven D. Mathewson. *Evangelical Quarterly* 77:2 (2005) 165–67.

Scripture Index

OLD TESTAMENT

Genesis
1:3—2:4	93–94
5:21–24	141
6–8	12–13
7:10—8:10	78–80
24	12
24:1–67	62–67, 107–12, 160–61
25:19–34	92–94, 147–52, 170–71
25:20–26	80–81, 103–17, 157–60
29:1–4	106
38:1–30	67–70, 204–14

Exodus
21:17	146

Leviticus
20:9	146
24:11–23	146

Judges
1:1:—2:5	74–77, 112–27, 161–65
2:11	30–31, 13
8:22–28	33–35
8:28	13
9:1–21	35–38
9:8–15	30–31
11:4–11	32–33
11:12–27	38–41

Ruth
1–4	4
4:1–10	91–92, 190–97

1 Samuel
1–2	9–10
1–31	13–14
1:1—2:11	6
29:1–11	5–6
30	8–9

2 Samuel
11:1–27	71–74
11	7, 11, 13, 15–19, 14
13:1–22	59–61, 97–100, 173–83
13:3–20	10–11
17:8–13	29

1 Kings
1–2	14
5:3–6	82–83

2 Kings
2:1–25	83–86, 138–47, 168–70
2:23–24	97
17:25–28	70–71
21:21–22	77–78

2 Chronicles
25:1–24	88–91, 225–31

Job

1:13–22	127–31, 165–66
1:14–22	57–58
1–2	11–12

Jonah

1:4–15	86–88

NEW TESTAMENT

Matthew

6:25–34	24

Galatians

4:4–5	24

Subject Index

Borden's approach, 52–53

Chisholm Jr's approach, 46–47
Closure, delimiting narrative text, 26, 42–44

Didactic format, 172–90

Exegetical idea
   definition, 155–56
   illustration, 157–71
Exegesis and narrative structure, 101–2, 103–52

Focus point
   definition, 102
Frame-Story format, 225–37

Green and Pasquarello's approach, 49–50

History, time, and repetition, 17–18, 20

Indentifying narrative constituents, 29–41, 57–100

Labelling text, 27
Levels of repetition, 1–2
Long's approach, 47–49

Main point
   definition, 103
   illustration 103–52
Marks text, 26–27, 29–41, 57–100
Matching units, 24, 29, 57–100

Mathewson's approach, 45–46

Narrative, 3
Narrative constituents, 1, 2, 4
Narrative exegesis, 101
Narrative text, 2, 3, 16

Preaching idea
   definition, 155–56
   illustration, 157–71

Repetition
   definition, viii
   and narrative constituents, 4, 16–17
   and structure, 2, 4, 16–17, 22–23
   and time, 20–21
   its dominance, 17–20

Single idea and sermon construction, 153, 154
Story-Reflection format, 204–25
Structure, definition, 22–23
Structure
   and communication, 21–22, 24, 54
   and meaning, 21–23, 25, 101–2, 153
   and narrative constituents, 4, 16–17
   and rhetorical criticism, 54
   and theatre, 54
Structured-Repetition Approach, 25–28
Synchronic approach, 1

Types of structure
   definition, 2, 56–57
   illustrations, 57–100
Theological idea
   definition, 155–56
   illustration, 157–71
Third Person format, 190–203
Trible's approach, 50–52

Uncover narrative structure, 29–34, 57–100

www.ingramcontent.com/pod-product-compliance
Lightning Source LLC
Chambersburg PA
CBHW051105230426
43667CB00013B/2445